LEGENDARY LOCALS

OF

OGDEN

UTAH

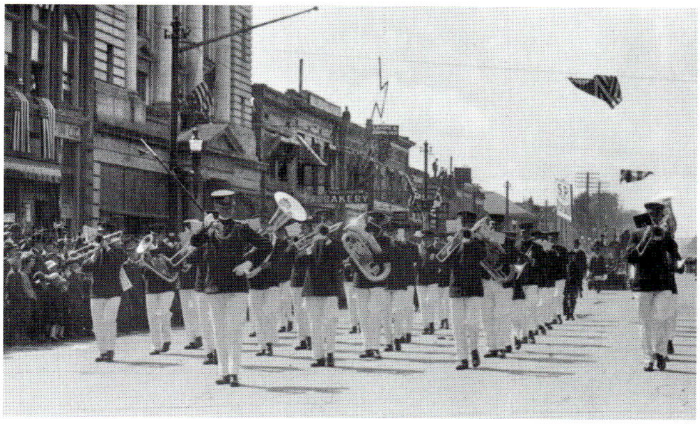

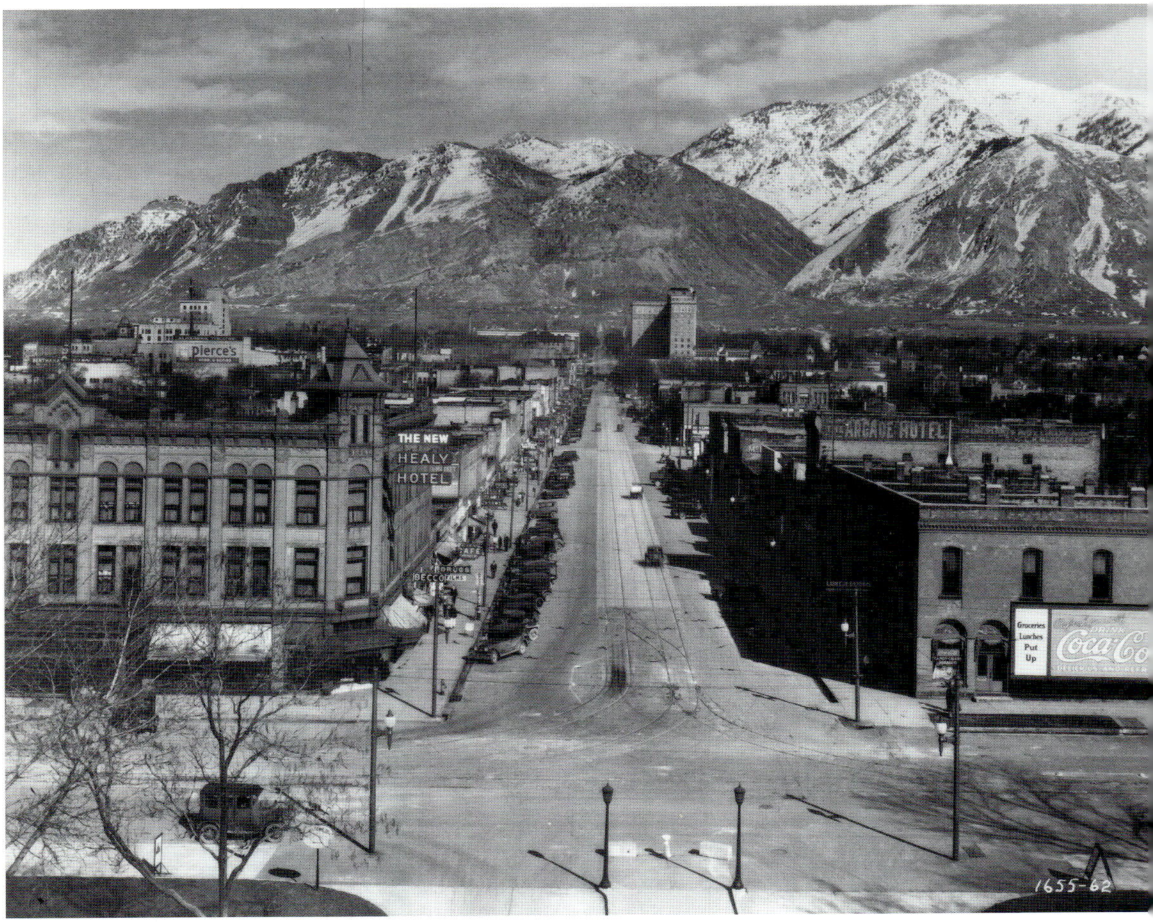

Page 1: Golden Spike Parade
On May 10, 1919, Ogden celebrated the 50th anniversary of the driving of the Golden Spike at Promontory Point. Thousands lined the streets as floats depicting various modes of transportation and marching bands like the one shown here paraded through downtown Ogden. After the parade, special ceremonies honored the pioneers who built the transcontinental railroad and celebrations continued into the night.

Page 2: Historic 25th Street
At the heart of Ogden's downtown area is Historic Twenty-fifth Street, notorious for its former saloons, gambling halls, and brothels. Today, the street is a thriving area with restaurants and stores where Ogdenites gather for the summer farmer's market, music festivals, and other special events. This photograph from the 1920s shows Twenty-fifth Street from the Union Station at Wall Avenue.

LEGENDARY LOCALS OF OGDEN UTAH

SARAH LANGSDON AND MELISSA JOHNSON

LEGENDARY LOCALS

ISBN 978-1-4671-0030-4

Legendary Locals is an imprint of Arcadia Publishing
Charleston, South Carolina

Printed in the United States of America

Library of Congress Control Number: 2012935503

For all general information, please contact Arcadia Publishing:
Telephone 843-853-2070
Fax 843-853-0044
E-mail sales@arcadiapublishing.com
For customer service and orders:
Toll-Free 1-888-313-2665

Visit us on the Internet at www.arcadiapublishing.com

Dedication
Sarah Langsdon: For my sister, Angel, who nurtured my love of books and to my children Cade and Sophie.
Melissa Johnson: To the memory of Lasha Ann Gale, because I said I would, and to my family for everything.

On the Cover: From left to right:
(TOP ROW) Willie Moore, barber (Courtesy of Charles Trentelman; page 116); Ted and Theron Littlefield, World War I veterans (Courtesy of Stewart Library Special Collections; page 62); Ida and Charles Maccarthy, photographer (Courtesy of Stewart Library Special Collections; page 13); Archie Bigelow, hotelier (Courtesy of Stewart Library Special Collections; page 28); Charles Trentelman, reporter (Courtesy Charles Trentelman; page 117).

(MIDDLE ROW) Lyle Richins, ammunitions inspector (Courtesy of Stewart Library Special Collections; page 67); Almira Rich (center), president DUP (Courtesy of Stewart Library Special Collections; page 17); Henry Aldous Dixon, congressman (Courtesy of Stewart Library Special Collections; page 77); Elizabeth and Donnell Stewart, philanthropists (Courtesy of Stewart Library Special Collections; page 21); Robert Joyce, doctor (Courtesy of Stewart Library Special Collections; page 46).

(BOTTOM ROW) Loring "Red" Nichols, musician (Courtesy of Stewart Library Special Collections; page 110); Thomas O. Smith, educator (Courtesy of Stewart Library Special Collections; page 57); Margaret Rostkowski, author (Courtesy of *Ogden Standard Examiner*; page 59); Bernard DeVoto, author (Courtesy of Stewart Library Special Collections; page 118); Rosanne King, entrepreneur (Courtesy of *Ogden Standard Examiner*; see page 115).

CONTENTS

ACKNOWLEDGMENTS

Since the special collections department was created at Weber State University's Stewart Library, the department has sought to document the history of Ogden City and the surrounding counties. The materials housed within the department offer a myriad of stories and information about the community's history in manuscript collections, photographs, and printed sources. This book documents some of those stories through photographs. Unless noted, all of the images we used are part of the collections at Weber State University. In particular, the chamber of commerce, Loni Prout, Richard Roberts, and Glenn Perrins photograph collections were utilized for their wonderful images. We appreciate several people for their help in obtaining photographs: Charles Trentleman, the *Ogden Standard Examiner*, Isaac Goeckeritz, photographer John Shupe, the Mount Benedict Monastery, Larry Leatham, and the Junction City Roller Dolls.

We thank our editors at Arcadia Publishing, Tiffany Fray and Erin Vosgien, who guided and prodded us through the process. We would also like to thank the staff in special collections: Alixe Ogden, Marci Farr, Erika Sisneros-Wood, Brook Lambert, and Matthew Limb, who helped with the photographs and picked up the slack. University librarian Joan Hubbard supported this process from the beginning, and we offer her our appreciation.

Several people have paved the way for this book through their research, writing, and enthusiasm for Ogden's history. First are Richard Roberts and Richard Sadler, who are responsible for the definitive histories on Ogden and Weber County. Next is Milton R. Hunter, who wrote the first history on Ogden under the direction of the Weber Chapter of the Daughters of Utah Pioneers. D. Boyd Crawford's *Ogden in Post Cards* was most helpful. Finally, we express our gratitude to the Mountain West Digital Library and its growing archives of digital Ogden newspapers. Without that resource and the microfilmed copies of the *Standard-Examiner*, and other Ogden newspapers, no chronicler—past or present—can tell Ogden's story.

INTRODUCTION

Ogden's first families began arriving in the Weber Valley in 1848. Previous to their arrival, the valley was a place for fur trappers, mountain men, and Native Americans to gather for trading. By 1850, the young settlement of mostly Mormon pioneers had grown to a population of over 1,000 and Lorin Farr was sent by Mormon leader Brigham Young to become the community's political and spiritual leader. Farr served as mayor of Ogden for 20 years, built the first saw and gristmills in the area, and prepared the community for the advent of the railroad.

The transcontinental railroad was completed in 1869 with the driving of the Golden Spike at Promontory Point. Soon after, Ogden became the "Junction City" between the eastern and western United States. The railroad had a dramatic impact on the community bringing with it a business boom and, more importantly, a wave of new settlers of diverse backgrounds who helped shape the history of Ogden.

As Ogden grew in size and diversity, mounting tensions between Mormons and non-Mormons began to alter the political landscape. LDS church leaders and members were suspicious of outsiders, and frequent boycotts of "gentile" businesses were called for by church leaders. Non-Mormons were fearful of the large political and commercial influence LDS leaders wielded and took issue with the Mormon practice of polygamy. Growing pressure from the federal government through the Edmunds-Tucker Act brought the political situation to head during Ogden's municipal election in 1889. Non-Mormon members of the Liberal Party swept the election, wresting power from the Mormon-led People's Party. It was the first such shift in political power in the Utah territory and Ogden's transition to a more secular government was closely watched, especially as the territory worked towards statehood.

After statehood was granted in 1896, Ogden continued to grow. No longer a rough, frontier town, Ogden became a thriving city. Elaborate homes were built along the east bench, public works were established, and hospitals were built. Women began to organize into clubs and other civic organizations, tackling social issues of the day, including child labor, education, sanitation, and women in the workplace. The Daughters of Utah Pioneers was established in Salt Lake City in 1901 to honor pioneers who settled the area before 1869. The Weber County chapter was organized in 1912 and four years later a special celebration was held to honor Ogden pioneers still living. This event was an annual celebration for many years after.

Resorts and recreation areas were established up Ogden Canyon, while theaters, dance halls, and a grand opera house were built downtown. The downtown area also provided entertainment of an entirely different sort, particularly along Ogden's Twenty-fifth Street. Saloons were numerous, and rail passengers could easily find gambling or prostitution only a short walk up from the train station. Belle London, one of Ogden's most notorious madams, ran several brothels at this time with her husband, Thomas.

Despite this continued growth, Ogden's economy was largely based in agriculture until the 1940s and the outbreak of World War II. Food processing companies, like Amalgamated Sugar and Utah Canning Company shipped locally grown produce around the region and were significant contributors to the economy for decades. But when the United States entered World War II, a large portion of the local labor force was sent overseas, causing a labor shortage that threatened the local economy. To help with this shortage, city and county officials petitioned for a prisoner of war camp in Ogden. From 1943 to 1946, seven thousand Italian and German POWs were held at the Utah General Depot, later named the Defense Depot Ogden. These POWs worked in orchards and farms up and down the Wasatch Front.

The Defense Depot was only one of several military installations in the area that helped shift the economy into a more industrial one. Ogden and its surrounding communities were chosen as sites for the Ogden Arsenal, Hill Field (later Hill Air Force Base), and the Clearfield Naval Supply Depot. A secure location and easy access to rail lines were both reasons why these sites were chosen. Not only were these military installations major employers, they were also built on condemned farmland, further drawing the economy away from agriculture. While the Arsenal was eventually closed, the Defense Depot and Clearfield Depot both continue to operate as business complexes. Hill Air Force Base also continues in operation, and all are a major part of the area's economy today.

Prostitution and gambling had continued to thrive in Ogden through the 1940s, especially as millions of soldiers stopped in Ogden while on their way overseas. But in the 1950s, growing pressure was put on city leaders to stamp out these vices. Police conducted frequent raids on brothels and illegal gambling halls, not quite driving them out of the city but at least driving them underground enough to satisfy Ogden's citizens.

After the Korean War, military spending decreased around the country, and in Ogden it was no different. About the same time passenger rail travel also decreased as air and car travel became more popular alternatives. As the hustle and bustle in Ogden's Union Station quieted down, Ogden experienced a dramatic economic lull that lasted into the 1980s. City leaders and community members worked together, however, to refurbish old business fronts and bring new businesses into the area. An Internal Revenue Service branch was established in 1956 and several manufacturing firms built factories in the 1970s. The Ogden City Mall opened in 1980 and was a major commercial center for two decades.

Today, Ogden continues its constant evolution. While freight continues to be transported through Ogden's rail yards, the Union Station now operates as a museum and gallery. Twenty-fifth Street is a thriving historic area with small businesses and restaurants, and the Ogden City Mall was torn down in 2002 to make way for the Ogden Junction, a 20-acre complex with restaurants, condominiums, a movie theater, and other entertainment areas. Ogden also continues its cultural evolution with growing Hispanic and Latino populations. From a mountain man rendezvous site to a frontier settlement to a booming city, Ogden's history has been one of constant change, but the future is bright for this community thanks in large part to its legendary locals.

CHAPTER ONE

A Family Venture

Ogden's Pioneer Portraits

Before the completion of the transcontinental railroad in 1869, Ogden was a rough frontier town surrounded by desert. Despite these harsh conditions, early pioneers like Ambrose and Minerva Shaw began their families in the Ogden Valley and laid the foundation for a thriving community that would rival many of the largest Western cities. The generations that came after would continue to build upon their legacy.

As Ogden grew and developed, several families came into prominence; Wheelwright, Scowcroft, Becker, Nye were all names that became synonymous with success and wealth. Their homes began to dot the eastern edges of Ogden while their businesses expanded throughout the region.

Other families, while less wealthy and prominent, still provided great service to the community and shaped its history. Charles Maccarthy worked as a railroad clerk but was also an avid sportsman, setting records in races and exploring Ogden Canyon. Almira Rich, the wife of Dr. Edward I. Rich, faithfully kept a diary for decades. While much of her account is full of her daily housekeeping tasks, she also writes about her involvement within the community, painting a picture of Ogden's women in service to each other.

Much of Ogden's history was also shaped by the generations of these families building upon one another. Gilbert and Adeline Belnap were some of the earliest settlers in Ogden, where generations of their family have continued to live. Their son, Hyrum, worked with Gilbert as a sheriff in Weber County, and Hyrum's daughter, Marion, was a school teacher in Ogden for many years. Building on the foundation provided by his parents, Ambrose A. Shaw further developed the family's dairy farm as well as branching out into other businesses. Elizabeth Stewart, his daughter, culminated the family's work and became one of Ogden's greatest philanthropists.

Ogden's early pioneers paved much of Ogden's history with their hard work and fortitude, carving their existence from a harsh desert. Their children and grandchildren reaped many of the benefits of their hard work, but these later generations also continued the pioneering spirit, shaping a legacy for today's Ogdenites.

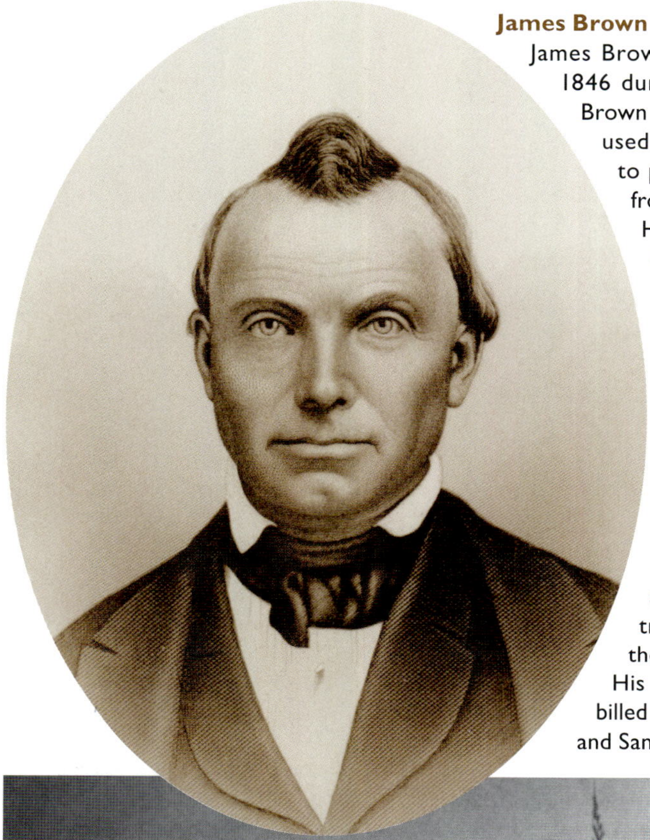

James Brown

James Brown joined the Mormon Battalion in 1846 during the war with Mexico. In 1847, Brown returned to Utah from California. He used funds from the federal government to purchase cabins, lands, and livestock from Miles Goodyear in Weber County. He named the settlement Brownsville before it was changed to Ogden. He died in 1863 after getting his arm caught in a molasses mill.

John Broom

John Broom arrived in Ogden in 1851 from England and was involved in a variety of businesses. He sold a wagonload of molasses and dairy supplies to a detachment of US troops and then took the remains of the wagon train to trade with John Browning for the lot, which became the Broom Hotel. His lavish hotel opened in 1883 and was billed as the grandest hotel between Denver and San Francisco.

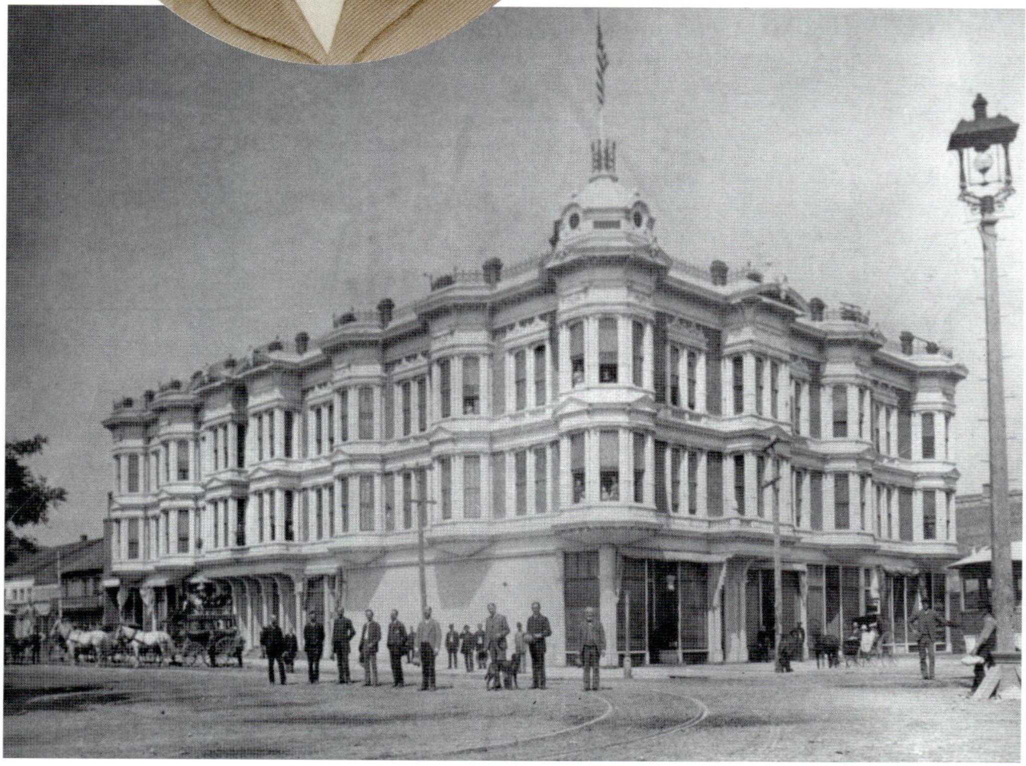

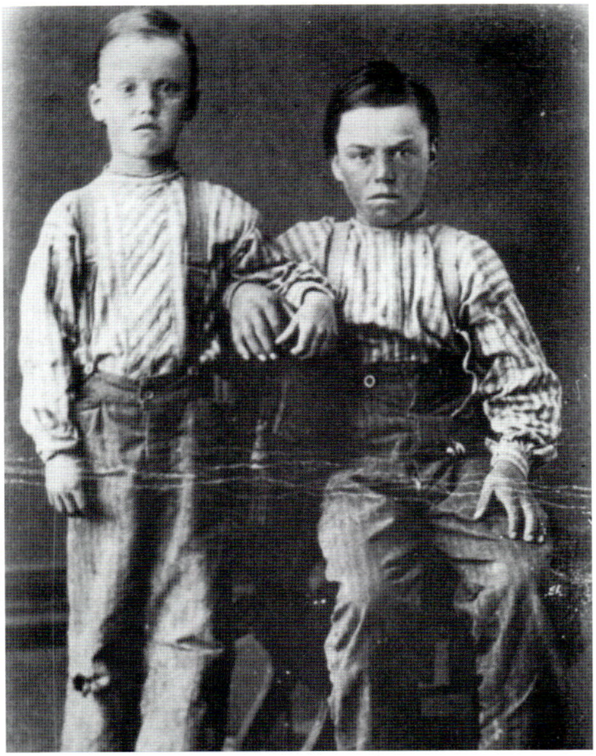

Wheelwright Brothers

Solomon and Thomas Wheelwright were born in the 1860s to Matthew and Catherine Wheelwright. In 1896, the Wheelwright brothers opened a mercantile shop on Twenty-fourth Street and Washington, where they sold all manner of household items. In 1906, the company expanded to a construction company with the mercantile shop dissolving in 1910. The company ventured into the lumber business in 1912. The lumber used for the construction projects was delivered by horse and wagon. The company advertised about the brothers' connections to Ogden and that they worked united for the building up of Ogden. Pictured here are the brothers at a very young age (left) and the Wheelwright Brothers store located at 2476 Washington Avenue in 1900 (below).

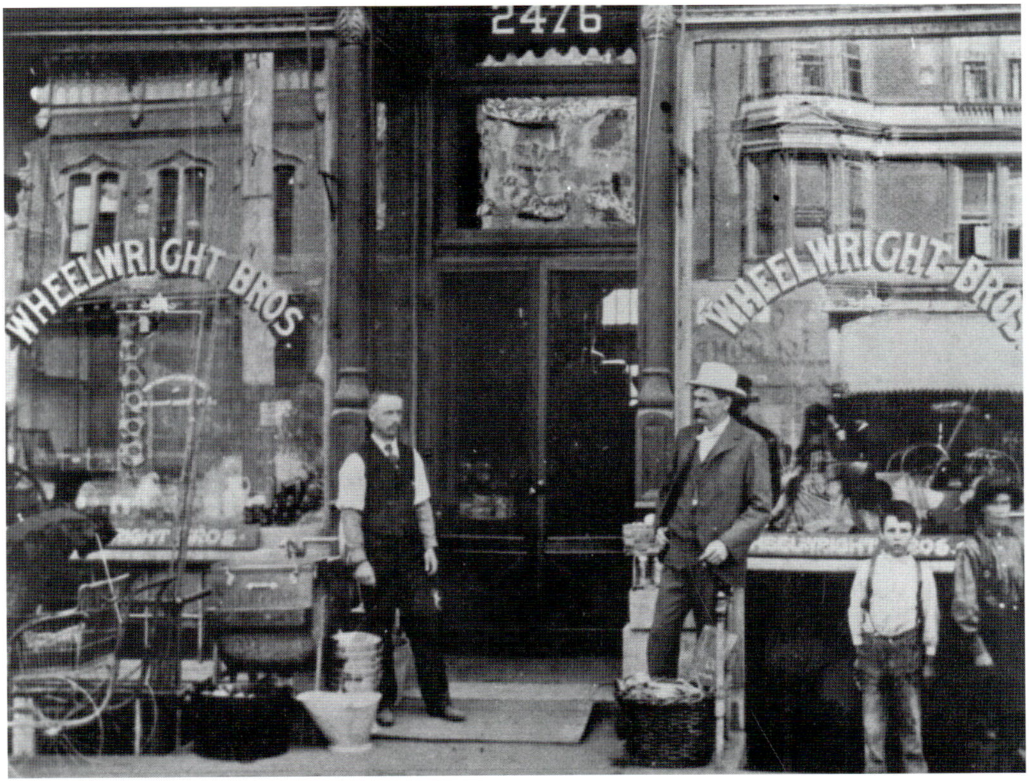

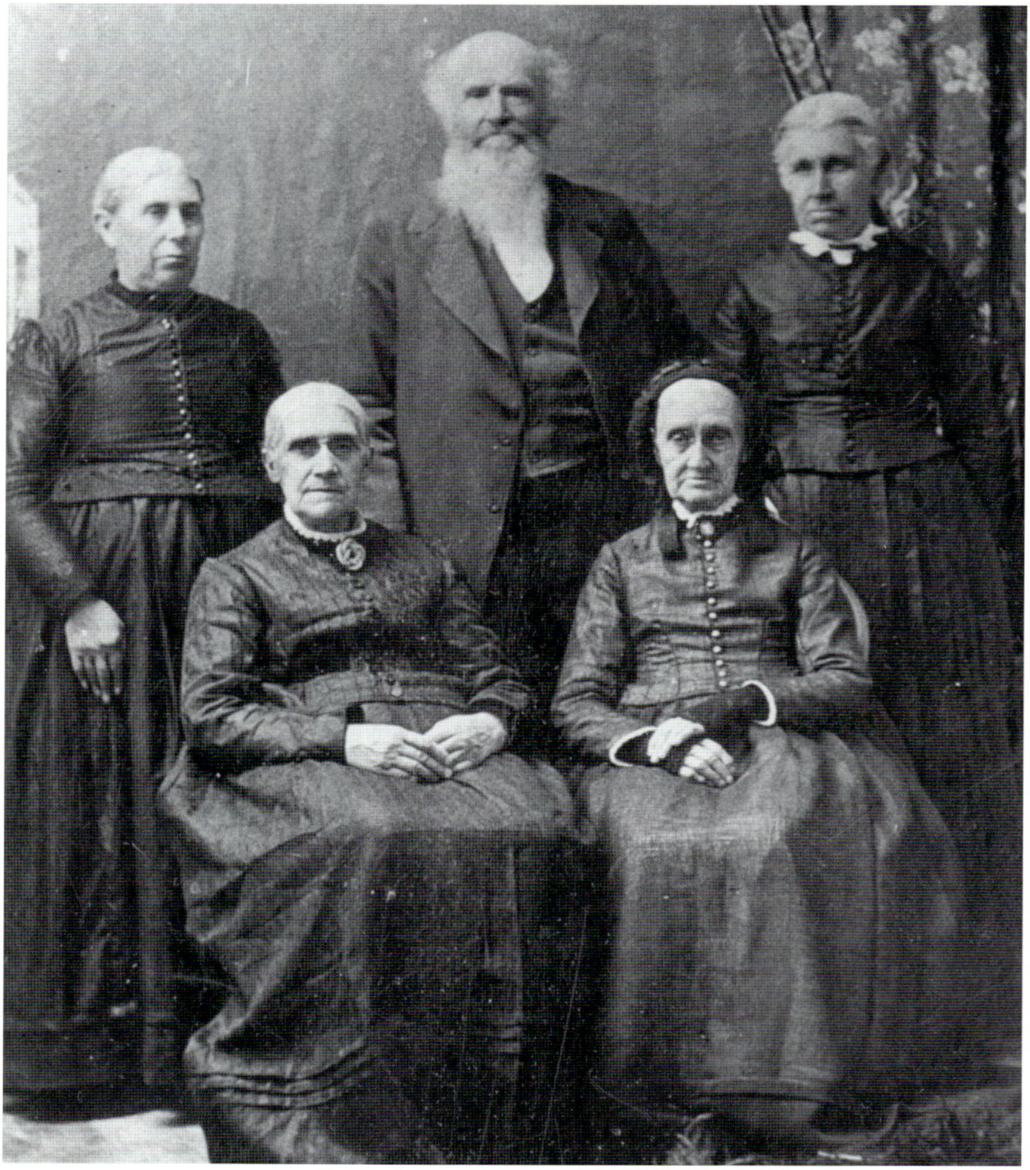

Belnap Family

Gilbert (back row, center) and Adeline Belnap (back row, left) were married in Nauvoo, Illinois, in 1845. After traveling across the plains with other Mormon pioneers, they arrived in the Salt Lake Valley in September 1850. Two weeks later, LDS church leader Brigham Young sent the small family to settle the Ogden Valley. Their first home was a dugout near present-day Thirtieth Street and Madison Avenue. Gilbert was a longtime law enforcement officer, serving as city marshal and as Weber County sheriff. His most famous arrest was that of Joseph Nay and E.K. Fisher, who robbed a Denver and Rio Grande train in September 1889. Gilbert captured the two in an Ogden pool hall. In 1852, Gilbert polygamously married Henrietta McBride, (back row, right) Adeline's first cousin. Henrietta was a school teacher and Adeline worked as a midwife. Both women had large families: Adeline had 13 children and Henrietta had five children. Gilbert and Henrietta both died in 1899, while Adeline lived until 1919. Also pictured here are Adeline's mother and sister, Martha and Rizpah.

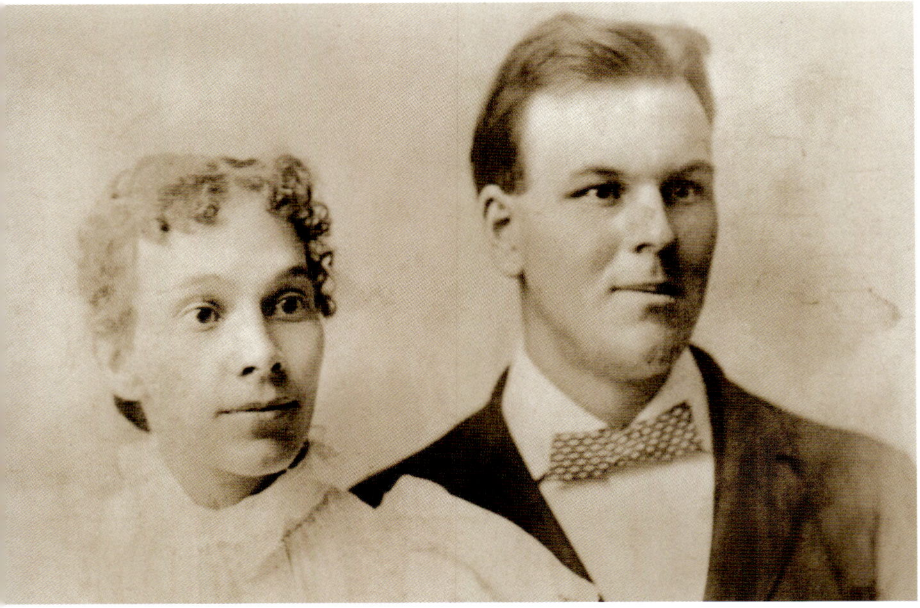

Charles and Mary Agnes Marriott

Charles and Mary Agnes Marriott were married in Ogden in 1894. Charles worked for the Ogden City Schools as a building custodian throughout his career. Mary was the mother of seven children and an active member of the Daughters of Utah Pioneers in Weber County. Charles passed away in 1945 and Mary lived until 1957.

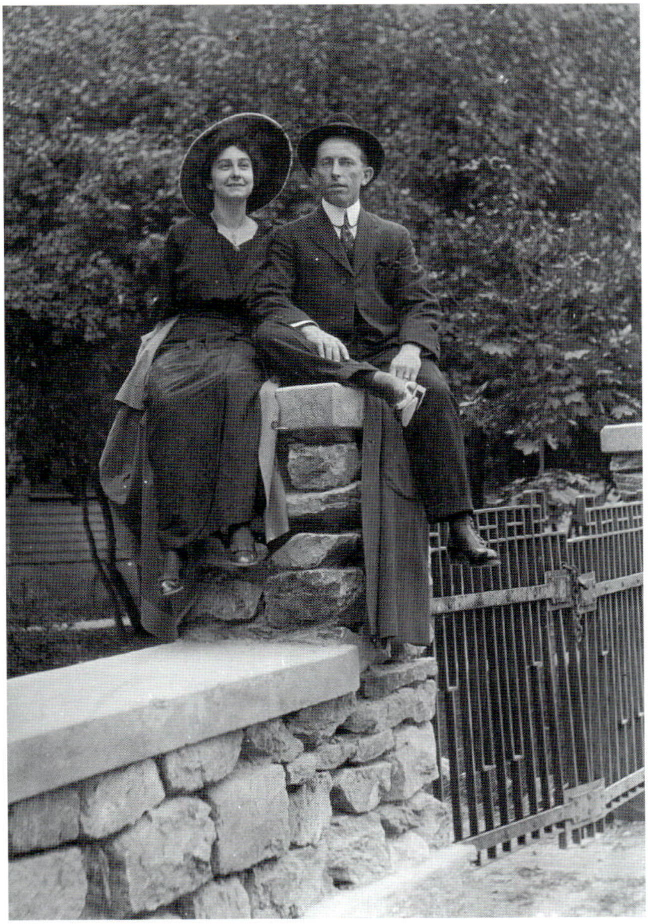

Charles and Ida Maccarthy

Charles Maccarthy was an amateur photographer and avid outdoorsman. One of his favorite activities was bicycle racing at the Ogden track where he set several records. He also loved exploring Ogden Canyon in the company of his wife, Ida, and other friends and family. Ida passed away in 1912 after giving birth to their twin sons. Charles later married Corly Coombs and worked as a railroad clerk until his retirement in 1951.

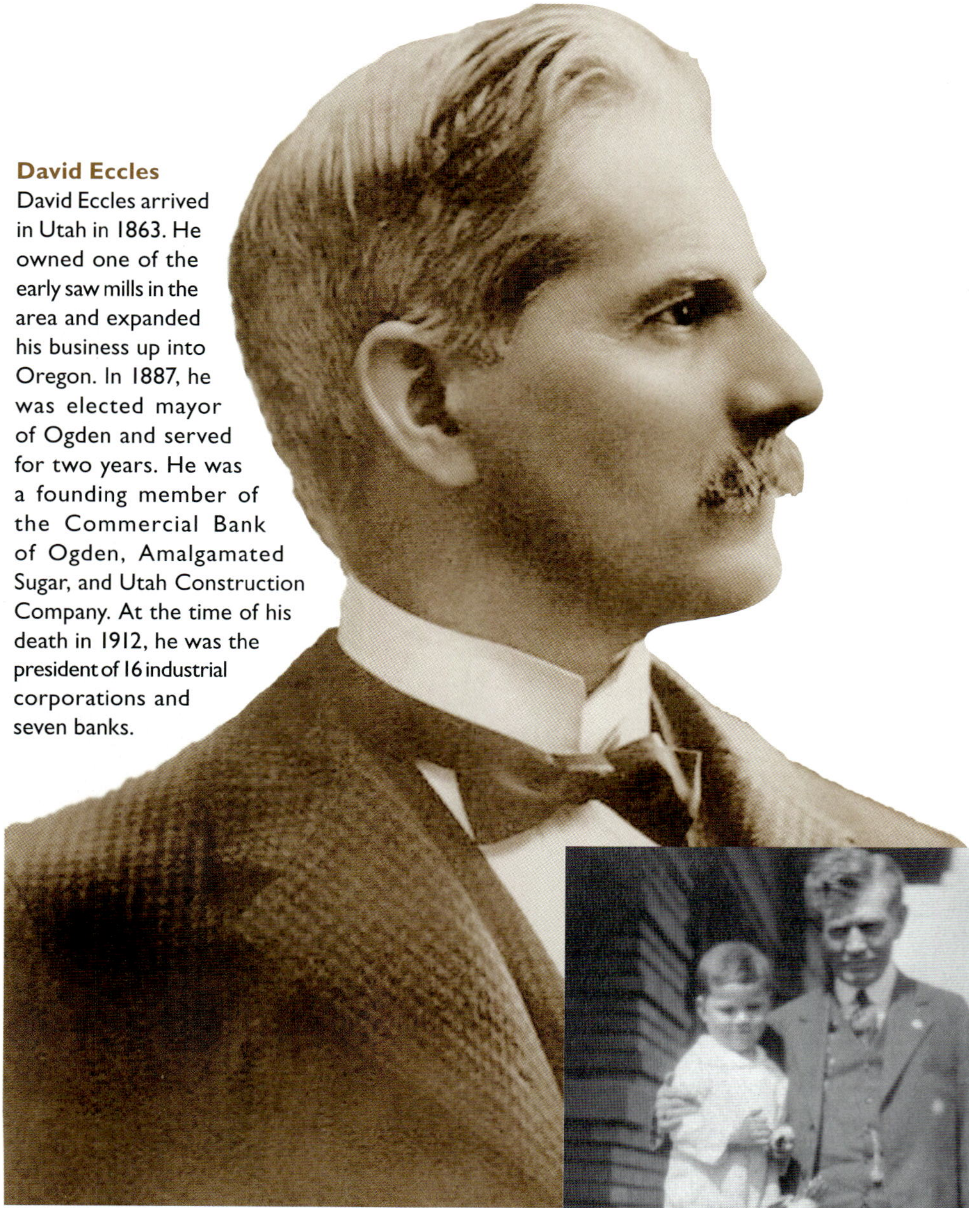

David Eccles

David Eccles arrived in Utah in 1863. He owned one of the early saw mills in the area and expanded his business up into Oregon. In 1887, he was elected mayor of Ogden and served for two years. He was a founding member of the Commercial Bank of Ogden, Amalgamated Sugar, and Utah Construction Company. At the time of his death in 1912, he was the president of 16 industrial corporations and seven banks.

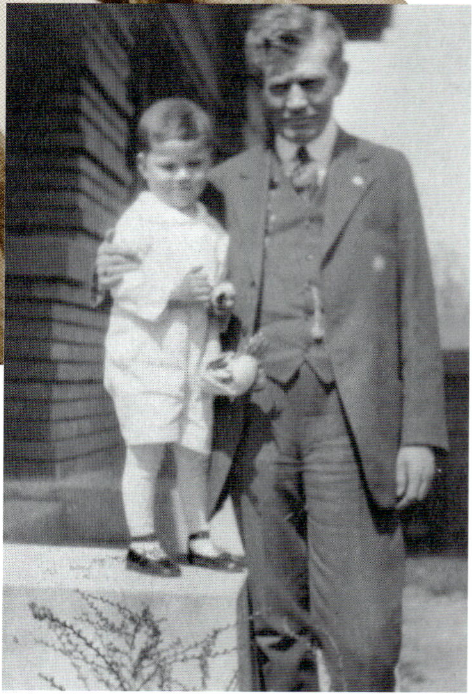

E.O. Wattis and Edmund Littlefield

Born in 1855 in Uintah, Edmund Orson Wattis went on to become a successful businessman. In 1900, he was one of the founding members of Utah Construction Company (UCC) with his brothers, Thomas Dee and David Eccles. He was the chairman of Six Companies as they built the Hoover Dam, but died in February 1934, before the dam was completed. He is pictured here with his grandson Edmund Littlefield, who later became head of UCC.

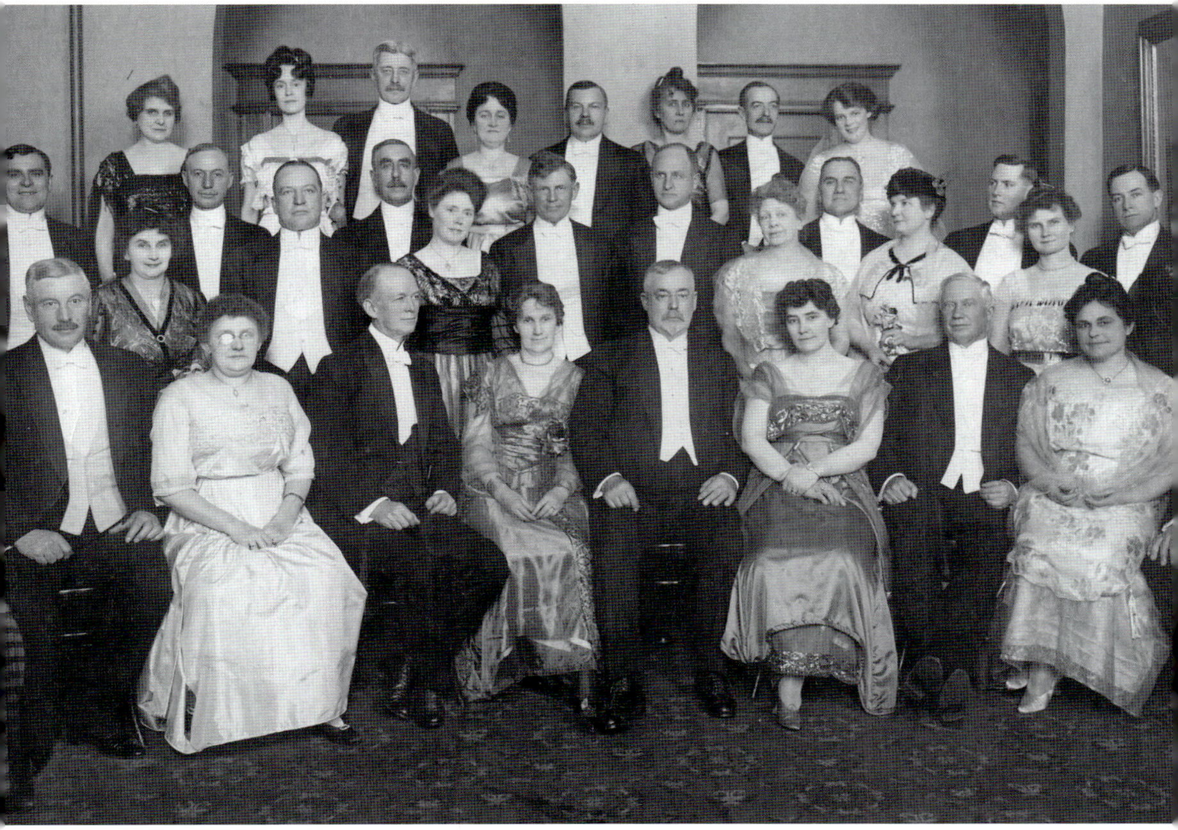

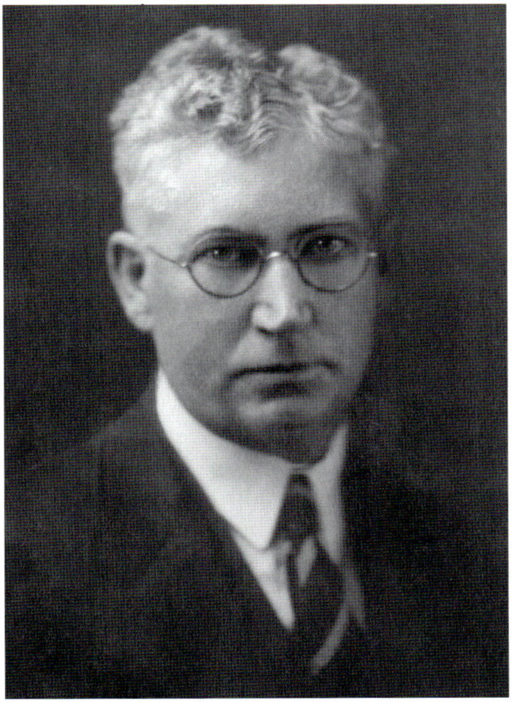

William H. Wattis

William H. Wattis was the fourth child born to Edmund and Mary Jane Wattis. He worked along with his brothers Edmund O. and Warren for their uncle's construction company building railroad lines. In 1900, the Wattis Brothers founded Utah Construction Company. W.H. served as president of the company until his death in 1931. Here he is pictured (seated, second from right) at a dinner for former governor William Spry in January 1917.

Warren L. Wattis

Warren L. Wattis was the third Wattis brother responsible for the founding of Utah Construction Company. His interests went beyond his secretary/treasurer position at UCC. He was a board member for the Red Cross and president of the Ogden Chamber of Commerce from 1919 to 1920. When he was younger, he won a $1,000 prize for a short story, and later worked as a newspaper reporter in his 20s. He died in 1928.

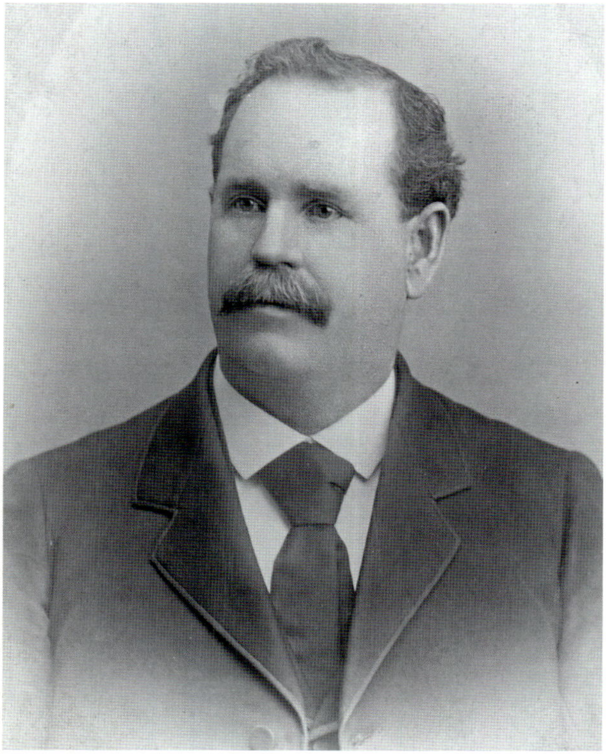

Thomas D. Dee

Born in Wales in 1844, Thomas D. Dee came to Ogden in 1860. He was very active in politics, serving as tax assessor, councilman, and judge. He owned a number of businesses, including Ogden Sugar Company, Ogden Savings Bank, and Utah Construction Company. He was also president of the Ogden City Board of Education. He died in 1905 of pneumonia after falling into the Ogden River while searching for a potential dam site.

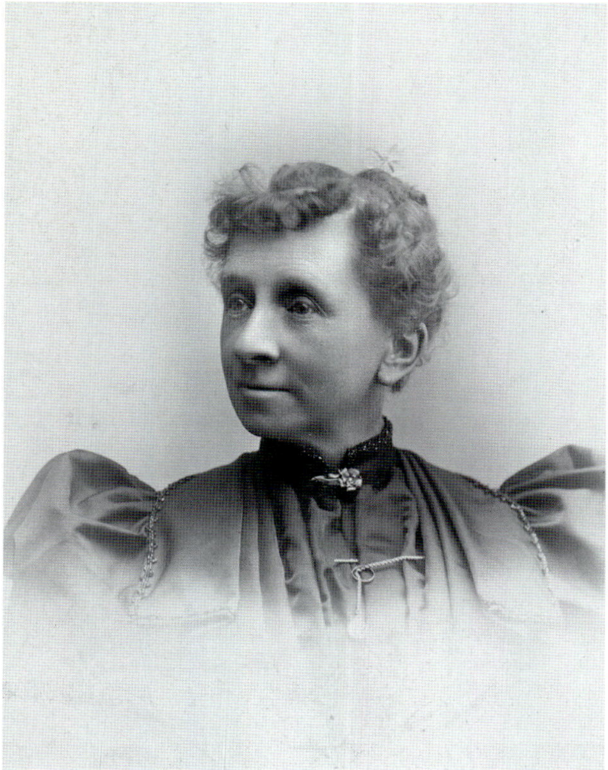

Annie Taylor Dee

Annie Taylor Dee came across the plains to Utah in 1860. By 1871, she had married Thomas Dee and went on to have seven children. After the death of her husband and oldest son Reese, she opened the Thomas D. Dee Memorial Hospital in 1910. She also owned the Berthana Ballroom with Bertha Eccles. She was a founding member of the Child Culture Club, Martha Society, and Daughters of Utah Pioneers.

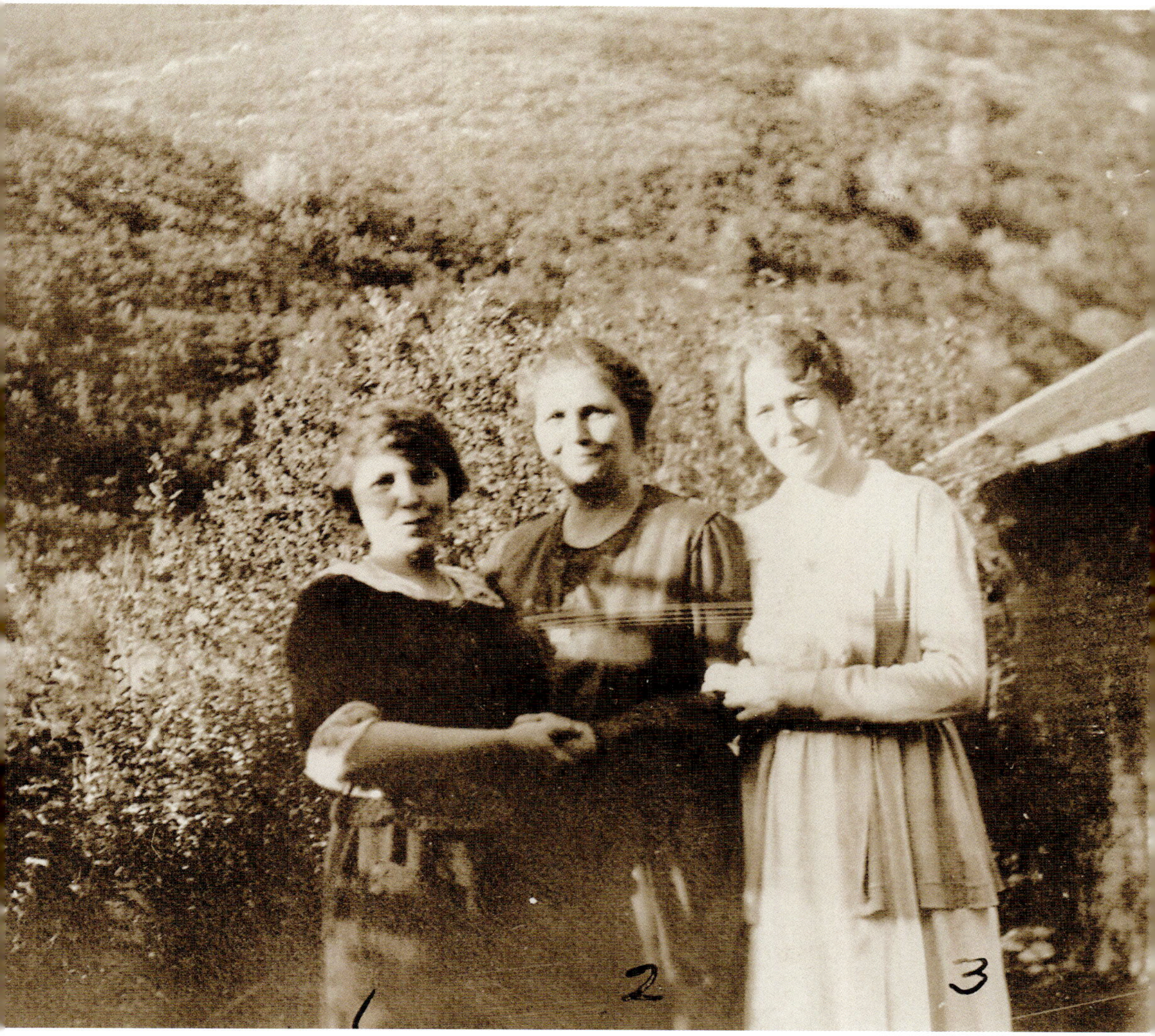

Almira Rich
Almira Cozzens Rich was born in 1871 in Montpelier, Idaho. A talented singer, she studied and taught music in Logan, Utah. In 1894, she married Edward Rich and they settled in Ogden where he opened his medical practice. Edward and Almira were the parents of seven children. They loved traveling and the outdoors, often visiting extended family near Bear Lake. Almira was heavily involved in the local community, organizing Liberty Bond drives during World War I, serving on the Weber County Red Cross executive board, and serving as vice chairman of the Utah Republican Committee. In 1928, she ran for the state legislature, but lost. Almira is shown here (center) at a social for the Daughters of Utah Pioneers, an organization of which she was president for two years.

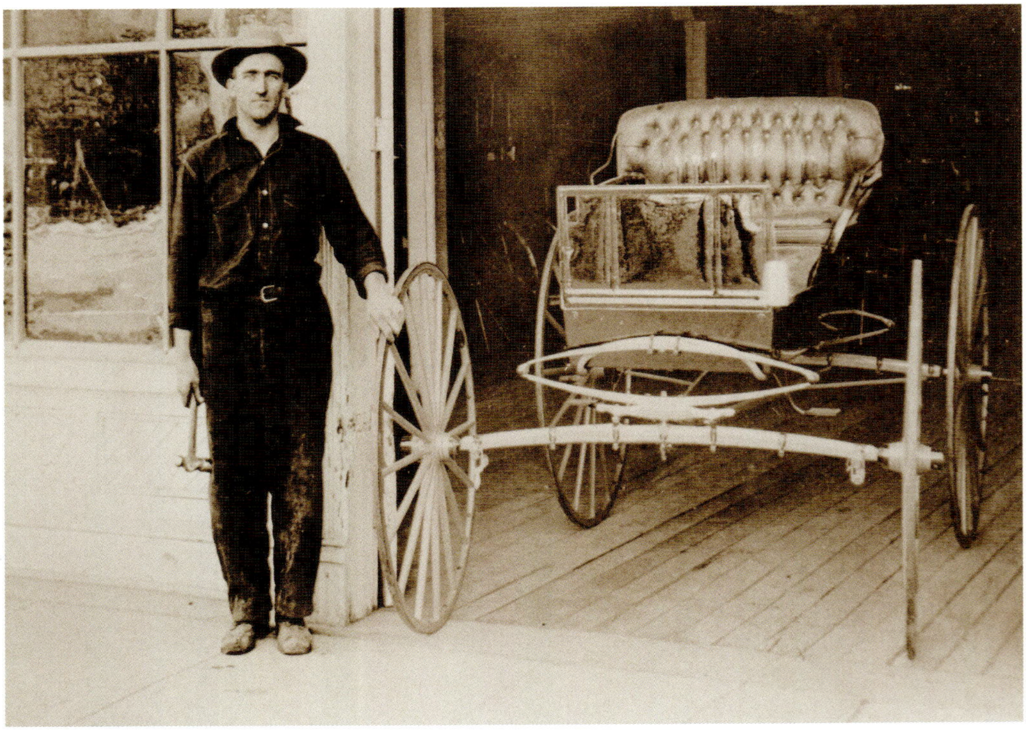

Asael Ipson
Asael Ipson, shown here in front of his carriage shop, married Lucy Knight in 1913. He owned his carriage shop until the early 1910s then served in the Navy during World War I. Asael and Lucy had two children, Harold and Beth, and were married for almost 70 years, until Asael's death in 1981. Lucy died in 1989.

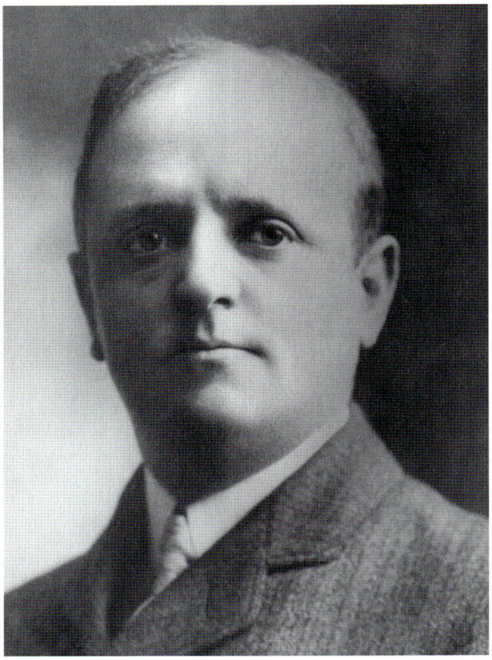

Joseph Scowcroft
Joseph Scowcroft was born in 1863. He began working with his father in the family store making candy and doing the baking. The family store grew from a grocery store to a wholesale warehouse. When his father died, Joseph became president of Scowcroft and Sons. He also had roles in banking, transportation, and sugar refining. By his death in 1931, he had been director of nine companies.

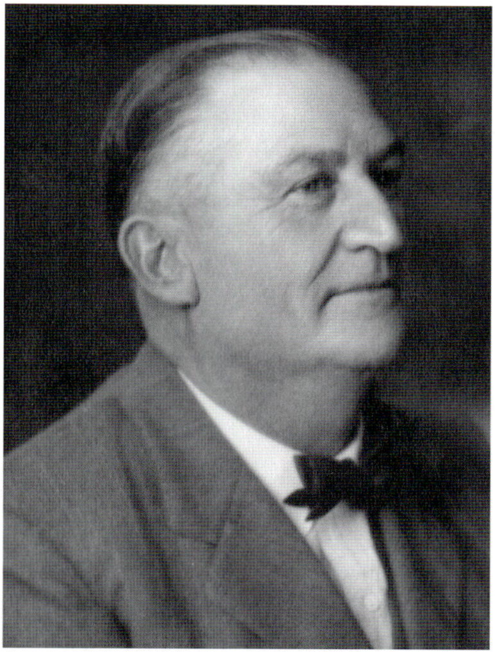

Albert E. Becker

Albert E. Becker was born in 1871 and had moved to Ogden by 1893 to serve as the vice president of the Becker Brewing Company. Becker was active in the Ogden Chamber of Commerce and served as director of Wasatch Insurance and the Rotary Club. In 1929, he ran for the Utah House of Representatives. After the death of his brother Gus Becker, Albert became the president of Becker Brewing Company.

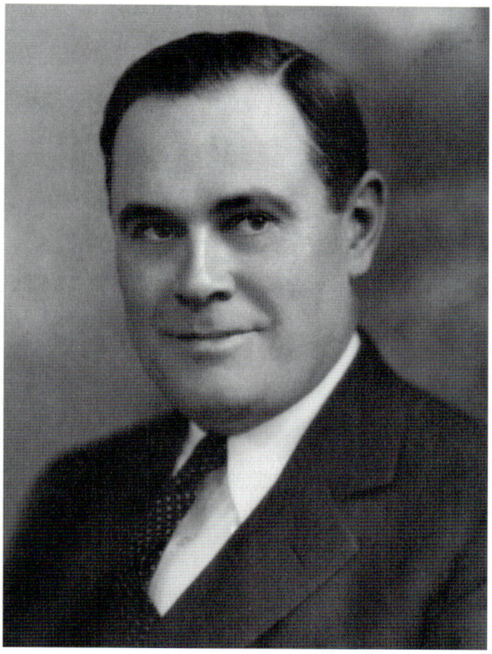

Fred M. Nye

Fred M. Nye arrived in Ogden in 1891 and opened a clothing store in 1898. He was active throughout Ogden, serving as president of the Ogden Retail Merchants Credit Bureau and chamber of commerce. He was on the Ogden City Board of Education and took a leading role in the construction of Ogden High School. His interests also extended into sports; he was the president of the Pioneer Baseball League from 1925 to 1928.

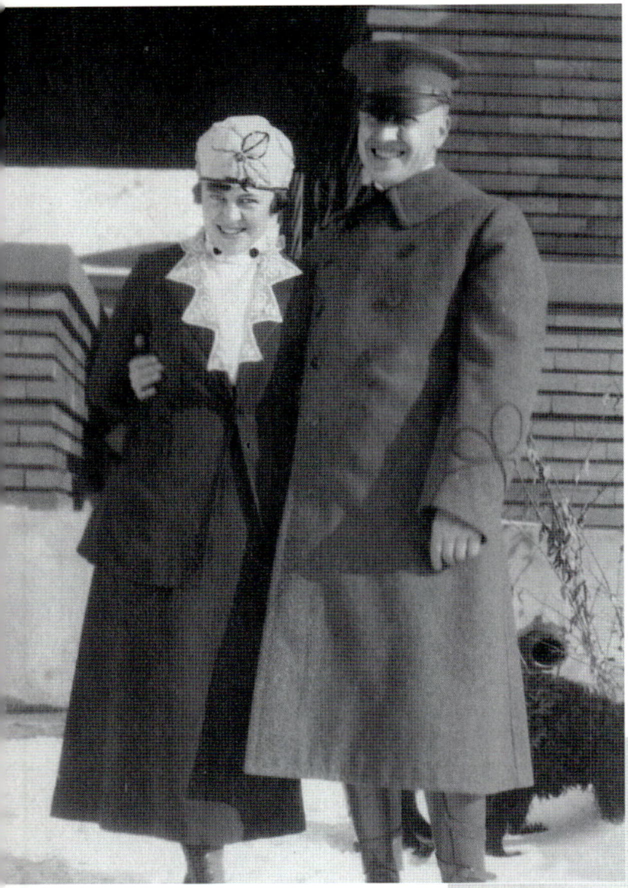

Ezekiel and Edna Dumke
Ezekiel Dumke came to Ogden in 1911 to practice medicine with Dr. Ezra Rich. By 1917, he had opened his own practice and married Edna Wattis. He served as the surgeon for the Utah Idaho Railroad, Bamberger Railroad, and the Utah Power and Light Company. He was very generous and often did not charge patients if he knew they could not afford medical care, and he helped young men attend medical school.

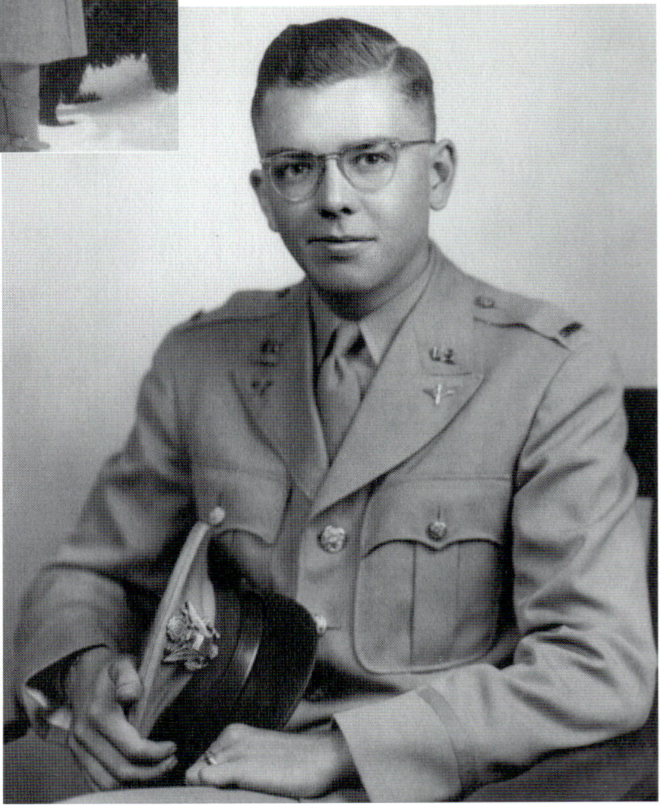

Thomas D. Dee II
Thomas D. Dee II was the son of Lawrence and Janet Dee. During World War II, he served in the Army Air Corps and was severely wounded in a plane crash in the Egyptian Desert in 1944. When he returned home, he was in management at the Utah Canning Company, vice president of the Ogden branch of First Security Bank, and a director of Utah International. He passed away in 2009.

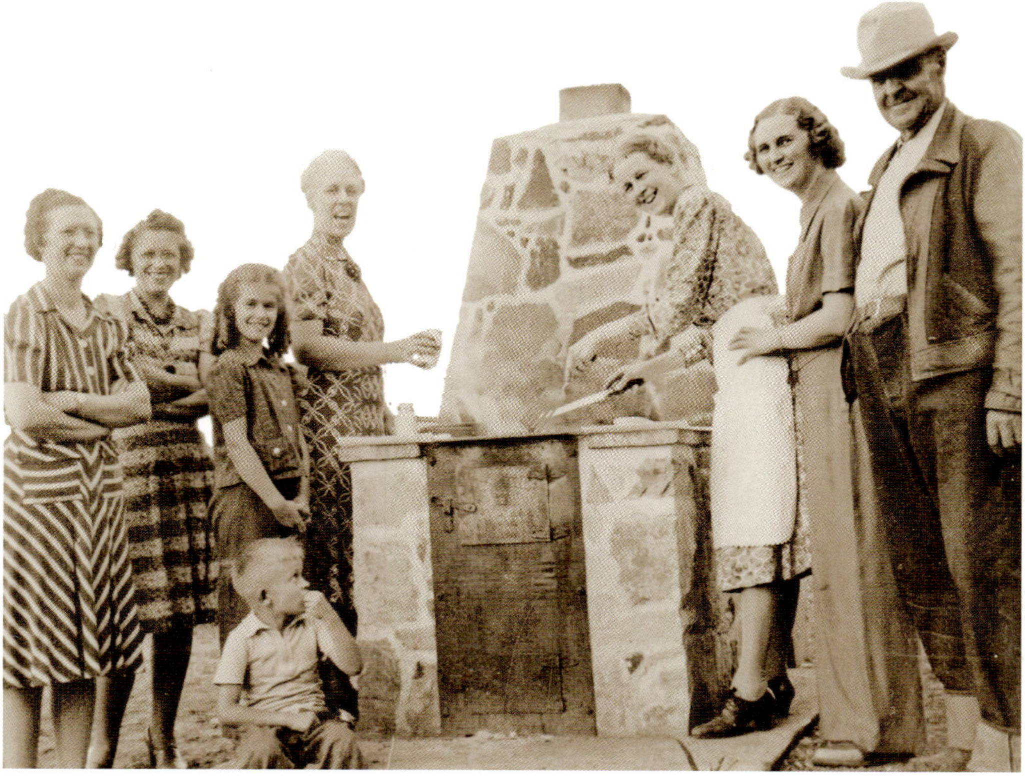

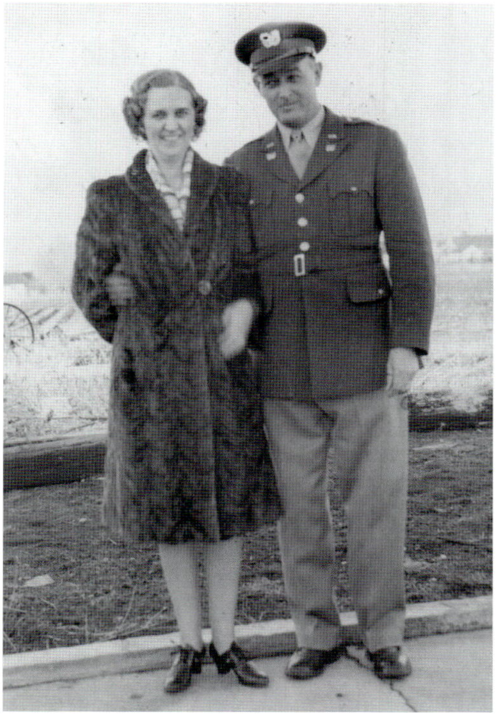

Shaw Family

The Shaw family, led by Minerva and Ambrose, were early pioneers in Utah. They settled in the Ogden Valley and began raising cattle. Their son, Ambrose A. Shaw, married Mary Elizabeth Dee, and while he worked in other industries, he continued to raise cattle in Eden. The Shaw Canyon home was also a gathering place for family and friends where they would barbecue, ride horses, and play games together.

Donnell and Elizabeth Stewart

Donnell and Elizabeth Stewart were married in 1943, and were known for their generous support of the community; together they donated millions of dollars to Weber County institutions. Elizabeth often volunteered at the hospital and loved to cheer on Weber State's athletic teams, even when confined to a wheelchair. For his service, Donnell was awarded the Alumni Distinguished Service Award from Weber State. He passed away in March 1996 and Elizabeth passed away later that year.

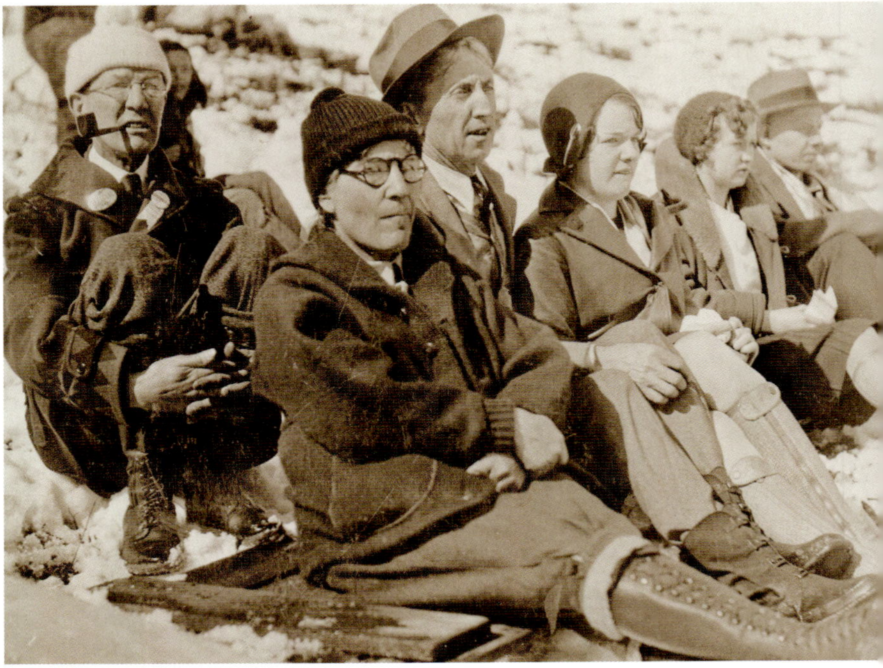

Shearman/Paradise

Wilhelmine Kiesel Shearman (front row, far left) was the only daughter of Fred J. Kiesel. As a young woman she traveled extensively around the world, something she continued to enjoy even after her marriage to Harry Shearman (back, far left) in 1918. The couple also enjoyed the outdoors—they are shown here watching ski jumping. They greatly supported the Boy Scouts of America, donating land for Camp Kiesel, which is still in use today. Wherever Wilhelmine traveled, her constant companion was Keitaru "Paradise" Kikuraku (below). Paradise "jumped ship" in Seattle during the Russian-Japanese war and soon after came to Ogden where he worked for the Kiesel and Shearman families until Wilhelmine's death in 1961. Wilhelmine provided for Paradise in her will, and having no family, he stayed in Ogden until his death in 1968.

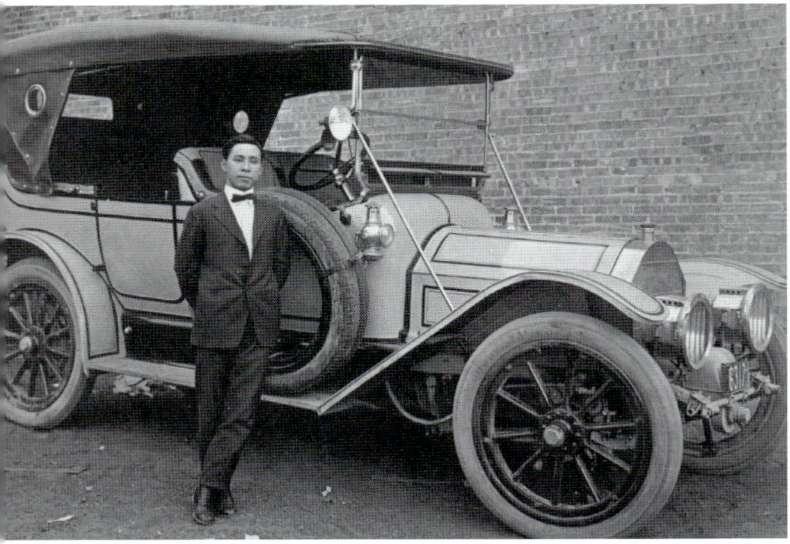

CHAPTER TWO

Business Booms

Ogden's Industries

Like any community, Ogden's business history has been one of booms and busts. But these periods of growth and decline have perhaps been more dramatic than in other places because of the prominent role that the railroad played in shaping Ogden's history. When business boomed just after 1869, Ogden was a thriving freight and shipping hub, and wholesalers opened stores to serve the entire Western region. In the downtown area, dozens of saloons were supplied by local businesses like the Becker Brewing Company and the George H. Tribe & Company, wholesalers of wine, liquor, and cigars.

Restaurants, bakeries, candy makers, and ice cream shops also opened downtown, while the Hermitage Resort and The Oaks opened in Ogden Canyon. Some businesses, like the J.G. Read Company and Hinckley Dodge, started as small shops, but grew into large businesses that shaped Ogden for generations. Local architects Leslie Hodgson and Eber Piers left their mark on Ogden, building some of its most famous landmarks and homes.

Fortunes were made and lost in Ogden. David Eccles started a business empire that his sons, George, Willard, and Marriner further developed. Today, the Eccles family focuses mainly on philanthropy, supporting education, and the arts. Archie Bigelow was another of Ogden's most successful businessmen. He built the Bigelow hotel and amassed a large fortune, but when the Depression hit, his entire fortune was wiped out.

After the Depression, Ogden recovered economically through military contracts—contracts that were obtained because of the nearby railroad lines. In this new economy, new leaders arose, like Ezra Fjeldstead, who led the Ogden Chamber of Commerce and helped form the Weber Basin Conservancy District, and John Lindquist, who worked to improve the economy through the Weber Economic Development Corporation and the Ogden Industrial Development Corporation.

As passenger rail service declined, Ogden's economy suffered, but today city leaders are working with business leaders to create jobs and bring businesses back into Ogden. The downtown area is beginning to thrive again with a number of small businesses, shops, and restaurants. Through booms and busts, Ogden has continually reinvented and revived itself, and its businessmen and women have left an indelible mark on the community.

John S. Lewis

John S. Lewis established the first jewelry store in Ogden in January 1879. Lewis and his jewelers made jewelry from gold nuggets that were melted down and formed into watch chains, buckles, rings and buttons. Lewis's sons Hyrum and John Jr. joined the firm in 1882. The store served Ogden for 63 years until it was sold to the Anderson Jewelry Company in 1937. In this photograph, father and son stand outside the store at 2463 Washington Boulevard.

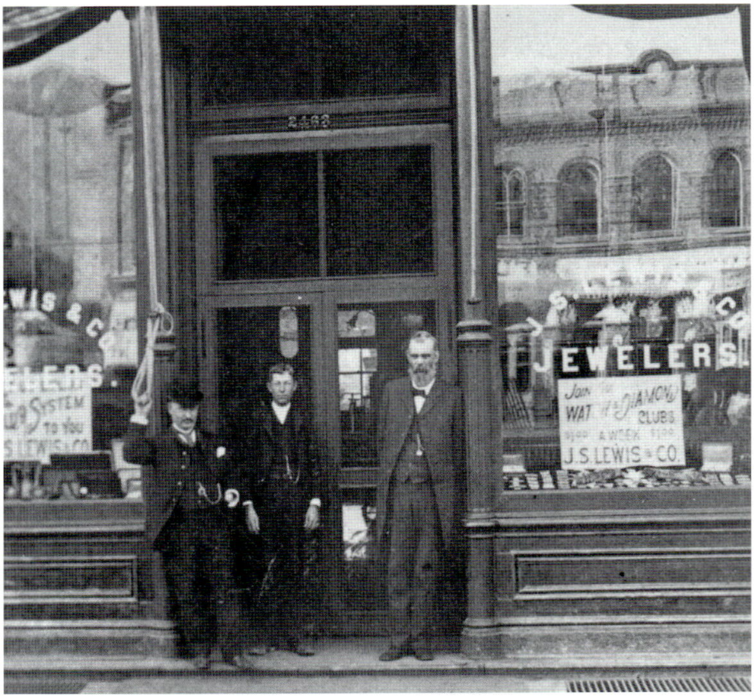

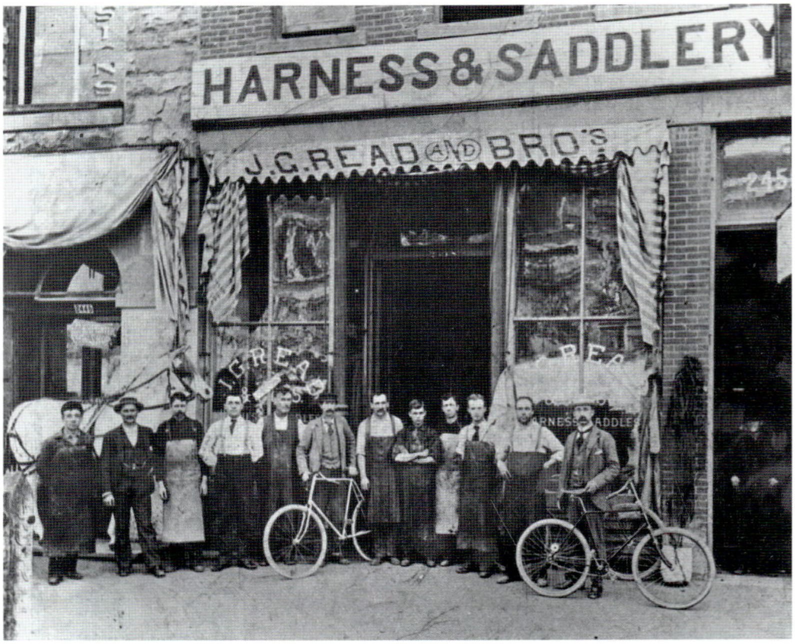

J.G. Read and Brothers

The J.G. Read and Brothers saddle shop was founded in 1876 by Josiah, William, and Oscar Read. Their original shop, shown here, stood on Washington Boulevard between Twenty-fourth and Twenty-fifth Streets. Here, they sold saddles, harnesses, and other leather products. In 1905, a new store was built on the corner of Kiesel Avenue and Twenty-fourth Street. This store, where they also sold automotive tires, stood until the 1970s.

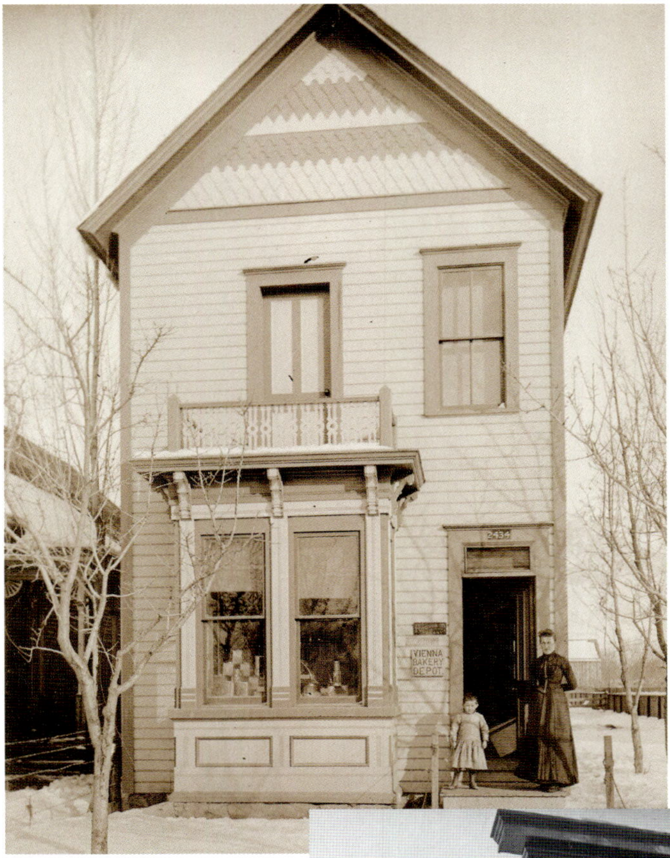

Vienna Bakery Depot
The Vienna Bakery was one of Ogden's earliest businesses. J.W. Keeney owned the bakery with various partners, and eventually opened a branch in Five Points (near present-day Second Street). The new branch, possibly shown here, was managed by Selma Olson. Keeney also operated the Keeney House Hotel, and later turned the Vienna Bakery into a restaurant.

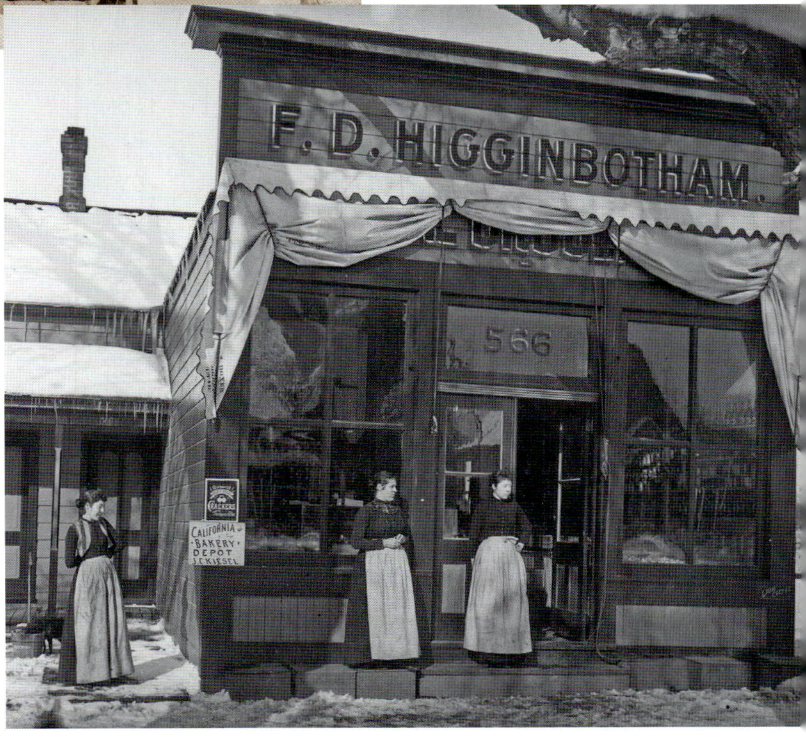

California Bakery Depot
Julius C. Kiesel came to Ogden from Germany in the 1870s, where his brother Fred Kiesel had also settled. Julius quickly opened a bakery and became known as a first-class baker. His wedding cakes were very popular and many commented on the artistry of his creations. Kiesel's baked goods were also sold in local grocery stores, as shown in this photograph of F.D. Higginbotham's grocery store and Kiesel's California Bakery Depot.

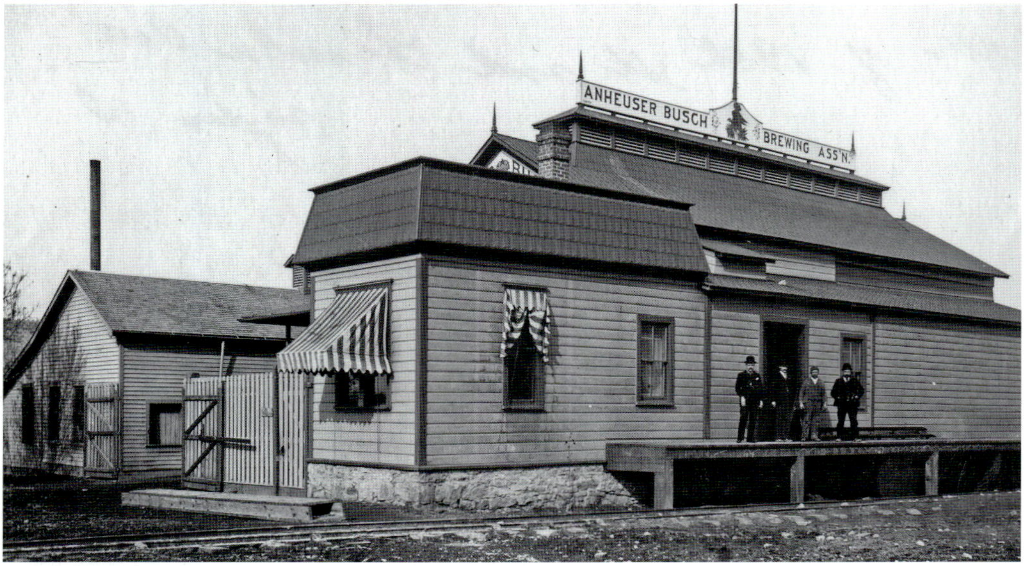

Anheuser-Busch Brewery

Anheuser-Busch's bottling plant stood on the corner of Nineteenth Street and Lincoln Avenue and did steady business bottling beer that was shipped directly from St. Louis. In 1891, plans were announced to build a brewery in Ogden that would serve the western United States. These plans never came to fruition, but under the direction of plant manager G.A. Elbring, bottling operations continued to grow steadily.

George. H. Tribe and Company

George Henry Tribe traveled across the plains to Utah in 1855, arriving in Salt Lake City the next year. Later he settled in Ogden, opening his own wholesale wine, liquor, and cigar store in 1869. Some of his employees are shown here in 1911. Tribe was also involved in several other businesses, including the First National Bank where he was a vice president. He died in 1914 after a four-year battle with cancer.

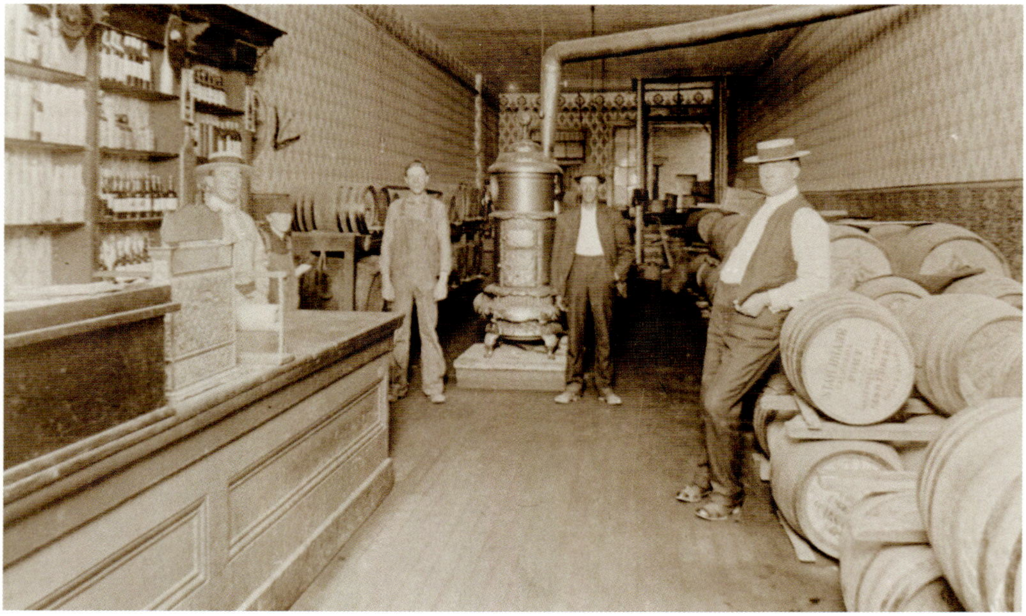

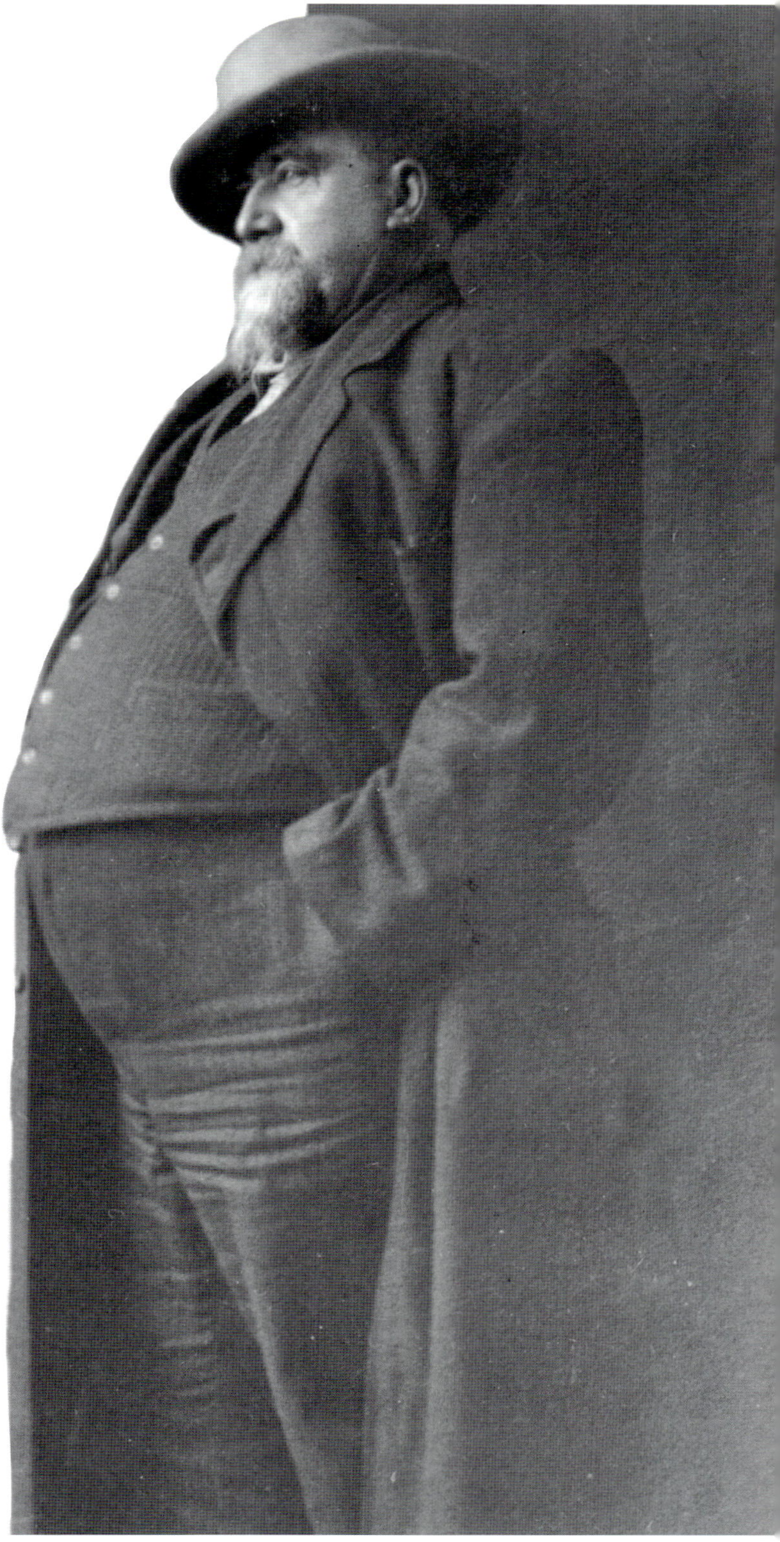

William Gibson Wilson
William G. Wilson came to Utah in 1869 as an 18-year-old immigrant from Scotland. He settled in Ogden and took over the Hermitage Camp, located halfway between Ogden and Huntsville. Known affectionately as Uncle Billy, he turned the camp into a first-class hotel and resort with boating, swimming, picnic areas, and a merry-go-round to amuse guests. The Hermitage also hosted summer concerts and held dances every night except Sunday. Uncle Billy served as county commissioner for nearly a decade and also had a thriving lumber business. He died in 1918, a victim of the influenza epidemic, and was greatly mourned by his family and the community. The Hermitage remained in business until 1939 when it burned down.

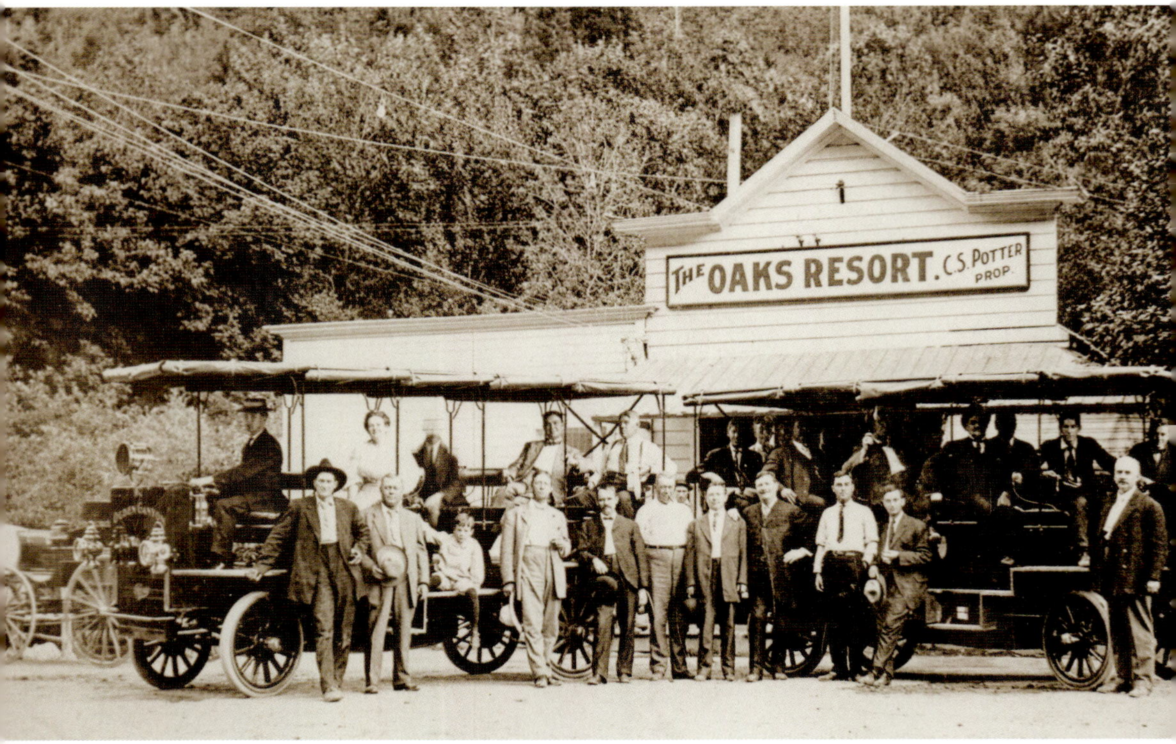

The Oaks Resort
Clifford S. Potter operated the Oaks Resort with his brother, Lewis, for several years. The resort was known for its immaculate camping grounds and was popular for parties and picnics. In 1908, Potter opened a restaurant on Twenty-fifth Street called The Potter, which he owned and operated for about 25 years. He was also a farmer, raising prize-winning dairy cattle. He died in 1914 at the age of 66.

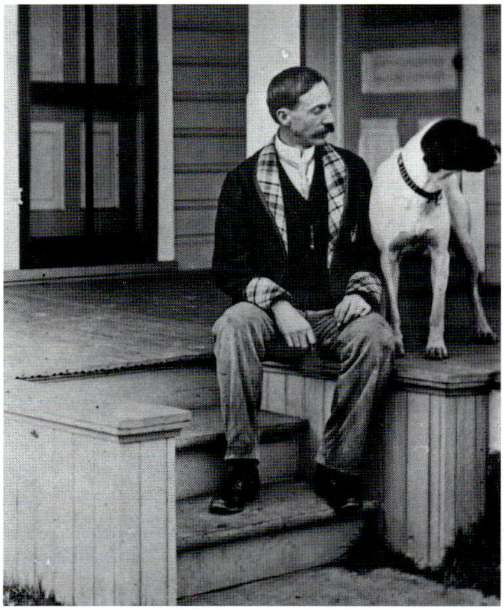

Archie P. Bigelow
Archie P. Bigelow was a prominent and respected businessman in Ogden. He was the owner of the Bigelow Hotel, known as one of Ogden's finest hotels in the 1920s. Bigelow became a renowned sportsman. In the 1890s, Bigelow teamed up with John and Matthew Browning and Gus Becker to make up the Four B's, Utah's premier bird-shooting team. He was also the president of Ogden State Bank.

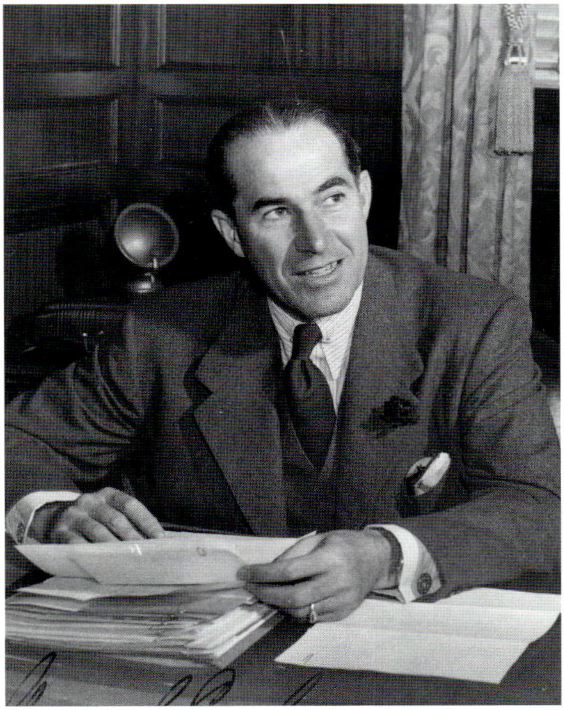

George S. Eccles
George S. Eccles was born in 1901 to David and Ellen Stoddard Eccles. After receiving his business degree from Columbia University, he became the secretary and treasurer of First Security Corporation. First Security was founded in 1928 with Marriner Eccles as president. George was active in national and international financial organizations, even purchasing Utah Rapid Transit in 1936. Eccles passed away in 1982.

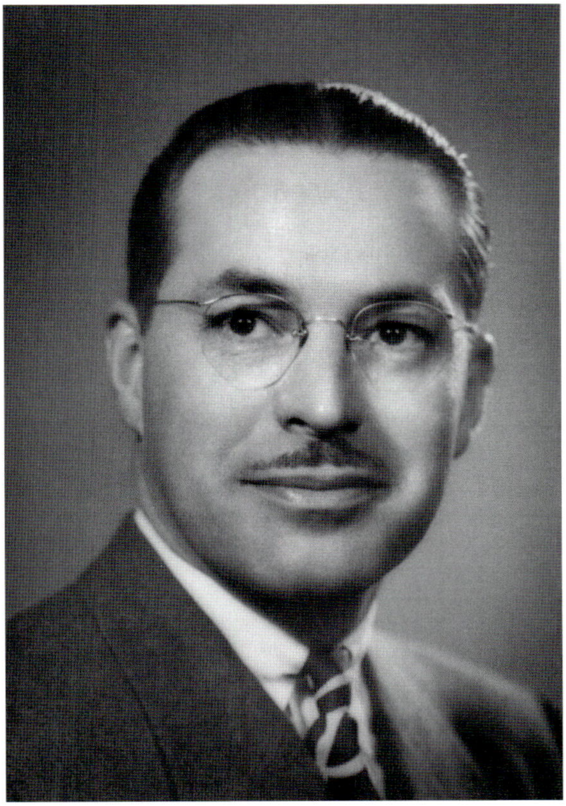

Willard Eccles
Willard Eccles was the youngest son of David and Ellen Stoddard Eccles. He was born in Logan, Utah, on February 12, 1909. He was very active in Ogden area businesses. He was vice president and secretary of First Security Banking Corporation, and president of the Ogden Chamber of Commerce from 1945 to 1946. He died in Ogden in March 1985.

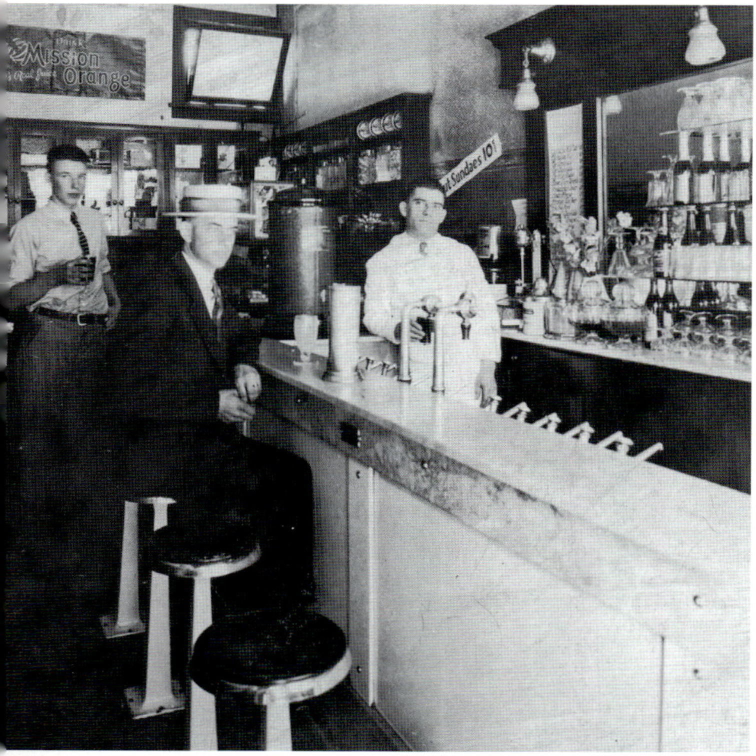

Little Sweet Shop

John Bockas arrived in Ogden in 1921. He began working as a candy maker for the Orpheum Candy Company located at 2522 Washington Boulevard. By 1922, he opened the Little Sweet Shop at 406 Twenty-fifth Street with Theodore Poulos. Bockas is on the right in the photograph below. The Little Sweet Shop advertised that it made candy fresh every day. The photograph at left shows the interior of the shop after a remodel. It was the smallest sweet shop in Ogden. In 1926, Bockas, an emigrant from Greece became a United States citizen. From 1931 to 1940, the name changed to John's Sweet Shop. By 1940, Bockas left the candy business to his partner John Dokos. Bockas, a sports enthusiast, passed away in Ogden in 1975.

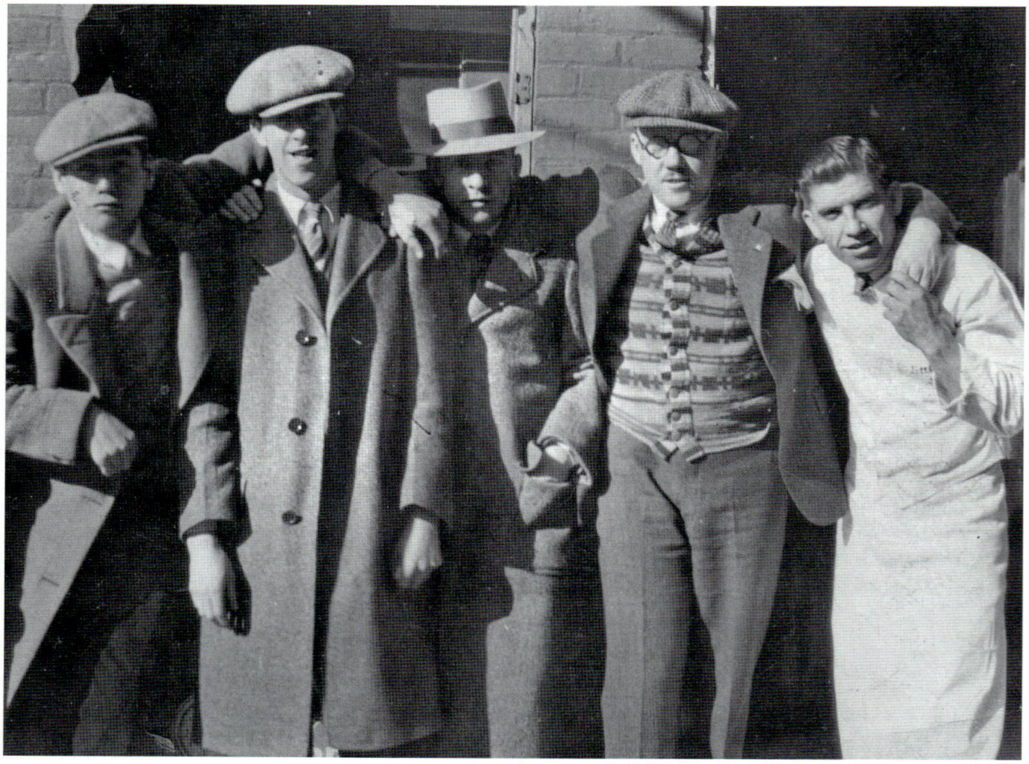

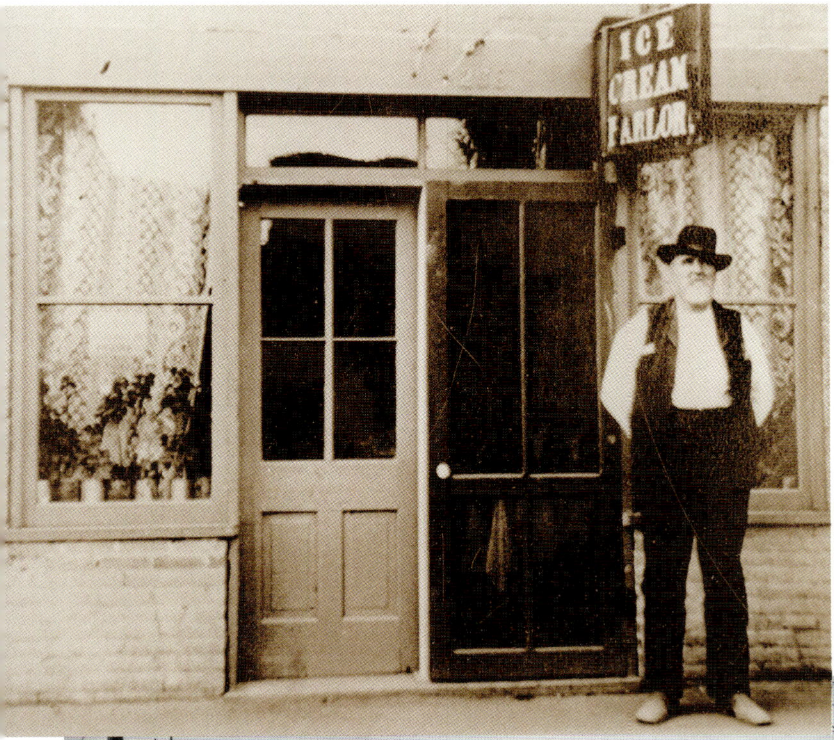

David H. Stephens
David H. Stephens was one of the first settlers, arriving in Ogden in 1852. He built an ice cream parlor at 268 Twenty-fifth Street with his wife, Albertine, in 1869. In the summers it was a profitable business with eight tables, homemade ice cream and a piece of hot yellow cake for sale. Albertine also made and sold fancy leather gloves from the store. Stephens died suddenly in 1905.

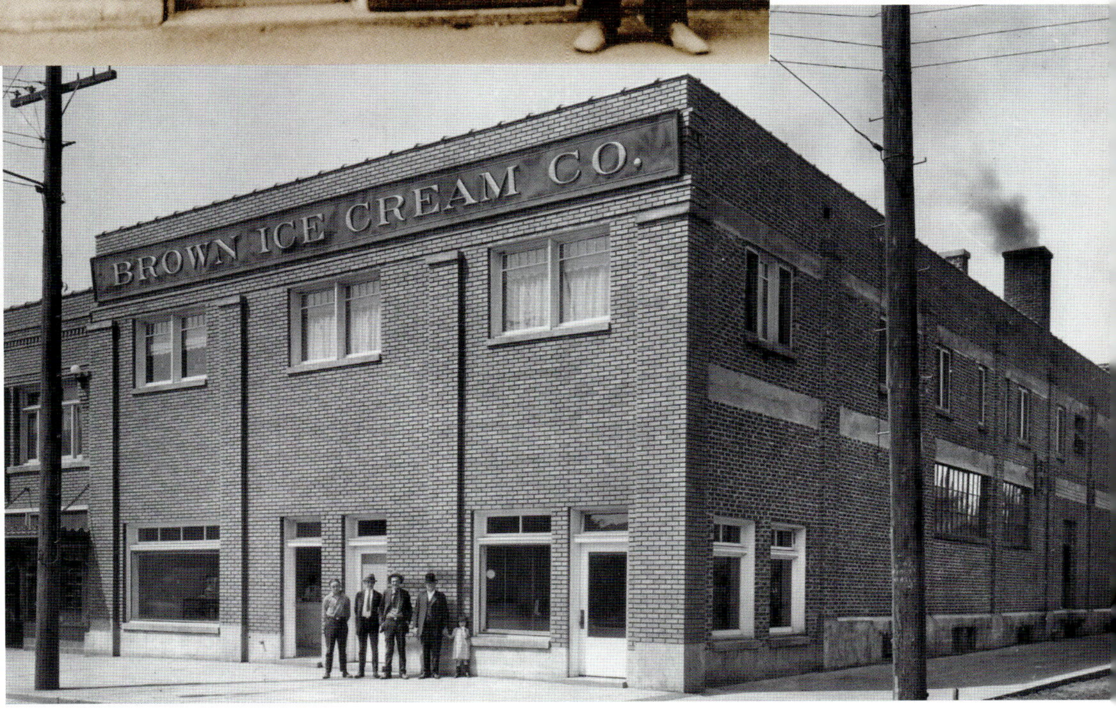

John Brown
John Brown built Brown Ice Cream in the early 1900s on the corner of Twenty-fifth Street and Lincoln Avenue. In 1922, the company created the Eskimo Pie, which was a combination of ice cream covered in chocolate. The plant was one of the busiest places in the city year-round. Workers prepared, packed, and sold ice cream, sherbets, and other dairy products.

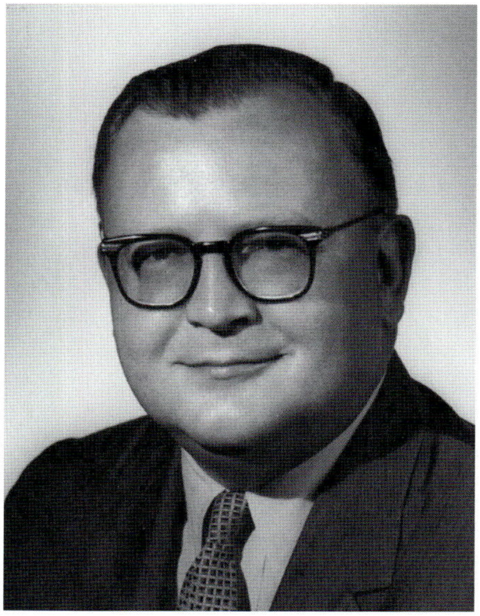

Robert Hemingway
Robert Hemingway was the son of Harold and Isabel Hemingway. He served as president of Commercial Security Bank in Ogden and chairman of the board of the Idaho Bank and Trust Company. He was very active in civic endeavors in Ogden, including a charter member of Weber State College Board of Trustees and the Weber County Industrial Bureau. He was an important proponent of the Urban Renewal Program for housing in Washington Terrace.

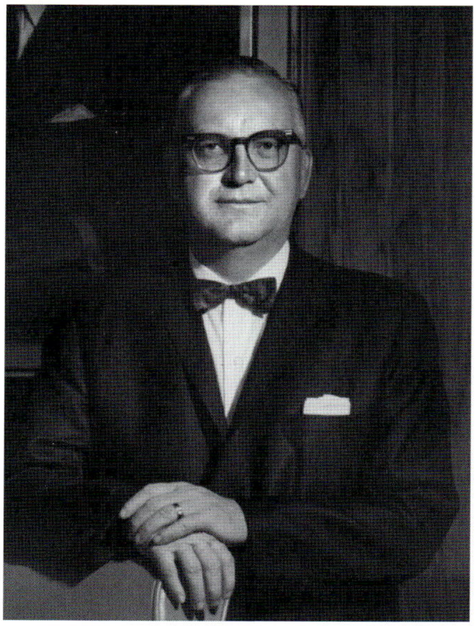

Richard Hemingway
Richard Hemingway, along with his brother Robert, directed Commercial Security Bank after the death of their father, Harold, in 1949. The bank merged with Key Bank Corporation in 1987. In 1954, he was named the chairman of the Weber County Industrial Development Bureau that helped bring businesses to Ogden. He was also involved in obtaining the land in downtown Ogden to build the Ogden City Mall in the late 1970s.

Robert H. Hinckley

Robert H. Hinckley founded his first Dodge dealership in 1915 in Mount Pleasant, Utah. In 1927, he moved to Ogden and here found his greatest success, founding several subsidiary companies and opening further dealerships in Salt Lake City. In 1934, Hinckley began working for the federal government while his wife, Abrelia, took over as president and managed the company. Hinckley and his wife retired in 1973 to their Ogden Canyon home, the "Garden of Eden," where they raised Welsh ponies. He died in 1988, but the Hinckley Dodge dealership continues today in Salt Lake City. It is the oldest Dodge dealership in continuous operation in the nation.

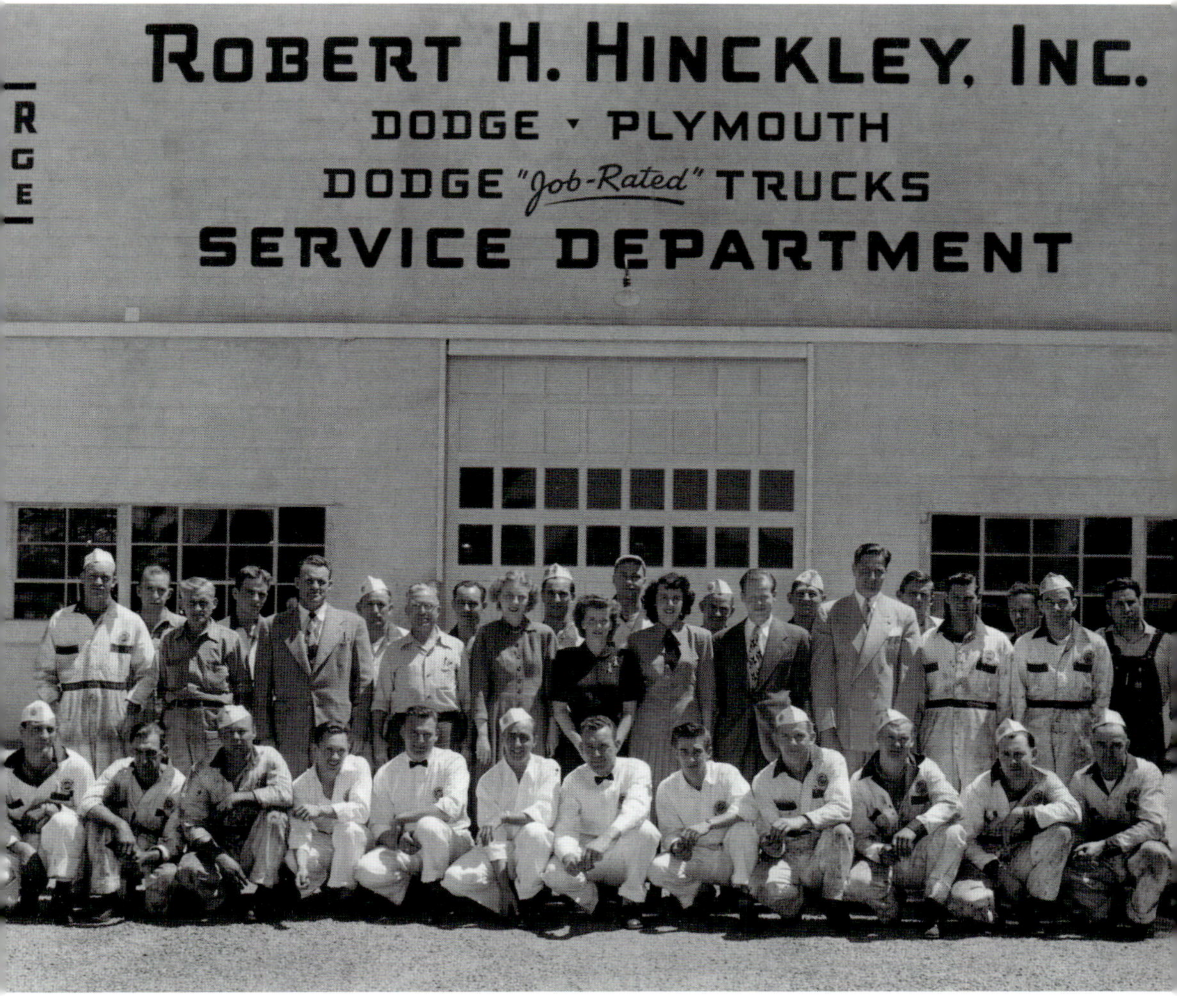

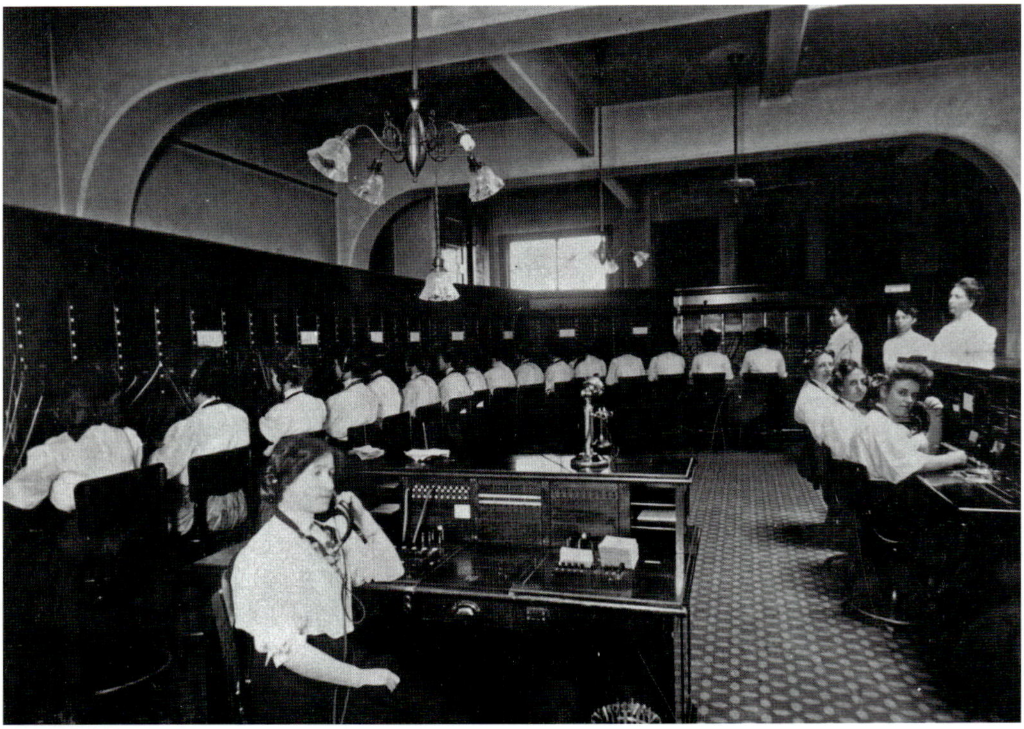

Ogden Telephone Exchange Employees
In 1880, Utah's first telephone exchange was built in Ogden with 24 lines and 30 telephones. It was also the first exchange in the Intermountain West and was managed by A.J. Pattison. In 1883, Sarah Martin became the first full-time operator in Utah and worked until her marriage three years later. Shown here is the Ogden exchange in 1909 with chief operator Janet "Nettie" Hunter Nelson standing in the background (far right).

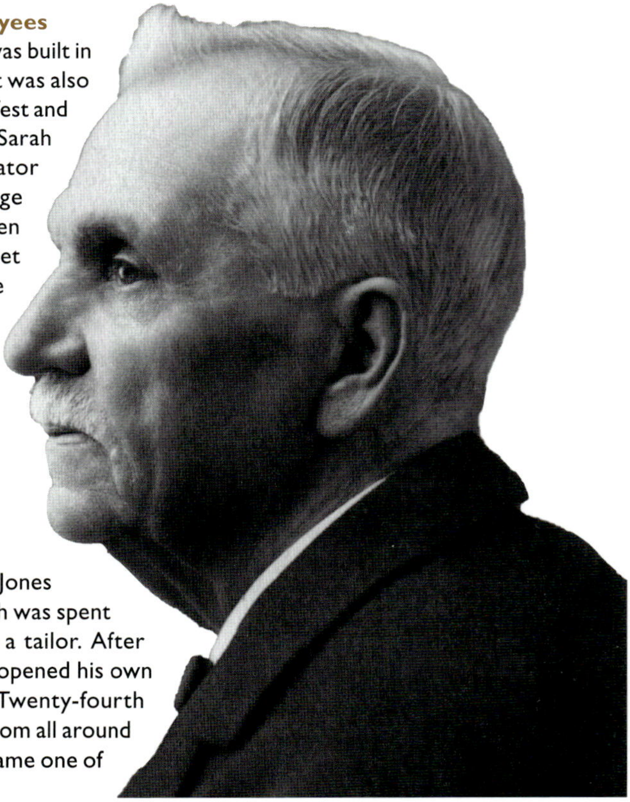

T.W. Jones
Born in Canada in 1834, Thomas Wilkins Jones settled in Ogden in 1854. Part of his youth was spent in Wales where he was apprenticed to a tailor. After serving in the Utah Militia for a time, he opened his own tailoring shop in 1870 on present-day Twenty-fourth Street and Washington Boulevard. Men from all around the West patronized his shop, which became one of the largest in Northern Utah.

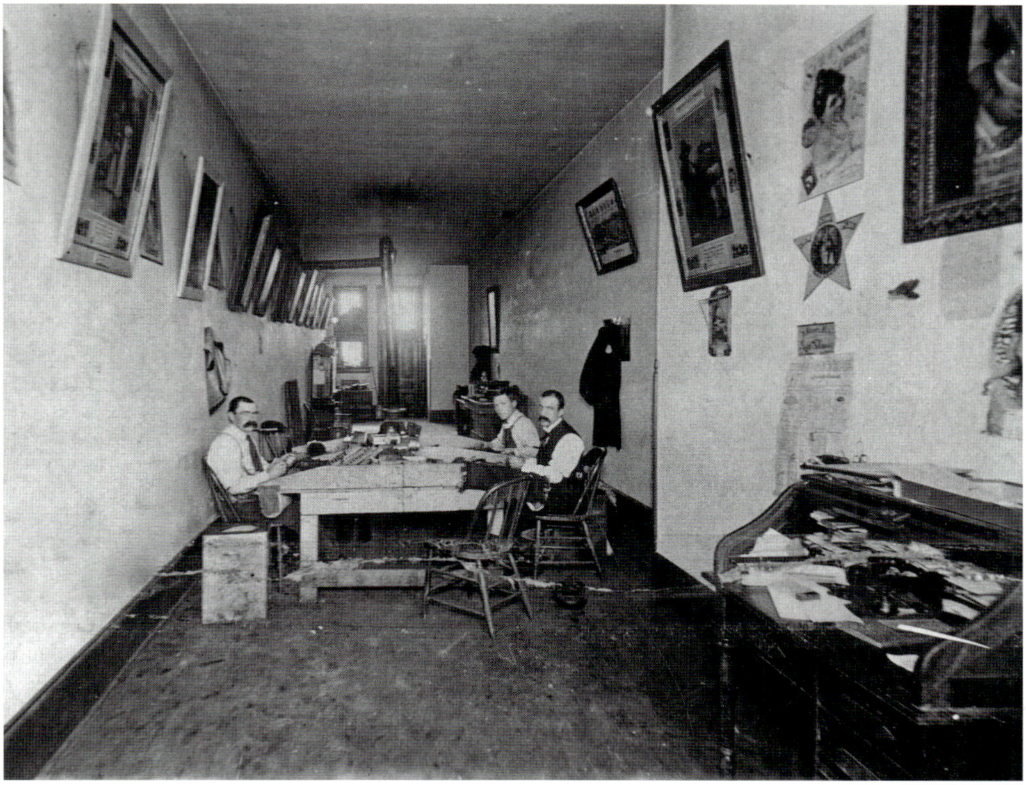

Max Davidson

Max Davidson opened the Columbia Club Cigar Company on Grant Avenue. In 1902, the local newspaper declared it the largest factory in the state, with 25 employees and a monthly payroll of $1,800. In 1905, demand for Davidson's cigars had grown to such an extent that he built a new two-story factory, including temperature-controlled vaults to preserve the quality of the tobacco. Shown here are Columbia employees in the original factory.

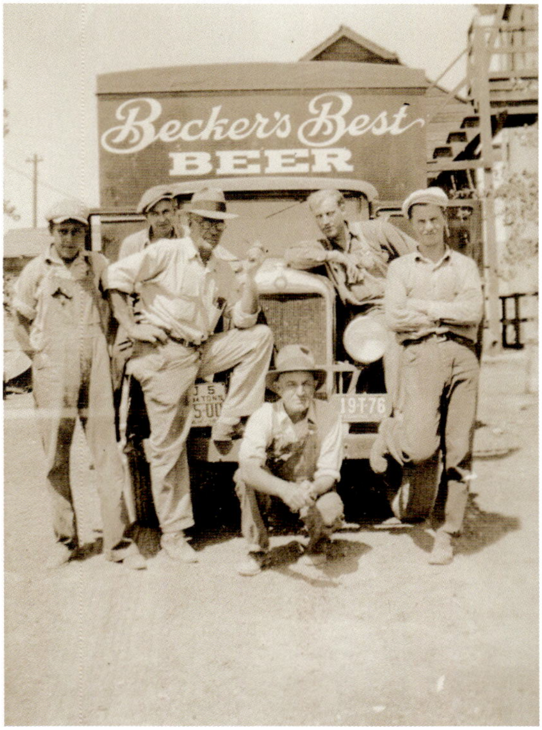

Becker Brewery

Founded by Gus and Albert Becker, the Becker Brewery was one of the most well-known breweries in the area and a major bottling company in the early 20th century. During Prohibition, the company stayed afloat by selling its nonalcoholic drink Becco but later returned to selling regular beer after Prohibition. Becker Brewery stayed in business in Ogden until the 1940s.

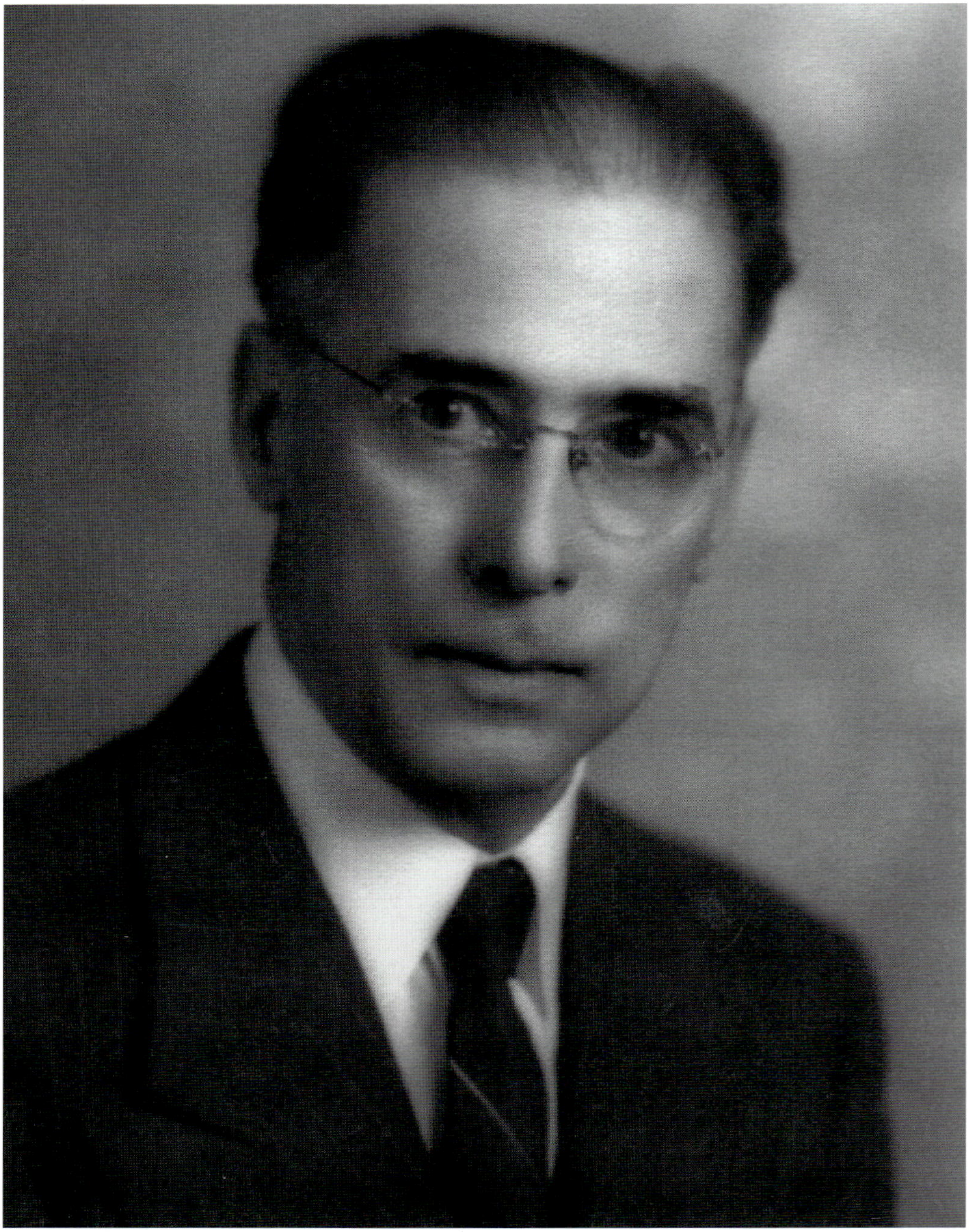

Leslie Hodgson
Leslie S. Hodgson began his career studying with Salt Lake City architects Samuel Dallas and Richard Klitting. Later, he went on to work in San Diego with Irving Gill who was in turn heavily influenced by Louis Sullivan and Frank Lloyd Wright. Returning to Ogden in 1906, Hodgson went on to establish himself as one of the leading architects in the area. Using classic Art Deco and Prairie-style architectural elements, he designed 75 of the major homes and buildings in Weber County, including the Forest Service Building, the Municipal Building, and his masterpiece, Ogden High School—the nation's first $1,000,000 school.

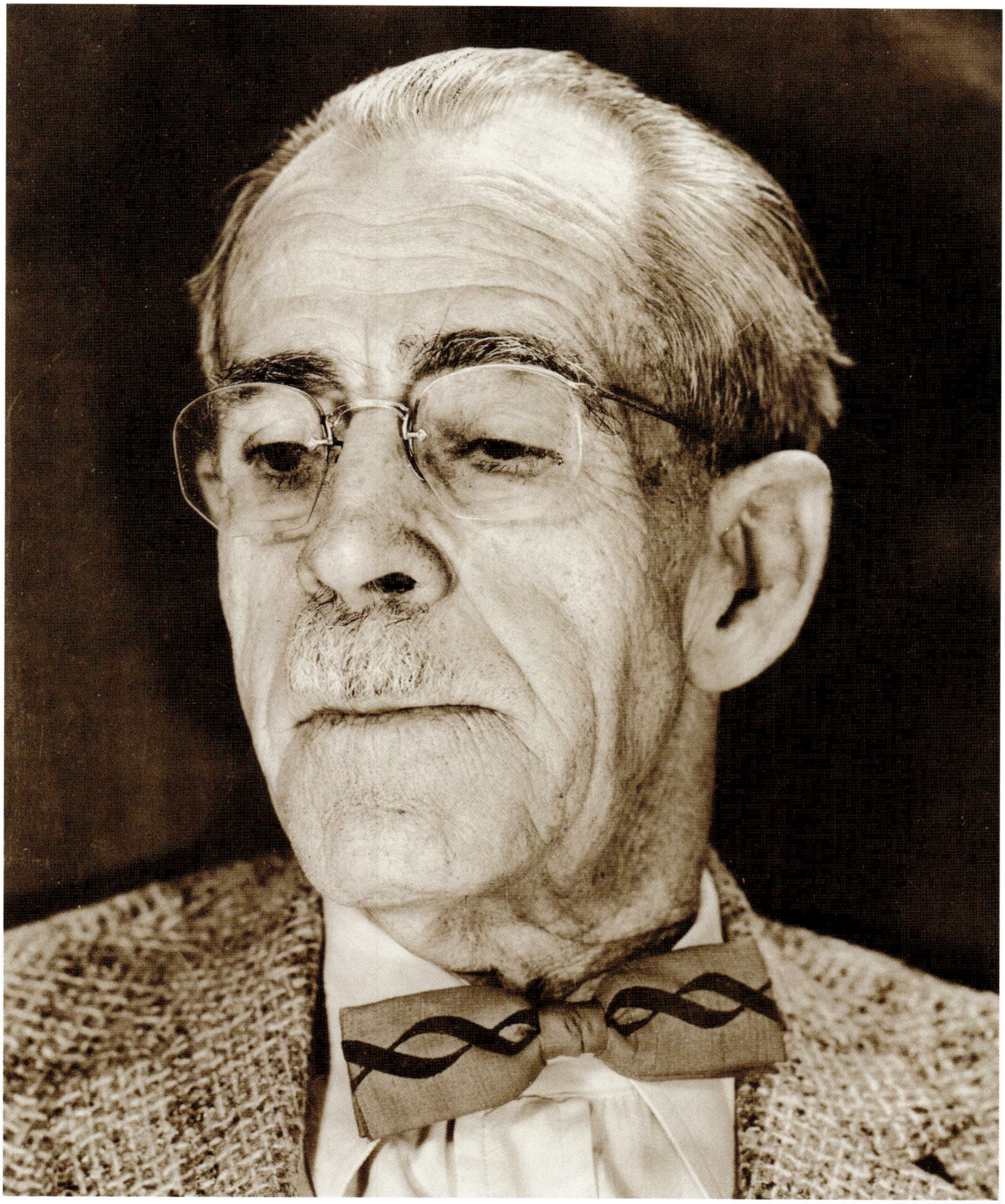

Eber F. Piers
Another prominent Ogden architect was Eber F. Piers. Born in Denver in 1889, he first worked as a draftsman then studied for a year at the School of Architectural Engineering at the University of Colorado. When he came to Ogden, he worked briefly for Hodgson's firm, then opened his own offices in 1911. Piers designed homes for several Ogden businessmen, including E.O. Wattis, Royal Eccles, and Marriner Browning. His greatest work is perhaps the First National Bank, which was a 12-story building constructed solidly on swampy land. His son described the foundation as "a continuous 'raft' of reinforced concrete in 12 feet of water, resting on a sea of mud," and called the building "a remarkable engineering feat."

John A. Lindquist

John A. Lindquist was born on July 14, 1919, to Charles and Ada Lindquist. He obtained his education at Weber College and served with distinction in the Army Air Corps in World War II. He began working at the family mortuary at an early age then took over the business and was president of Lindquist Mortuary until he relinquished the position to his son. Lindquist was also active in the Ogden Chamber of Commerce. As president of the chamber, he helped create the Weber Economic Development Corporation and Ogden Industrial Development Corporation—entities that helped build and fill the Weber Industrial Park. Lindquist worked to create the Ogden-Eccles Conference Center and helped to restore Ogden's Peery's Egyptian Theater and Union Station as well as save the Ben Lomond Hotel.

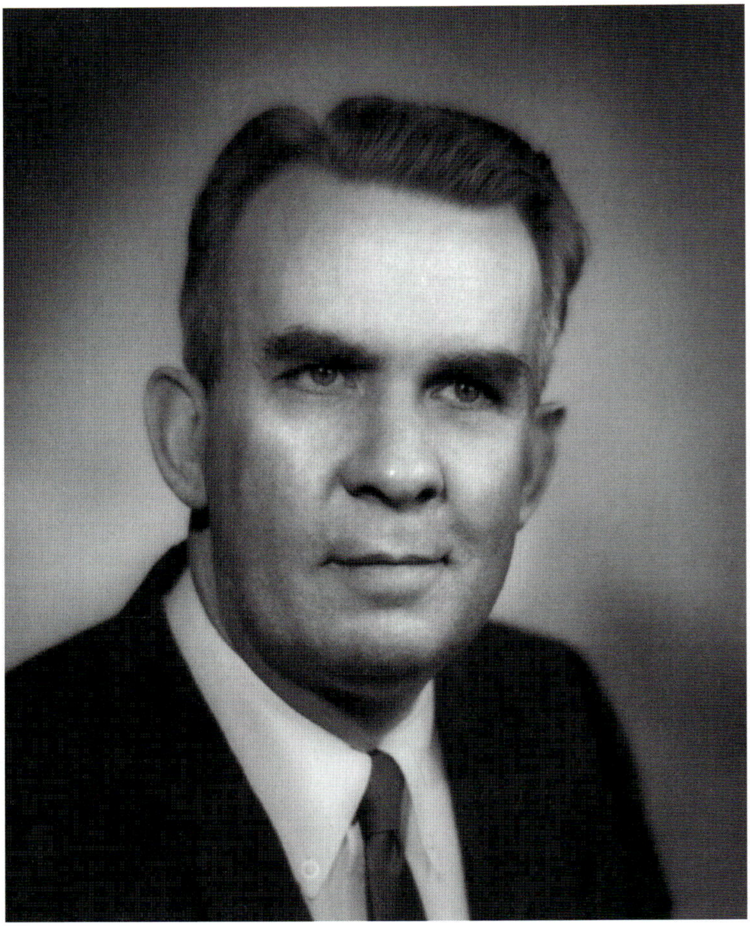

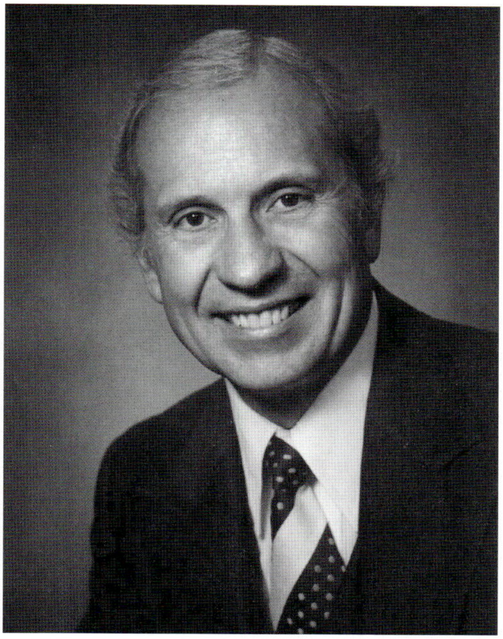

Richard Meyers

Richard Meyers is one of the founding members of Meyers Mortuary that first opened in Ogden in 1945. Myers has served as president of the National Funeral Directors Association. He is philanthropic in his community, volunteering his time and energy to the building of neighborhood, city, and state programs and resources. Meyers has served as chairman or president of many organizations, including the Weber State University Board of Trustees and Ogden Pioneer Days.

Ezra Fjeldsted

Ezra Fjeldsted was a giant among community leaders in Ogden. He served as executive director of the Ogden Chamber of Commerce where he promoted the Golden Spike National Livestock Show. He took the lead in surveying potential reservoir sites and helped form the Weber Basin Conservancy District. He passed away in 1974.

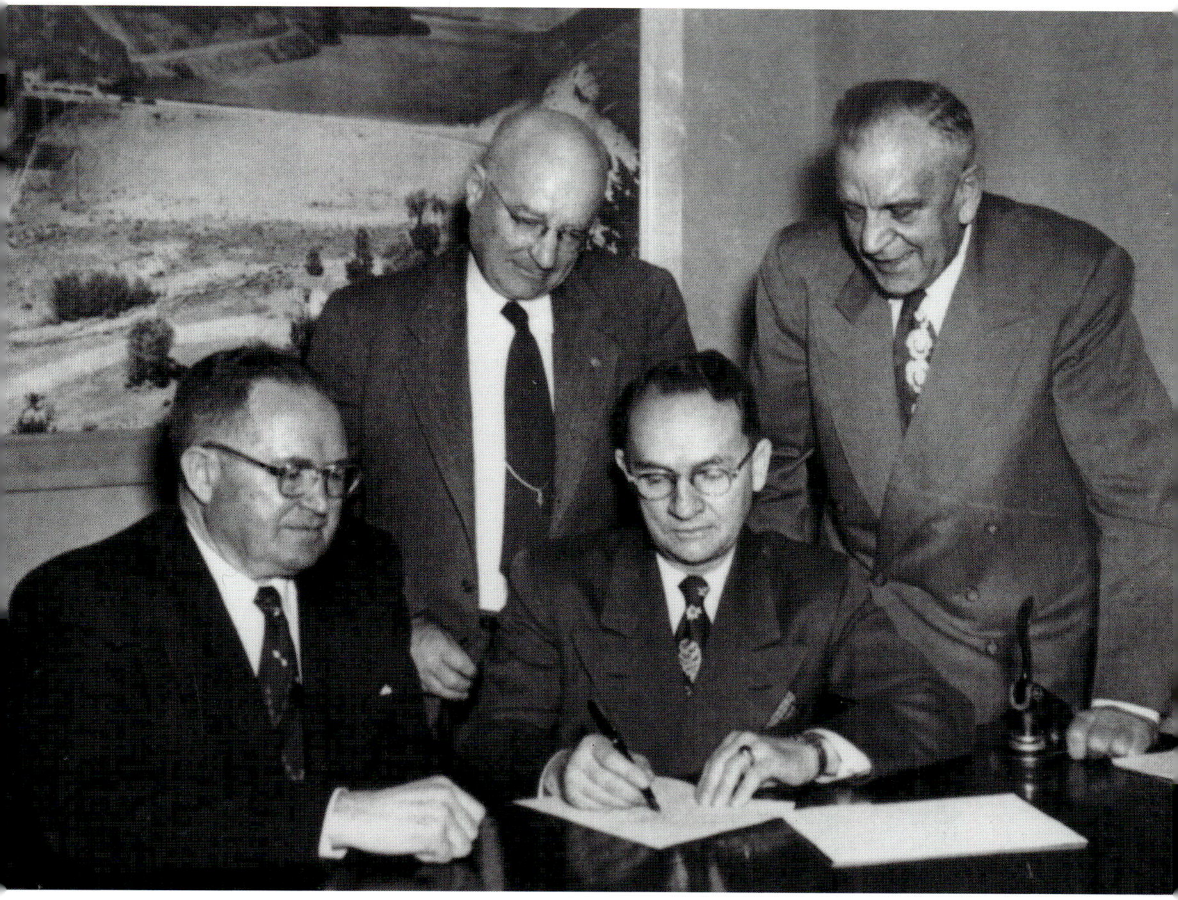

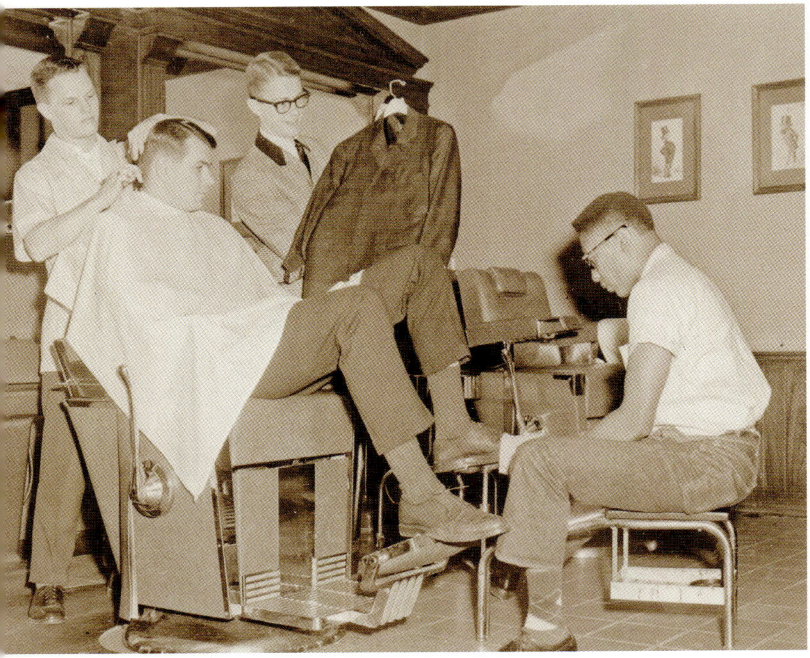

Nye's Cellar

In 1959, the Fred M. Nye Department Store decided to open a men's clothing department in the store basement where Ralph Dayton (barber on left) and Bud and Val Chase operated a barbershop, which became known as the Cellar. Ray Robinson shined shoes, and later Jim Oborn also joined the staff. Dayton and Oborn eventually bought out the Chase brothers, and although their location has changed, the Cellar is still in business today.

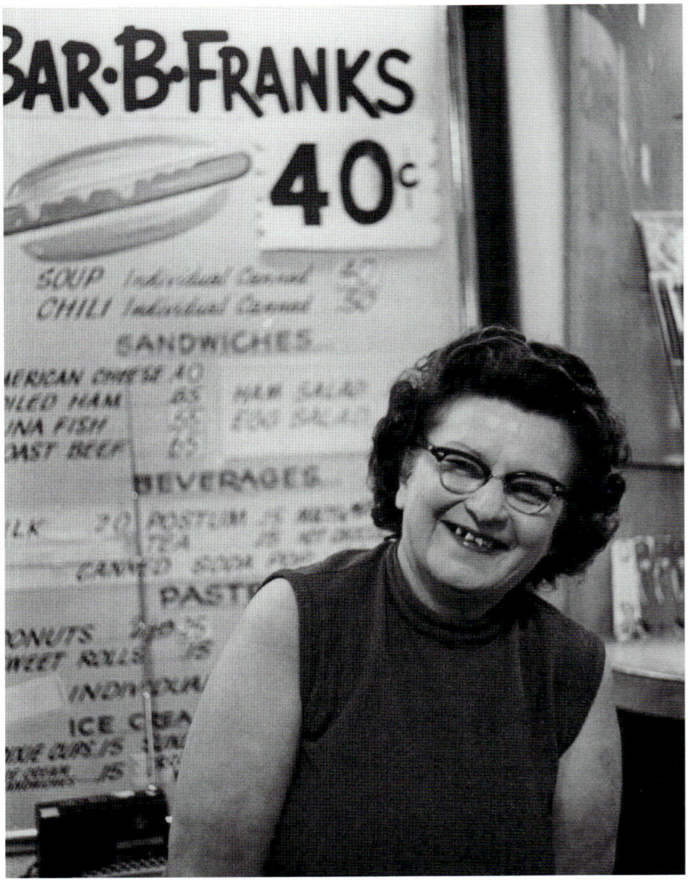

Hazel Smith

The Barkalow Brothers newsstand was located in the Union Depot Station and during the night was manned by Hazel Smith. John Shupe, local newspaper photographer, remembers her as a warm and caring person who knew everyone from police officers to active criminals. She kept a radio tuned to the police department frequency and consequently always knew what was going on in Ogden. (Photograph courtesy of John Shupe.)

CHAPTER THREE

Service in Aid and Need

Public Servants

Ogden's history of public servants goes back to the beginning of the city. The first law enforcement officer was B.W. Nolan, who was elected Ogden City Marshal on April 7, 1851. The city marshal and sheriff's office worked with the city and county courts to enforce the laws. The coming of the railroad increased crime and violence in Ogden from 1869 to the 1950s. The areas of Ogden closest to the railroad station became known for violence, crime, gambling, and prostitution. In 1884, Gilbert Belnap was elected sheriff and served in that position for 14 years. Over the years, Ogden has seen other law enforcement, including Mac Wade, Ernest Shaw, and Marshall White.

Medical care in the early days of Ogden consisted of local doctors performing surgeries on the kitchen table in the patients' homes. In 1910, Annie Taylor Dee changed all of that when she opened the Thomas D. Dee Memorial Hospital. After the death of her son Reese following appendicitis and her husband, Thomas, of pneumonia, the Dee family decided to provide the much-needed hospital to Ogden. The first 32 doctors on staff took care of 895 patients and performed some of the early medical procedures in the area. The hospital also started a school of nursing that educated over 700 nurses from 1910 to 1955. In 1946, the Sisters of St. Benedict opened a second hospital in Ogden that still serves the population today.

Ogden's growth also led to an increase in federal public servants. In 1908, Ogden became the hub of the Intermountain Region of the US Forest Service. Several gentlemen worked for the Forest Service and impacted Ogden like Chet Olsen, who was close friends with Bernard DeVoto, Julia Child, and George Nichols, an architect who designed many of the buildings and ranger stations. The public health nurses were closely monitored by the federal agency to keep the spread of disease to a minimum during World War II. These nurses were responsible for teaching both the soldiers and prostitutes about the prevention of spreading diseases. Public servants worked to better the community of Ogden.

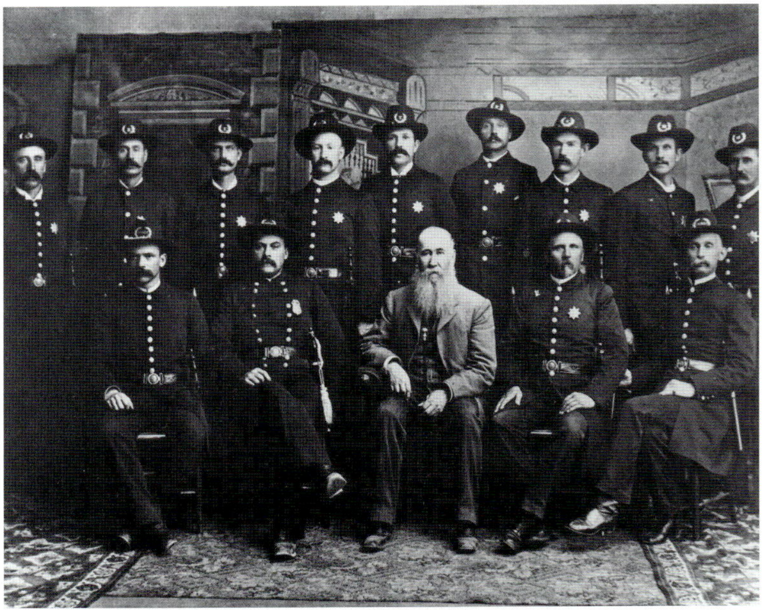

Ogden Police Force

Ogden's police force was organized in 1851, and was instructed to curb the sale of whiskey, clean the sidewalks, and to see that cattle did not roam though the streets at night. In the middle of the photograph, taken in 1891, is city judge S.M. Preshaw with police chief John W. Metcalf on his right, and on his left, officer William A. Brown, who was killed in the line of duty in 1899.

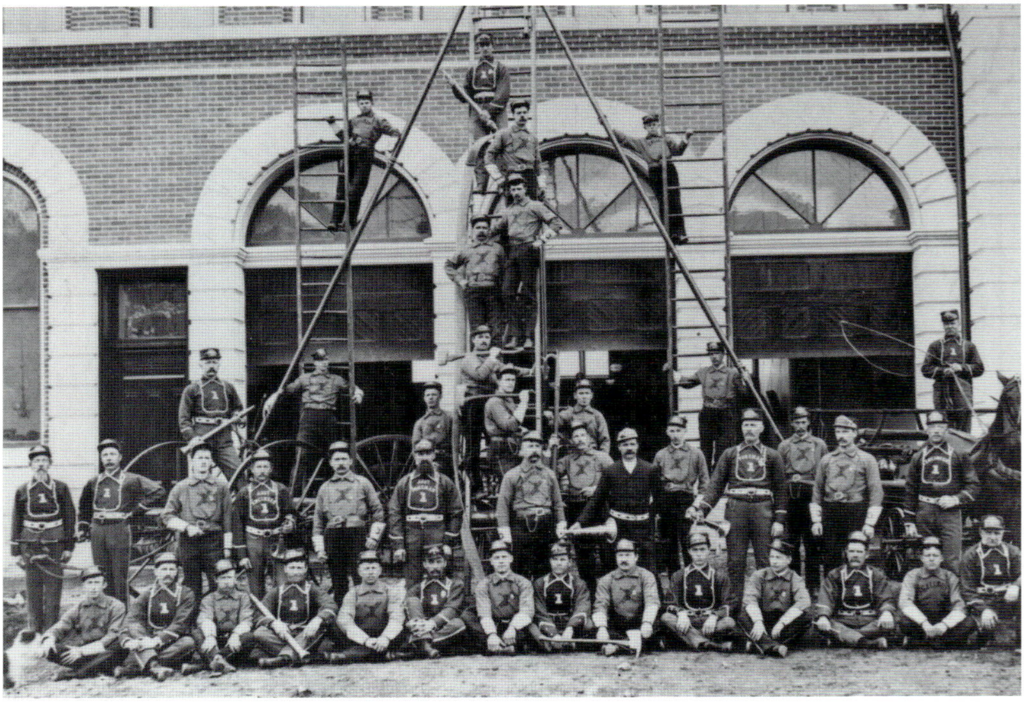

Ogden's First Fire Station

Ogden's first volunteer fire brigade was organized in the early 1870s with Joshua Williams appointed fire chief. By 1883, two companies of about 32 men each had been organized: Engine Company No. 1 and Hook and Ladder Company No. 1. They served in the downtown area until 1890, when a paid fire department was organized and the volunteers were moved to Five Points. Williams died in 1900, honored by his community and fellow firefighters.

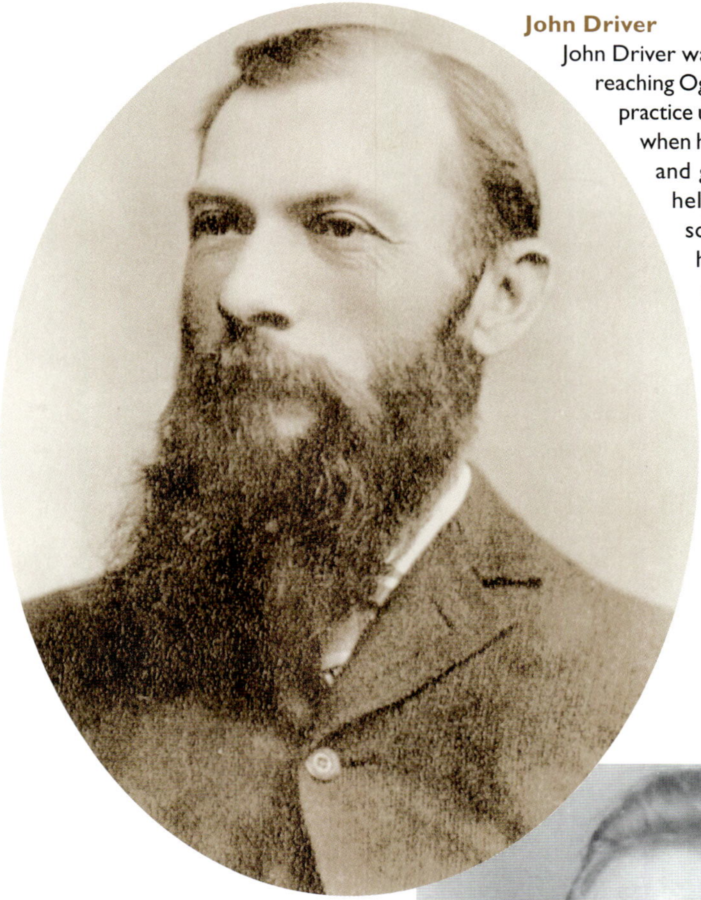

John Driver

John Driver was born in England in 1848. Upon reaching Ogden in 1875, he struggled with his practice until a diphtheria outbreak in 1880, when his treatment of carbolic acid, iron, and glycerine had great success. He helped organize the first medical society in Weber County. After he retired from active practice he spent much of his time working on a cure for skin cancer. He passed away on May 8, 1936, after becoming bedridden.

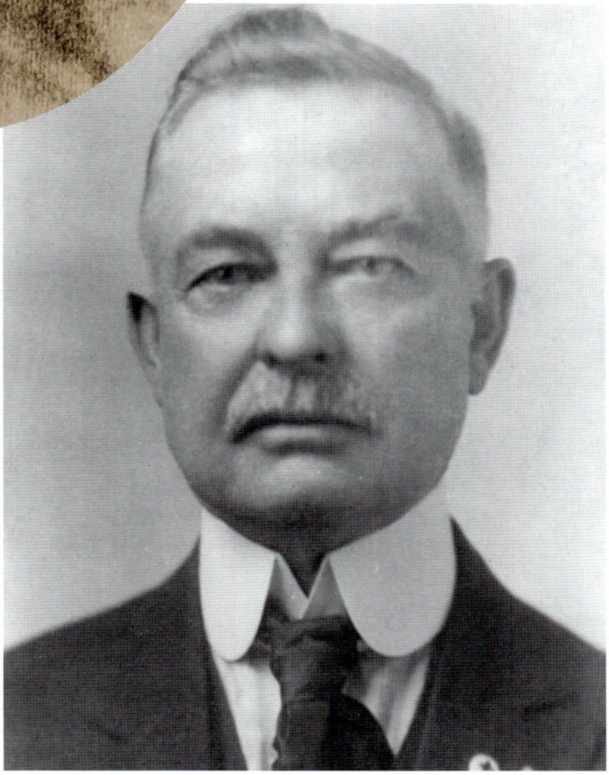

Edward M. Conroy

Edward M. Conroy moved to Ogden in May 1890, when he opened an office and started practicing medicine. During World War I, he never sent a bill to a service man or his family. While active in the medical field, he was also very involved in civic affairs. He was elected mayor of Ogden in 1905 and served as a member of the Ogden City Board of Education for 10 years.

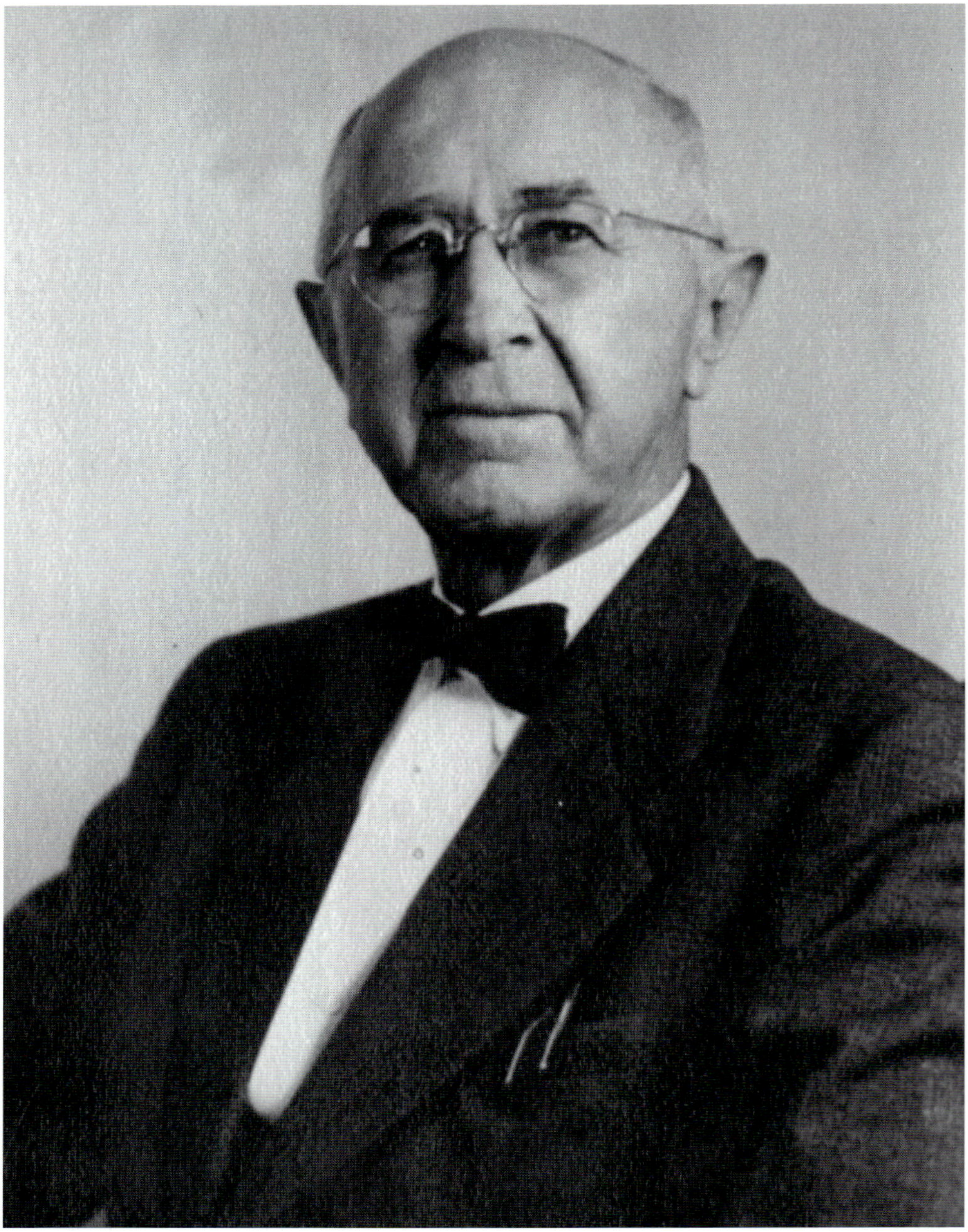

Dr. Edward Israel Rich

Dr. Edward Israel Rich was a prominent physician and surgeon in Ogden. He retired on May 2, 1947, after 54 years of practice. He was born in 1868 and came to Ogden in 1894 after receiving his medical degree from the Jefferson Medical College. He delivered more than 5,000 babies and performed many surgical operations in private homes before the Dee Hospital was established. He married Almira Cozzens and had seven children. His practice was a general one and he handled all kinds of cases from drug addiction to broken bones. During the influenza outbreak from 1918 to 1919, he traveled all over Weber County and even into Davis County to provide the needed medical care for his patients. He lived to be 100 years old.

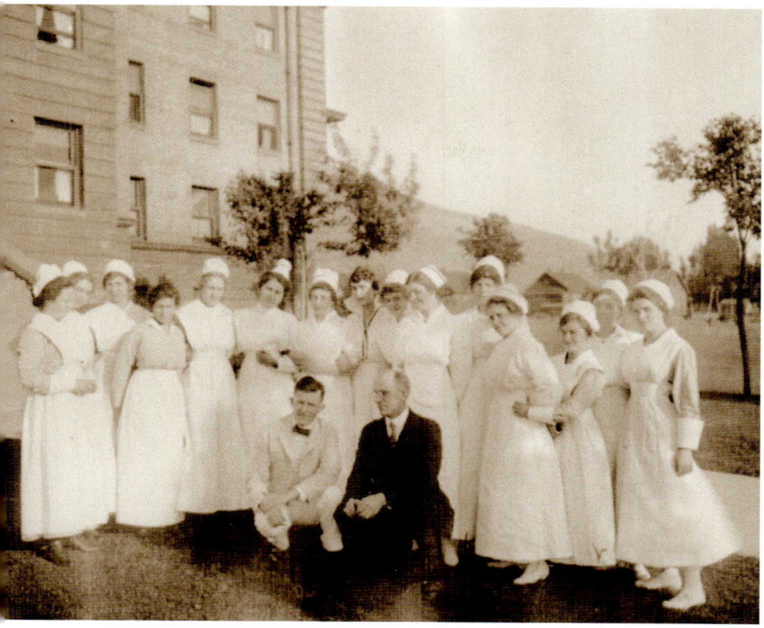

Dee Hospital School of Nursing Doctors and Nurses

The Dee Hospital School of Nursing was founded in 1910 with the first class graduating in 1913. In 1912, Annie Hall became superintendent and instituted the cap and uniform. By 1917, a home for the nurses was established. Here are nursing students in 1919 with Dr. H.G. Adams and Dr. J.R. Morrell. The students helped staff the hospital, especially during the influenza outbreak during 1919.

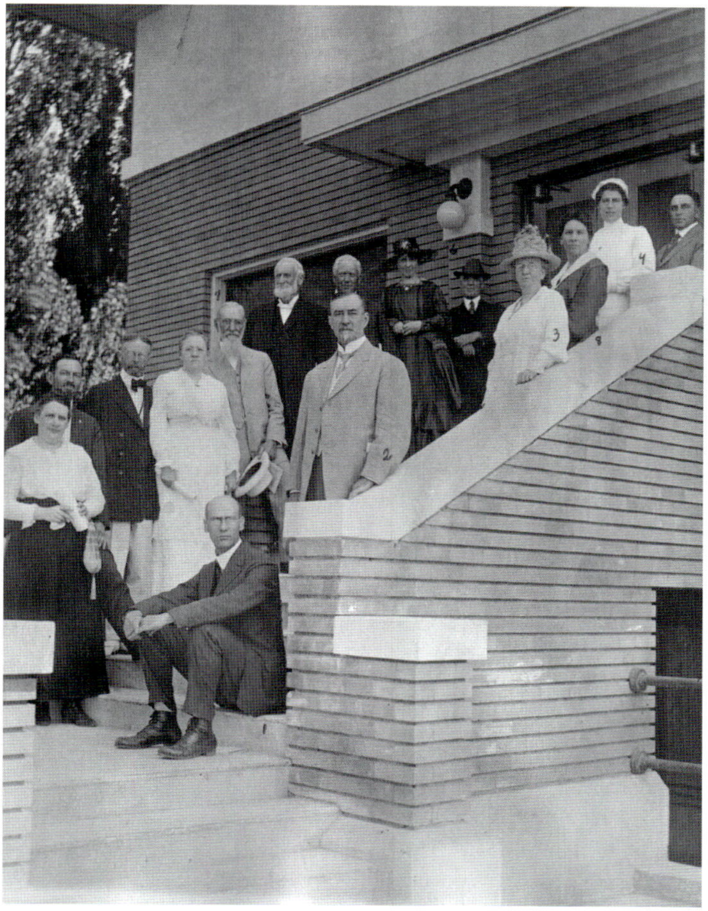

Nurses' Home Dedication

On August 24, 1917, the completed nurses' home for the Thomas Dee Memorial Hospital was opened to great fanfare. The home was completed for a cost of $30,000 and accommodated 50 nurses. Attending the opening were LDS president Joseph F. Smith (fifth on left), William H. Wattis (seventh on left), Annie Dee (third on right), and Stella Sainsbury, superintendent of nurses (fifth on right). The home included classrooms and laboratories.

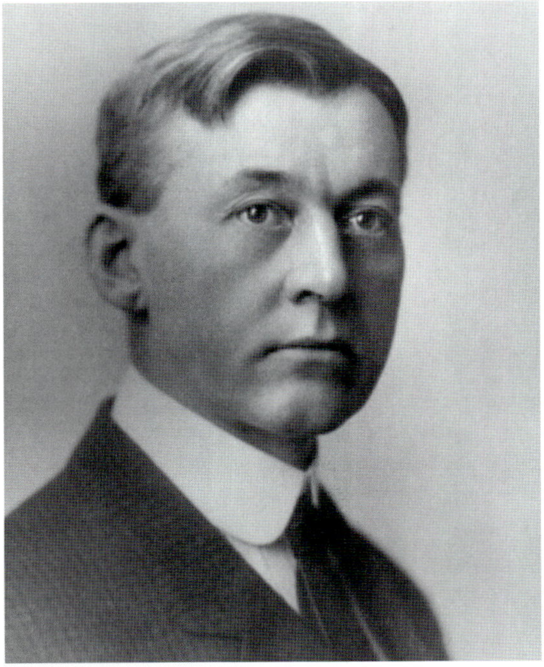

Dr. Robert S. Joyce

Dr. Robert S. Joyce came to Ogden in 1891 to practice medicine. His original methods in surgery brought him fame throughout the West. He was the personal physician to Thomas and Annie Dee. After Thomas Dee died of pneumonia, the family built the Thomas Dee Memorial Hospital with the help of Joyce. He was a prominent member of the staff when the new hospital opened in 1910.

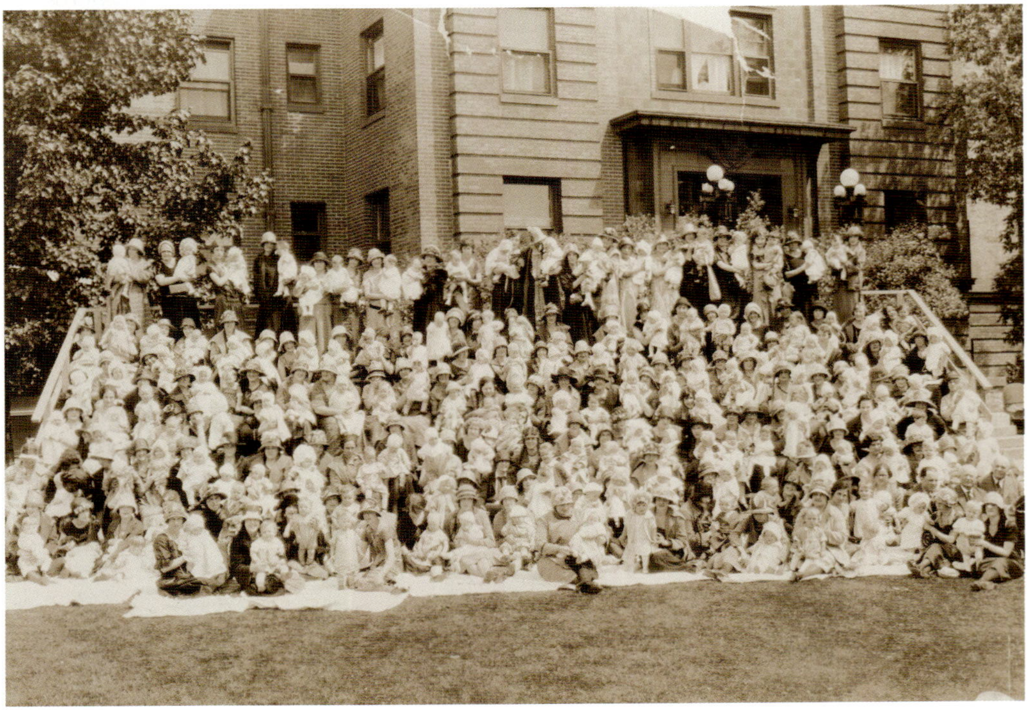

Dee Hospital Day

On May 13, 1923, the Thomas D. Dee Memorial Hospital celebrated Dee Hospital day. They had celebrations to honor Dr. Robert Joyce and the 100th birthday of Florence Nightingale. Pictured here are all the babies born at the hospital in the previous year. When the hospital first opened, all the births were paid for by Annie Dee to encourage delivery in the hospital so that student nurses could be trained.

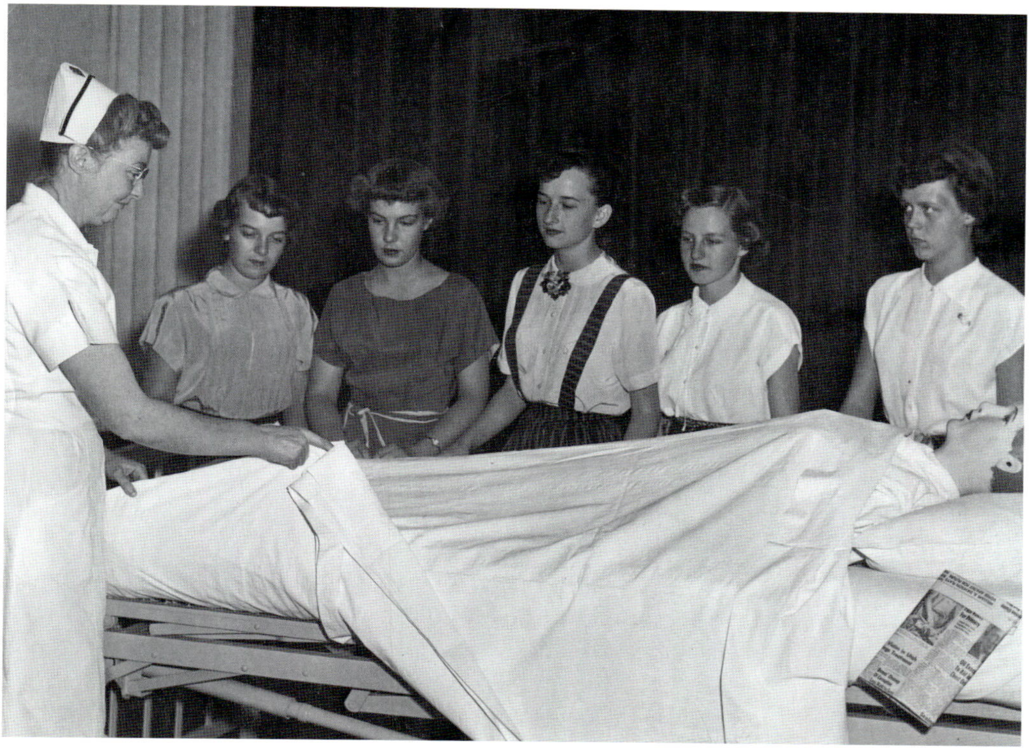

Dee School of Nursing Students

In 1952, the Dee School of Nursing admitted its final class. Pictured here are, from left to right, LaPrelle Neville, Louise Anderson, Diane Stowe, Edna Walchi, LuAnn Secrist, and Marion Cook. These students were recipients of the Bamberger Scholarship. During their training, nursing students worked 12-hour days between floor duty and classes. During their first three months, they were probies and had to follow the strict rules, including not being able to be married. The final class graduated in 1955.

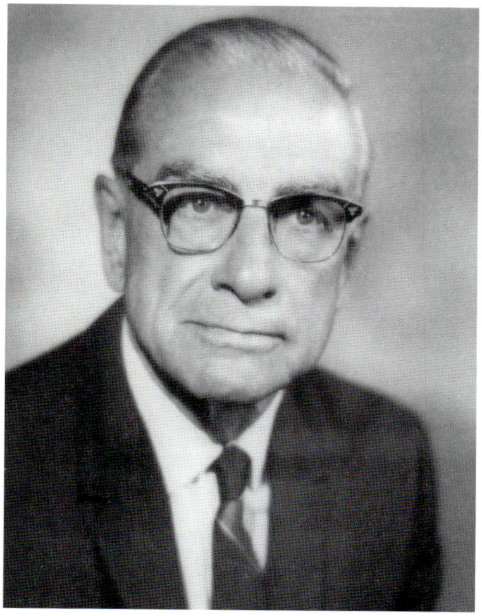

Dr. George M. Fister

Dr. George M. Fister graduated from Utah State Agricultural College. He earned his medical degree in 1919 from Rush Medical College in Chicago. He moved to Ogden to specialize in urology. Fister was president of both the Utah State Medical Association and the Ogden Surgical Society. He served as a member of the American Medical Association Board of Trustees until he was elected as the 116th president in June 1962.

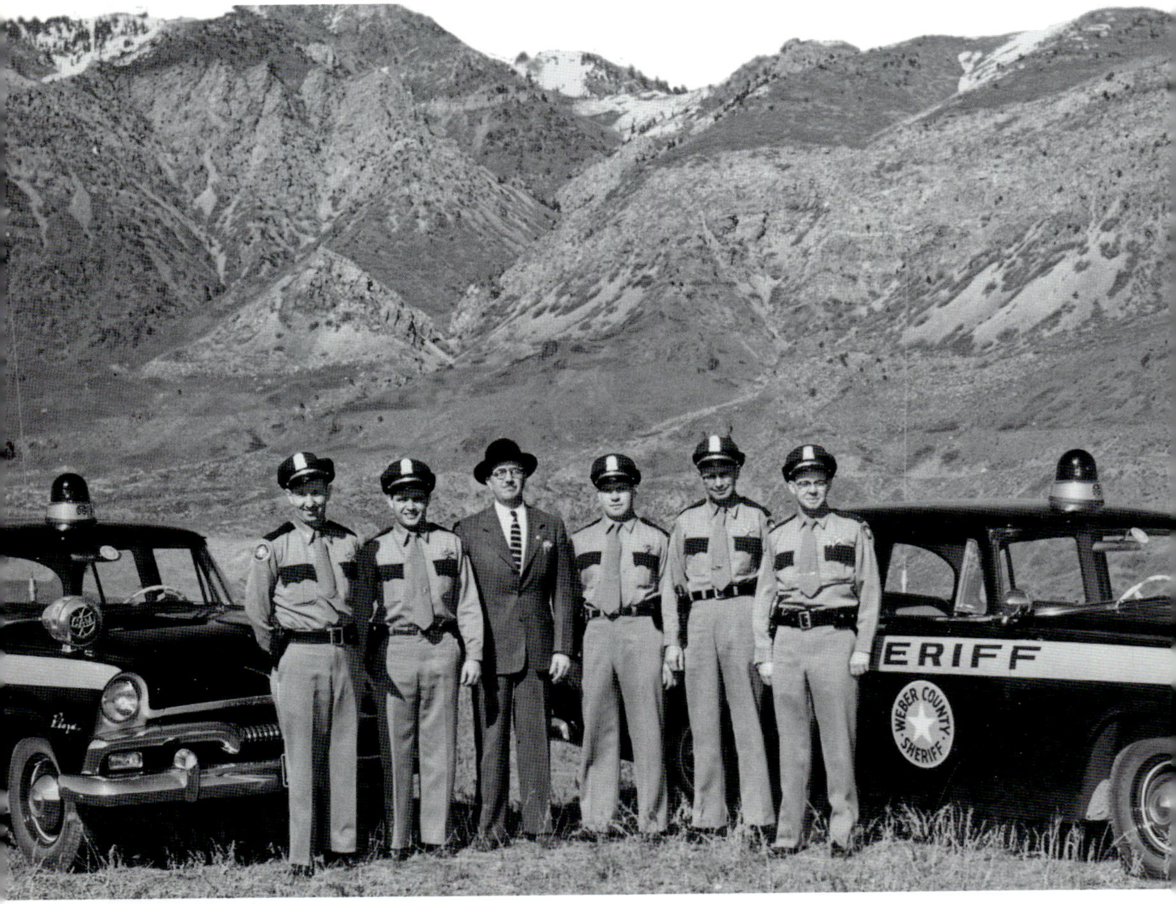

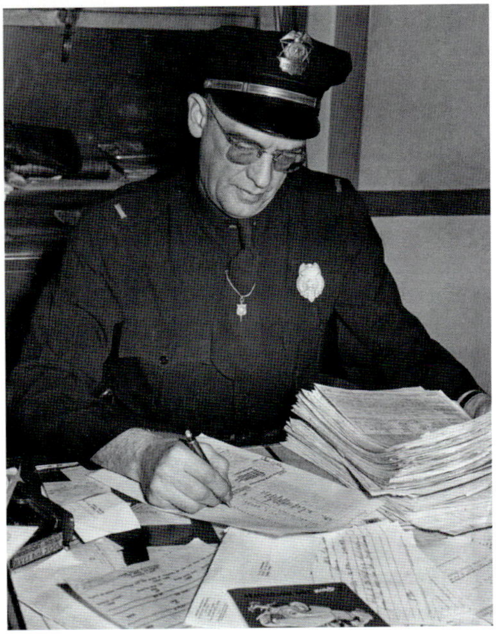

LeRoy Hadley

LeRoy Hadley (third from left) was elected as Weber County sheriff in 1962. In early 1966, Hadley was charged with three counts of malfeasance and perjury for failing to perform his duties as a sheriff by releasing a federal prisoner. After his trial, he was sentenced to 90 days in jail and a $500 fine. He was removed from his position as sheriff in 1966.

Ernest L. Shaw

Ernest L. Shaw was named chief of Ogden City Police on February 1, 1964. He served the department for 36 years prior as head of the traffic division. During his time as police chief, Shaw established the uniform division with five captains. Each captain was in charge of an eight-hour shift. He also started the police teletype system to provide rapid exchanges through the state and a fund for injured officers.

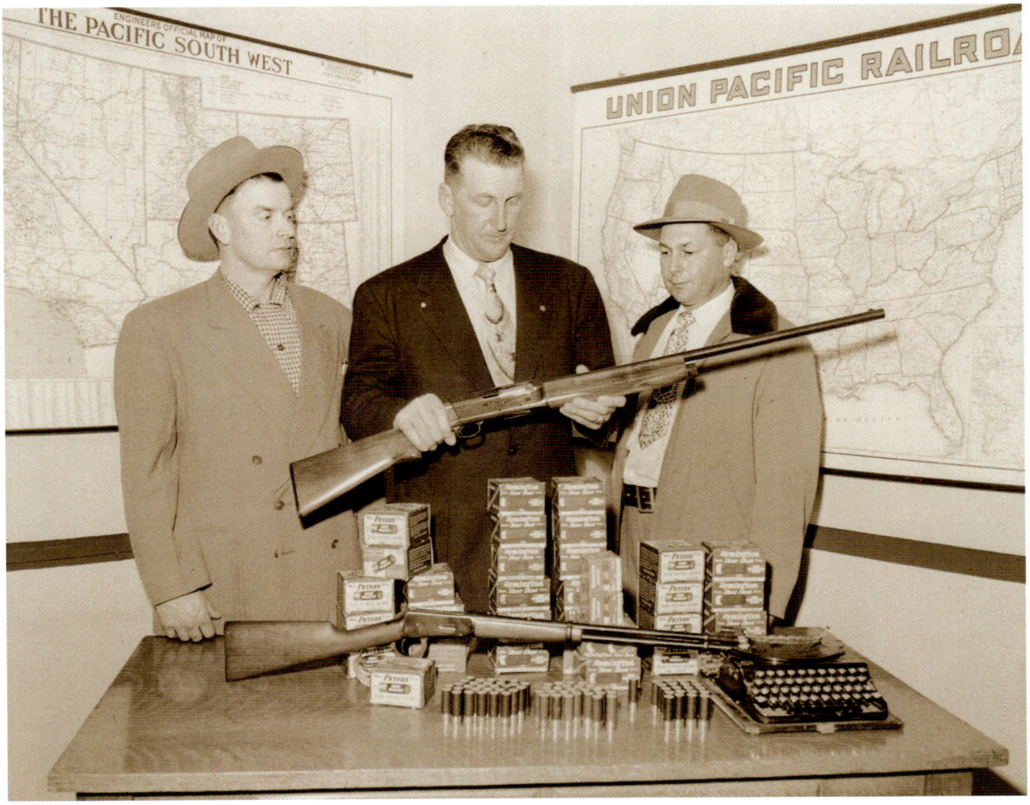

Mac Wade

Mac Wade served as the Weber County Sheriff from 1947 to 1954. During that time, he worked to try and clean up Ogden. Wade wanted to preserve the peace and make all lawful arrests. As a result, the sheriff's office carried on a successful campaign against crime and vice during his tenure. His biggest capture was that of murderer Ray Dempsey Gardner, who was wanted for killing a teenage babysitter. He was also responsible for the arrest and conviction of Rose and Bill Davies, who were known proprietors of a brothel on Twenty-fifth Street. Wade is pictured here in the middle of Blaine Farr and Ray Gibson after they arrested four men involved in a robbery in Plain City. (Photograph courtesy of *Ogden Standard Examiner.*)

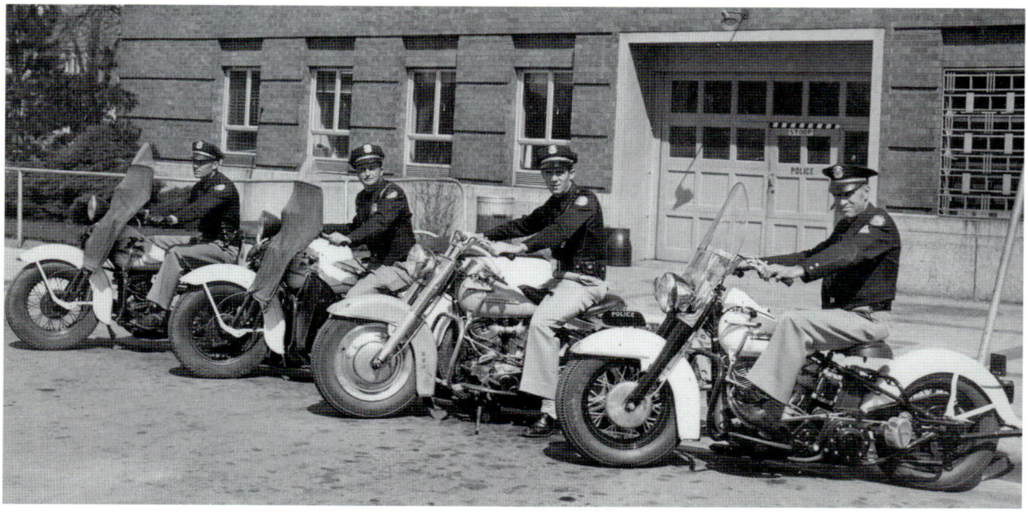

Ogden City Police Officers
These police officers are posed in front of the Ogden police station, located by the municipal building on Washington Avenue between Twenty-fifth and Twenty-sixth Streets in 1952. From Ogden's earliest days to the present, nine officers have given their lives in the line of duty. Officer Jared Francom, the most recent officer to fall, died on January 5, 2012, after being shot while executing a search warrant.

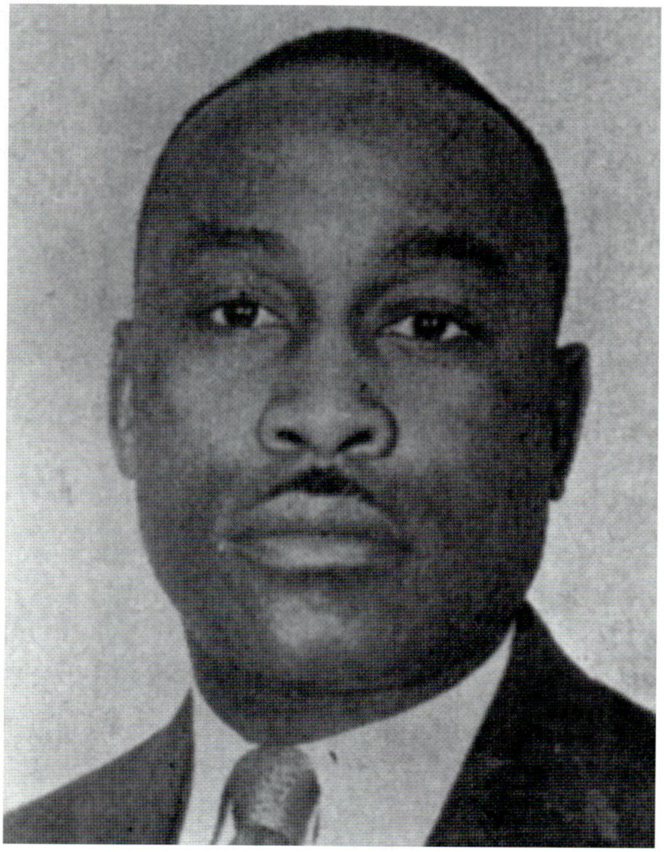

Marshall White
Marshall White was shot on October 15, 1963, while searching for a 16-year-old escapee from the State Industrial School. Michael Jones shot White in the stomach, and he died three days later. White had been a detective on the Ogden police force for 15 years. He was the president of the local chapter of the NAACP. Upon his death, the community of Ogden decided to name the newly constructed community center in his honor. (Photograph courtesy of *Ogden Standard Examiner.*)

Public Health Nurses

Pictured here are the Public Health Nurses in Ogden during 1952. The nurses were responsible for the health needs of the community and focused their time on the fight against communicable diseases. During World War II, the nurses worked to combat the spread of venereal disease by monitoring soldiers and working girls and educating the community on the dangers. In 1948, the public health department ran a VD clinic one night a week and saw between 20 and 25 patients. Most of the cases came from taverns and joints on Twenty-fifth Street. The police force brought in one to five women a week for examination. Those testing positive were sent to the rapid treatment center in Salt Lake City.

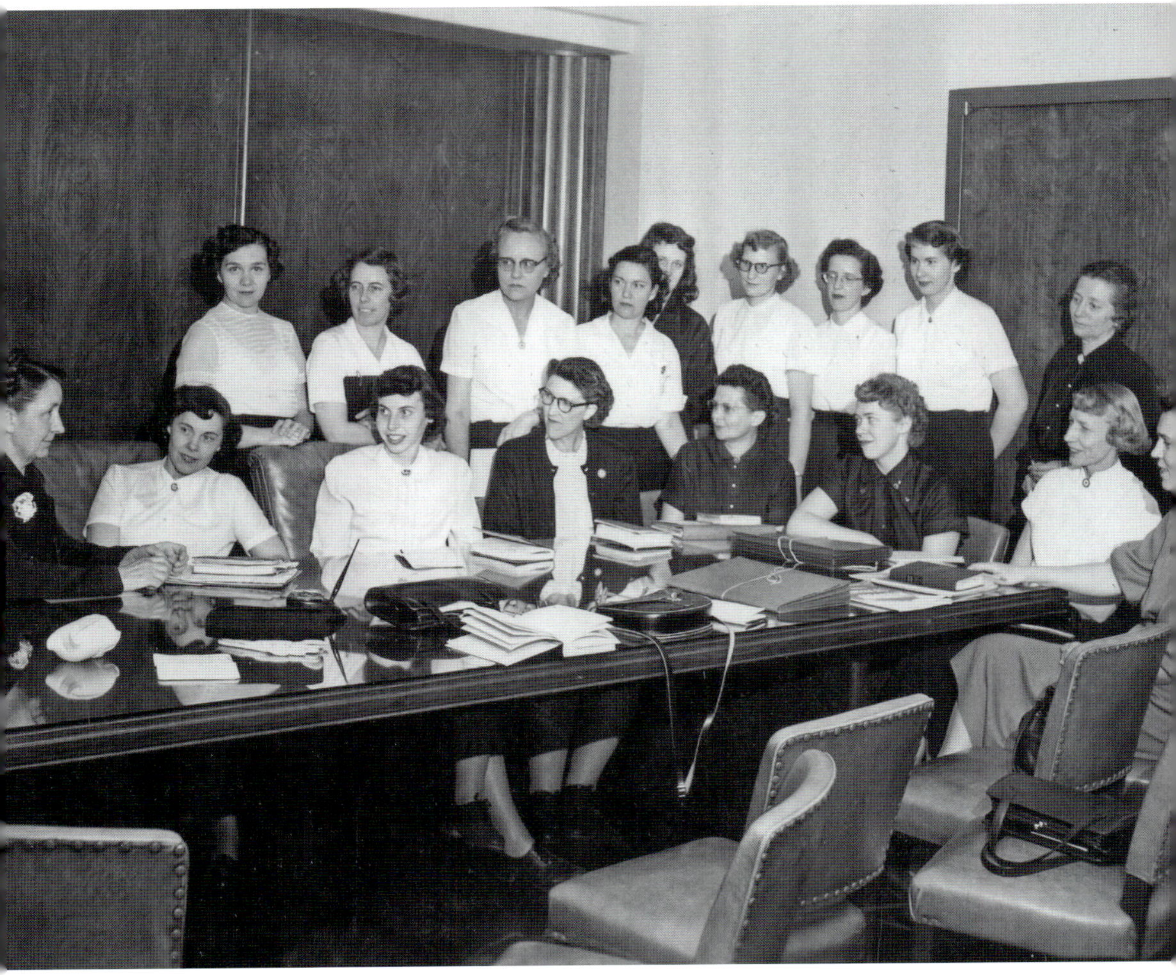

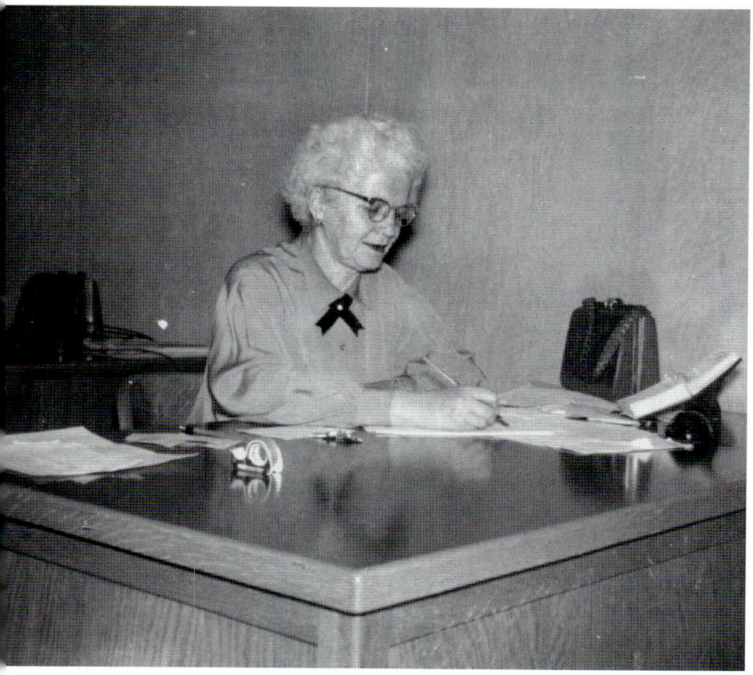

Willamelia Smith

Willamelia Smith was a caseworker for the Weber County Welfare Department for 28 years. She was the chief of welfare workers. Smith also became the head of the medical aid to the aged and dependent children department before she retired. In the 1950s, Smith was the president of the American Association of University Women. She passed away on May 28, 1994.

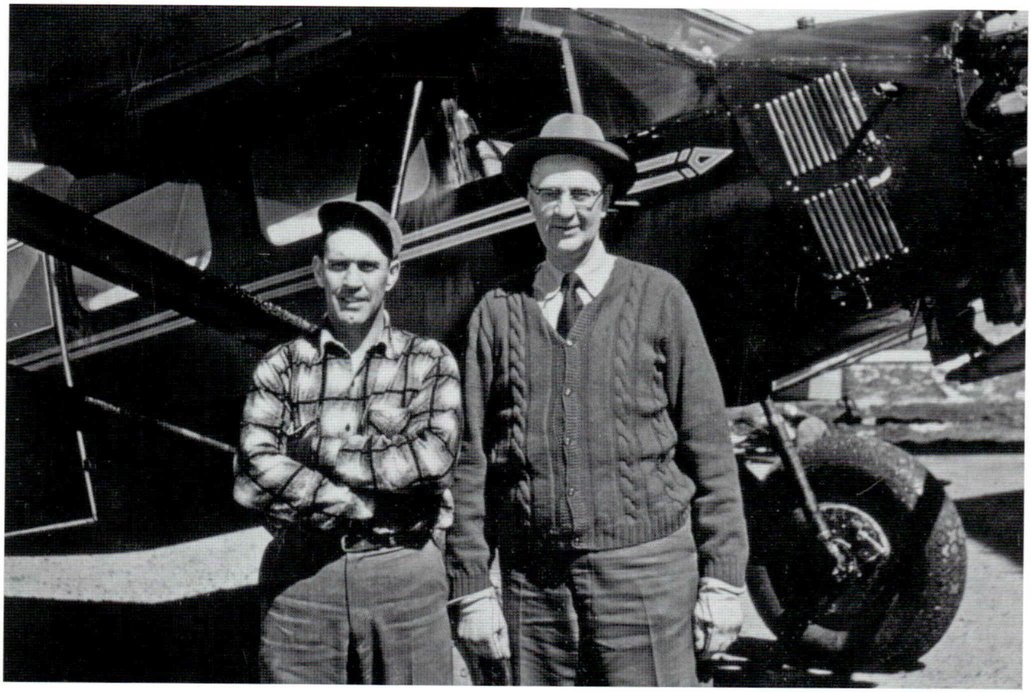

Chet Olsen

Chet Olsen (right) served most of his adult life working for the US Forest Service in Ogden. He was a close friend with author Bernard DeVoto and his wife, Avis. Avis even once wrote to Julia Child in 1953 about Olsen saying "his food tastes are exactly like B's, worse luck." When Bernard died, Olsen was responsible in spreading his ashes over the Clearwater National Forest.

CHAPTER FOUR

Give Us Teachers

A Rally for Education

Ogden's earliest schools were small classrooms with few supplies. While the city council worked to improve the school system, they found it difficult to collect taxes from the people, and for many years, the schools limped along as best they could. After 1869, the railroad brought in an influx of non-Mormon settlers, raising tensions in the community, especially concerning the education of children. Mormons were concerned about their children being influenced by outsiders, while non-Mormons were worried about their children being exposed to the practice of polygamy. Until the late 1800s, most of Ogden's schools were parochial, like the Sacred Heart Academy. But one election, set against the backdrop of mounting pressure against polygamy from the federal government, changed everything.

The 1889 Ogden municipal election marked a shift in political power from the People's Party, a conservative party closely allied with the Church of Jesus Christ of Latter-day Saints, to the Liberal Party consisting mostly of non-Mormon business leaders who advocated a strong separation between church and state. Despite accusations of unfair voting practices on both sides, the Liberal Party won every office on the ballot that year, including the office of mayor, which went to Frederick J. Kiesel, Ogden's first non-Mormon mayor. Shortly after his election, Kiesel decided to create the city's first board of education dedicated to providing free education for all of Ogden's children.

While there had been little cooperation across religious denominations in the past, Ogdenites rallied around Kiesel's education initiative and committed themselves to supporting their schools. Ogden became the first community in Utah to provide free education, but soon the entire territory adopted a similar system of education in order to improve its bid for statehood. Eventually, all of Ogden's private and parochial schools closed leaving only the free public schools.

Since that time, Ogden has taken great pride in its schools. An annual children's parade was started to show support of the schools, and today the Ogden School Foundation continues to raise funds to support Ogden's school system.

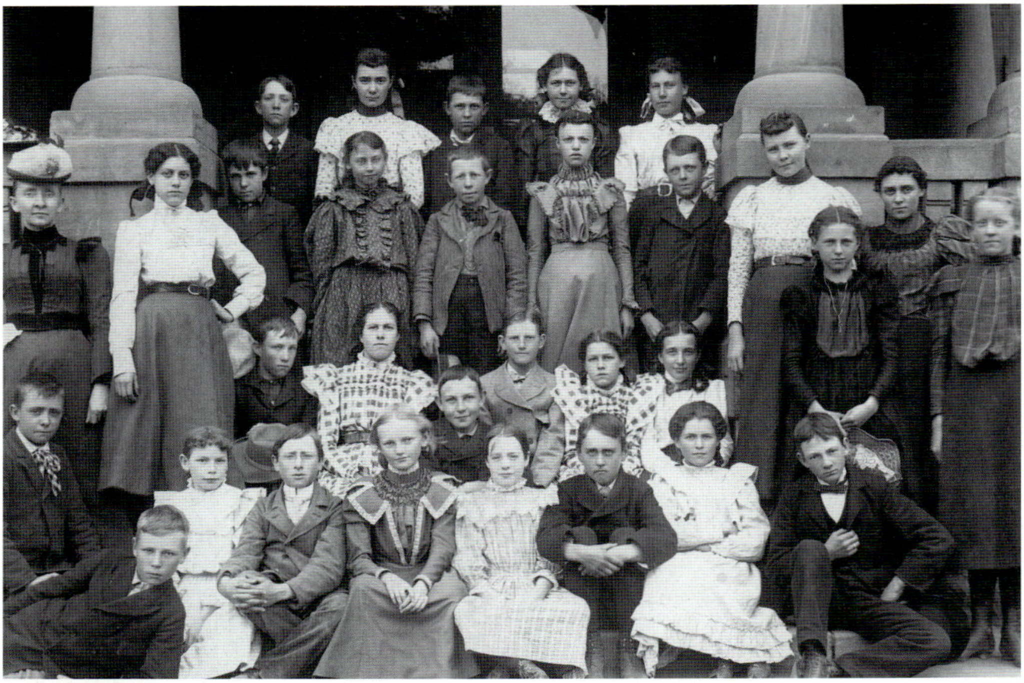

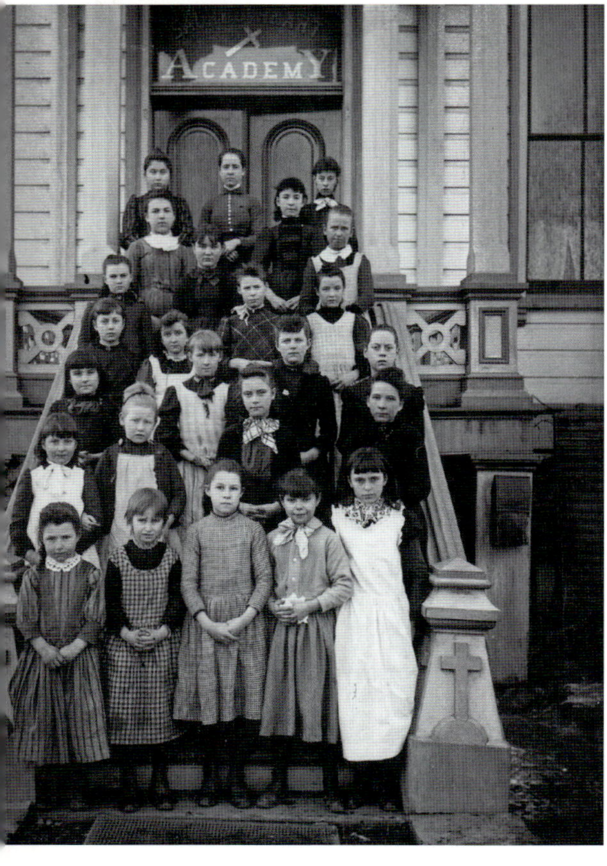

Linda Irwin at Grant School

Linda Irwin was one of Ogden's earliest and longest serving teachers. Born in New York, Irwin came to Ogden in 1891. She taught at several schools, including Mound Fort, Grant, Washington, and Central schools, until her retirement in 1929. She is shown here with one of her classes (second row, far left). She died in 1941 at the age of 89.

First Sacred Heart Academy

In 1878, seven nuns from the order of the Sisters of the Holy Cross arrived in Ogden to open a new Catholic school. Sacred Heart Academy opened on Twenty-sixth Street and Washington Boulevard, and by 1883, there were 200 students in attendance. In 1892, a larger campus was built on Twenty-fifth Street and Quincy Avenue. This school building could house as many as 600 students and had an increased faculty of 21.

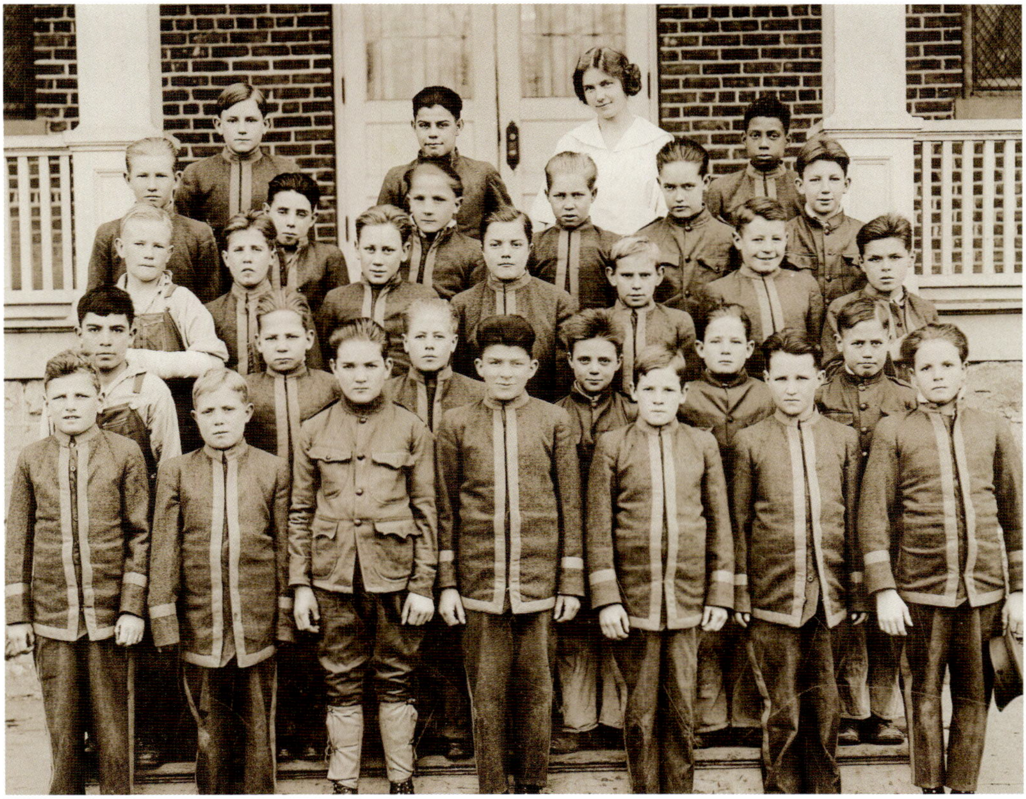

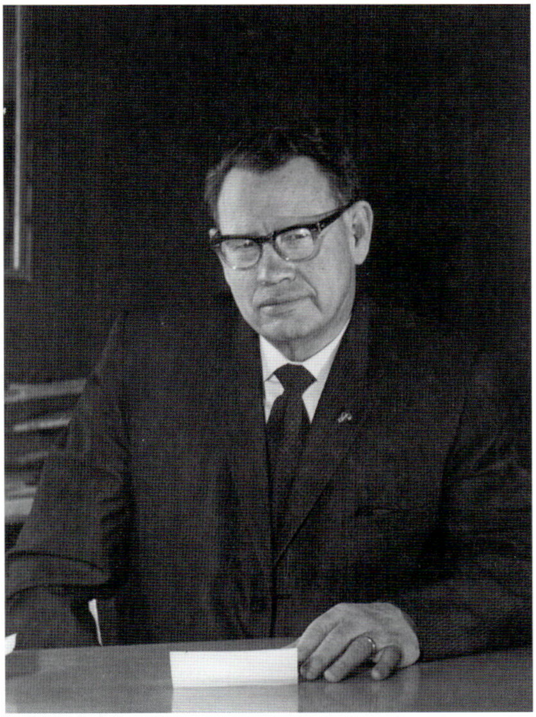

West Cottage Boys Group
On October 31, 1889, the Utah Territorial Reform School opened in Ogden with 23 inmates. Meant to provide education to troubled youth, the school curriculum had a heavy emphasis in vocational training. In 1896, the school changed locations and became known as the State Industrial School. By 1944, the school had 750 acres of land where students farmed and raised dairy cows.

Claud Pratt
In 1954, Claud Pratt was appointed superintendent of the State Industrial School. While students previously had received vocational training in farming, barbering, carpentry, bookkeeping, and other trades, Pratt broadened the educational program and in 1969, the school was accredited. During his 24-year tenure, Pratt helped over 7,000 students, modernized the grounds and buildings, and improved training for faculty and staff. He died in Ogden in 2001.

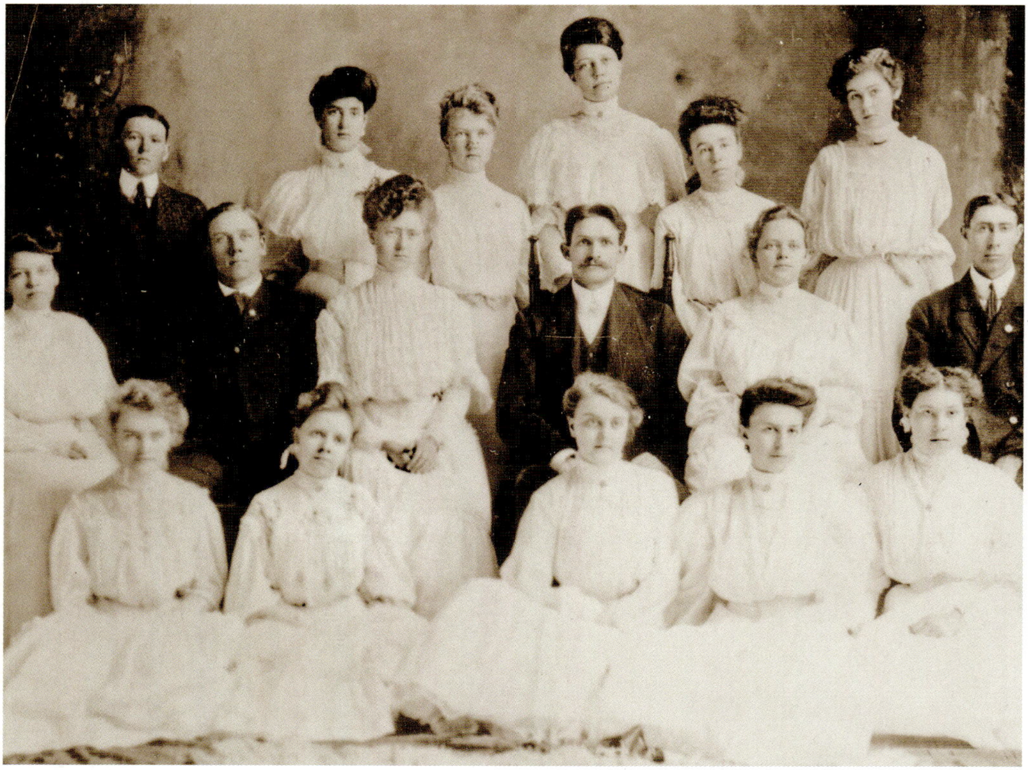

Weber Stake Academy
Weber Stake Academy was established in 1889, with Louis F. Moench leading 100 students as principal. The Academy continued to grow and in 1902, David O. McKay (seated, center) became the second principal. McKay began teaching at Weber in 1897 and served as principal until 1908. Standing behind McKay is Marion Belnap Kerr, granddaughter of Gilbert Belnap. She played on the academy's women's basketball team and later served as a teacher in Weber County.

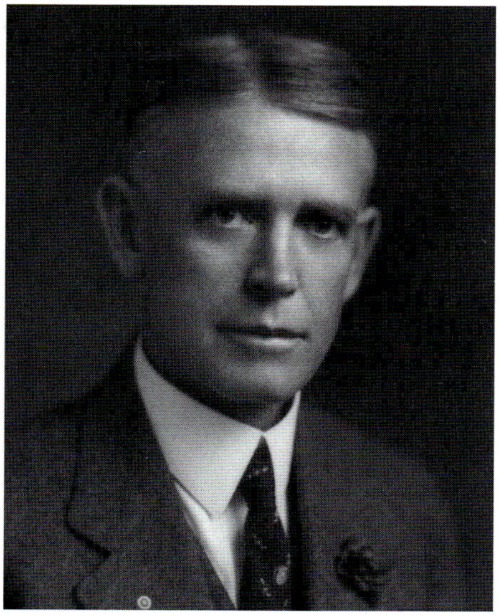

Frank M. Driggs
Frank M. Driggs began teaching deaf and blind students in 1889, and in 1901, was appointed superintendent of the Utah School for the Deaf, a position he held for 40 years. Driggs was a dedicated teacher, even participating with his students as they showed the cattle they raised. In 1939, Driggs was attacked by one of the bulls, breaking four ribs. He retired two years later but continued to work in the deaf community.

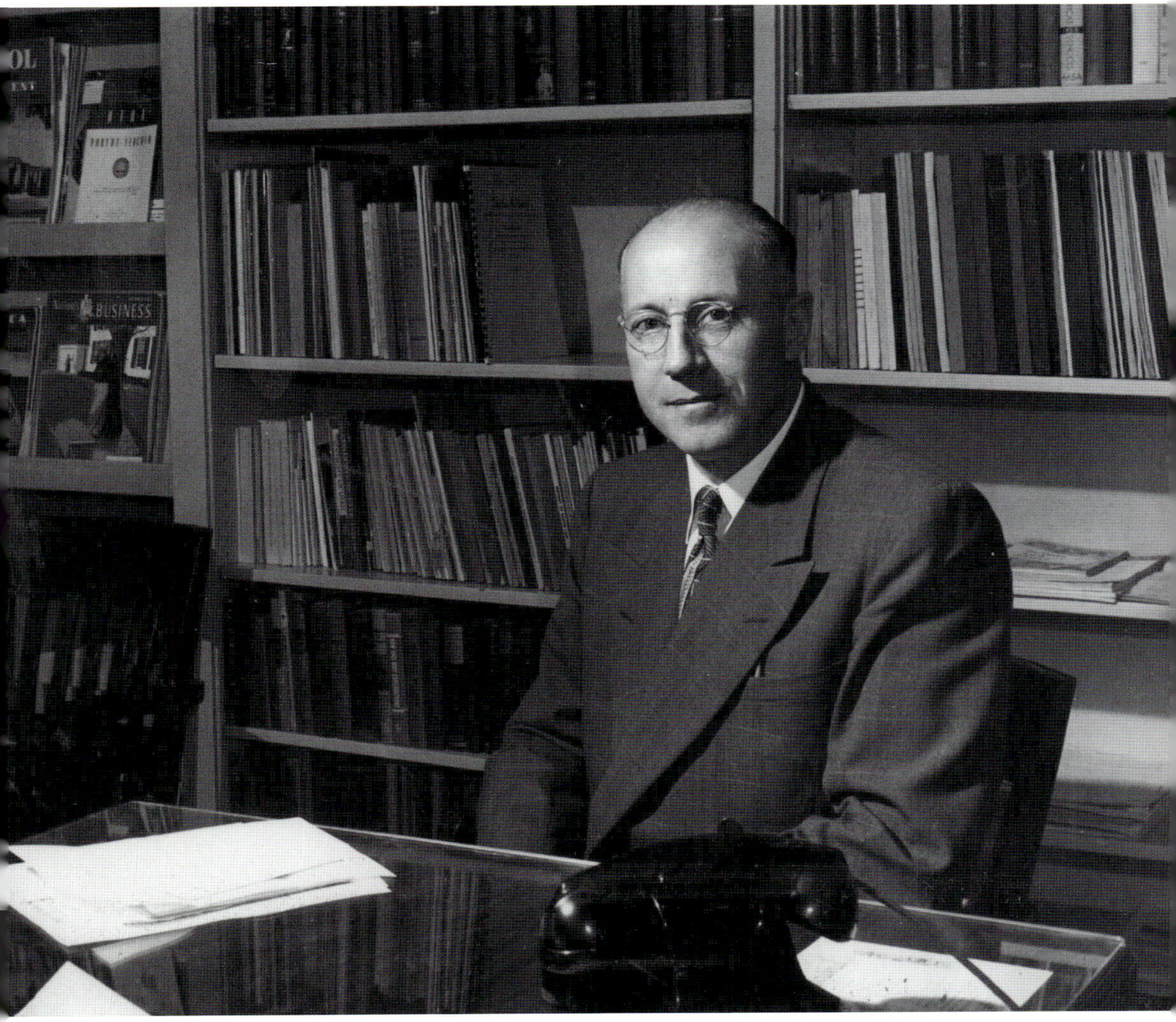

Dr. Thomas O. Smith

After studying at the University of Utah, Ogden native Thomas O. Smith began teaching in Weber County in 1929. Later he also became principal of Lincoln Elementary, Washington Junior High, and Ogden High School. In 1948, he was appointed superintendent of Ogden School District, a position he held for more than 20 years. Over 300 people attended his retirement party in 1969, where he told his guests, "If we can educate people, we can have the chance to serve world problems better than through any other avenue or means." Smith's dedication to education was passed on to his daughter, Olene Walker, who became Utah's governor in 2003 and continues to work to improve education. In 1956, the T.O. Smith Elementary School on Thirty-third Street and Gramercy Avenue was named in Smith's honor.

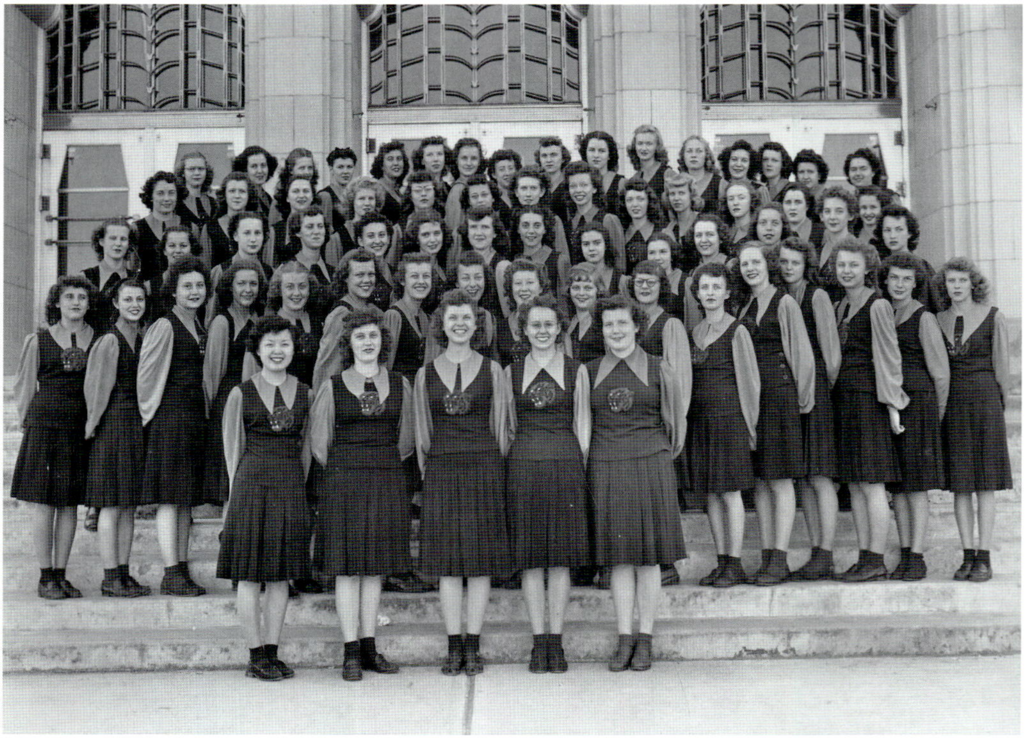

OHS Pep Club

Ogden High's pep club, under the direction of Helena B. Chase, was charged not only with supporting the school's athletic teams, but also with supporting a variety of school activities. Club membership was determined by scholarship, attendance, and conduct. The 1942 club (pictured) included 160 members and spent the year gathering almost 500,000 pounds of scrap metal for the war effort.

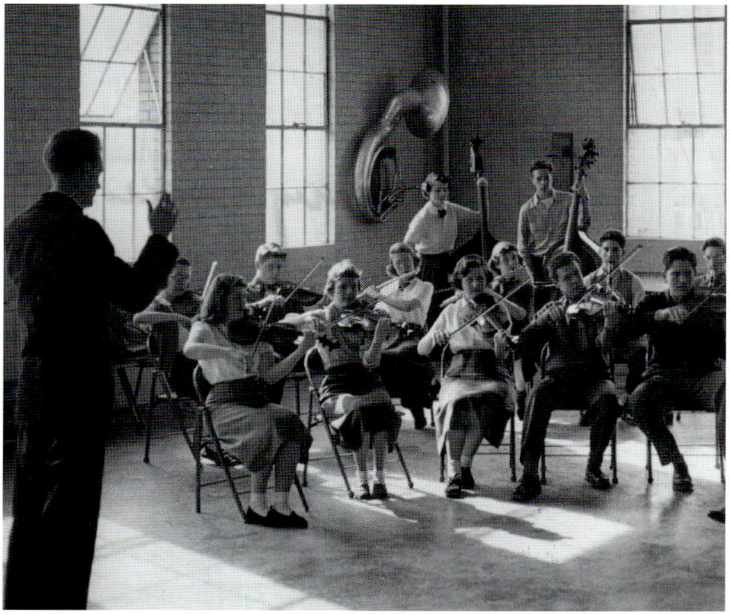

Max Dalby

After studying music at Brigham Young University, Max Dalby became the principal clarinetist for the Utah Symphony. In 1951, Dalby began teaching summer music lessons at Central Junior High School. Later that year, he took over for his brother as music director at Ogden High School, where he remained until 1955, when he became music director at Weber College. Later, he became music director at Utah State University until retiring in 1984.

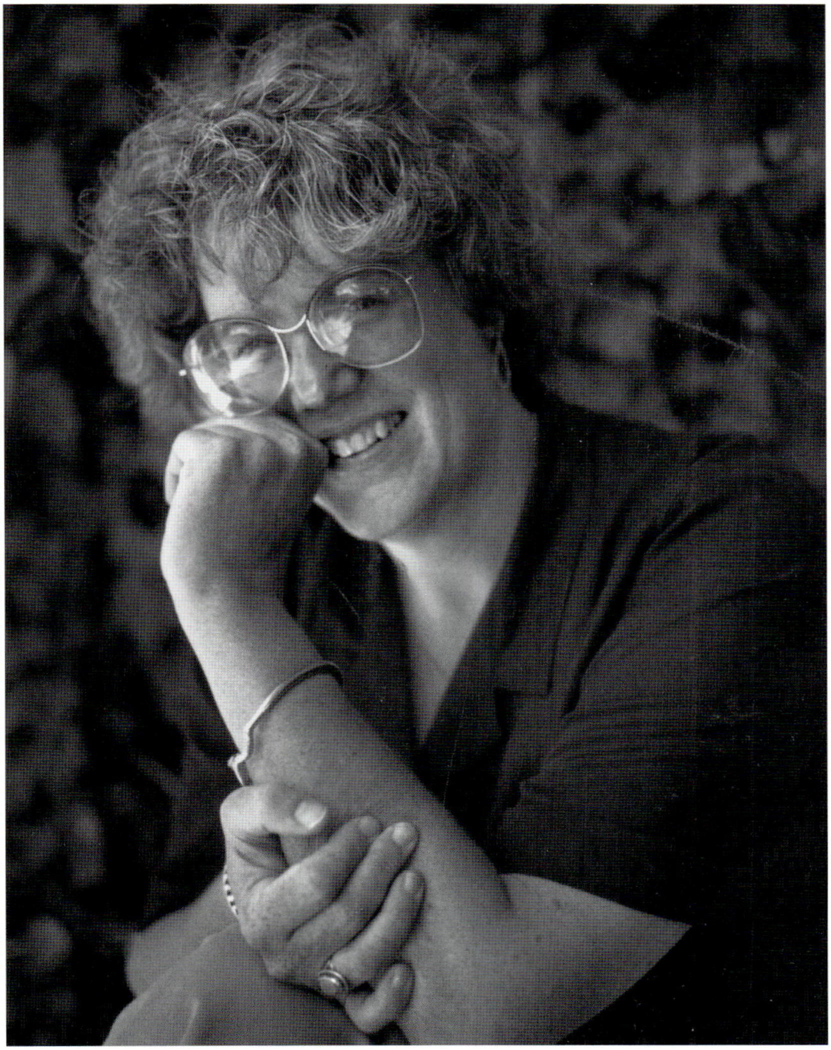

Margaret I. Rostkowski

Margaret I. Rostkowski was born in Little Rock, Arkansas, on January 12, 1945. Her family moved to Ogden in 1947 and she graduated from Middlebury College, Vermont, and the University of Kansas. She taught at Ogden High School and was the advisor for the *Literary Harvest*. Rostkowski has written three young adult novels: *After the Dancing Days, The Best Friends,* and *Moon Dancer. After the Dancing Days* was an American Library Association notable children's book in 1986 and won the Golden Kite award for excellence in children's literature that same year. Rostkowski, in an interview after winning the ALA award stated, "I find that my students are deeply interested in the issues of war and peace and duty to country and where one finds true heroism . . . This book grew out of those questions, many of which I haven't yet answered for myself." (Photograph courtesy of *Ogden Standard Examiner.*)

Bill Terry

Bill Terry was an Ogden High teacher of modern languages. He was also responsible for announcing Ogden High's football games. One night, the stadium PA system cut out and Terry was left to call the plays from the sidelines. Apparently, the fans still enjoyed the game, as the newspaper reported that Terry sounded just the same.

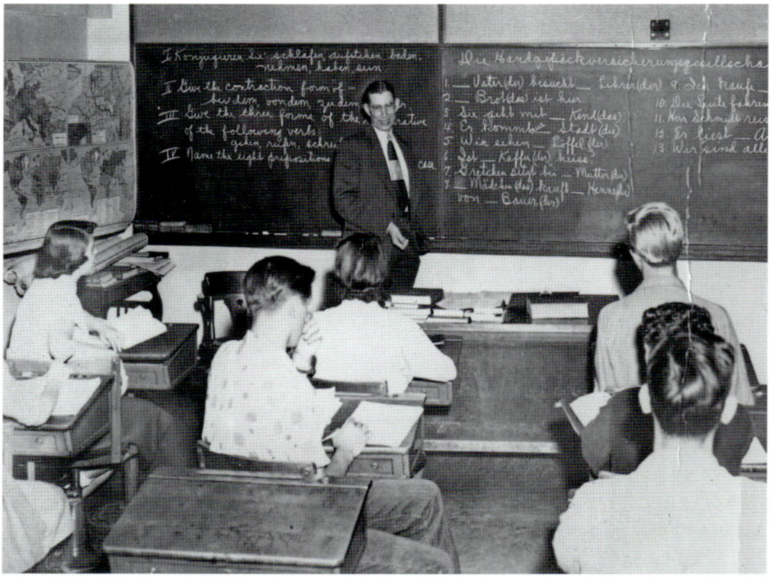

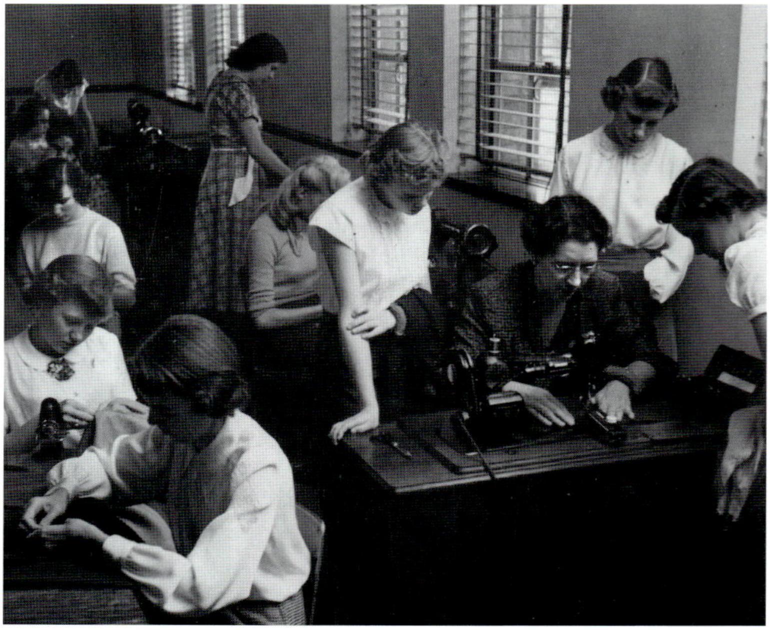

Sara Nicholson

Sara Nicholson was the domestic arts teacher at Ogden High School. She taught the girls about home living, sewing, and food. One of her students said of Nicholson's class, "In home nursing and home living, I not only discovered how to get a man, but also how to keep him."

CHAPTER FIVE

Military Service
At Home and Abroad

Wartime had a strong influence on the economic and social history of Ogden. The procession of countless soldiers who stopped in Ogden on their way to war stands out in the memory of longtime citizens. In World War I, a number of Ogden's young men volunteered or were drafted for duty. The soldiers saw action across the European front and some were even awarded medals of valor. When the regiments began to return in 1919, they were met with a hero's welcome with the biggest parade in Ogden's history. The troops were initially ordered to march down Washington, but no crowds were allowed to gather or to speak with the troops because of the threat of the influenza epidemic. The citizens of Ogden had other plans. At the depot, families and friends ran to greet their returning soldiers.

Between World War I and World War II, several federal and military installations were established in the Ogden area. The city was chosen because of its inland location, railroad system, and workforce. In early 1920, the Ogden Arsenal was constructed to store ammunition. During World War II, the Arsenal was expanded to include storing and shipping of vehicles, small arms, and artillery pieces. In 1940, The Utah General Depot, later known as Defense Depot Ogden, was established as a general warehousing facility. During World War II, the depot became home to a German and Italian prisoner of war camp. The facility housed approximately 7,000 prisoners who worked at farms and construction jobs throughout the county.

With over 4,700 men from Ogden serving in the military during World War II, the work force shortage hit the home front hard. There were over 50,000 civilians that worked at the federal and military installations in Ogden. Many of the workforce was young women who became training in driving forklifts, shipping, and packaging as well as office duties. The war years changed the economy of Ogden from agriculture to industry and commerce and set up Ogden for years to come.

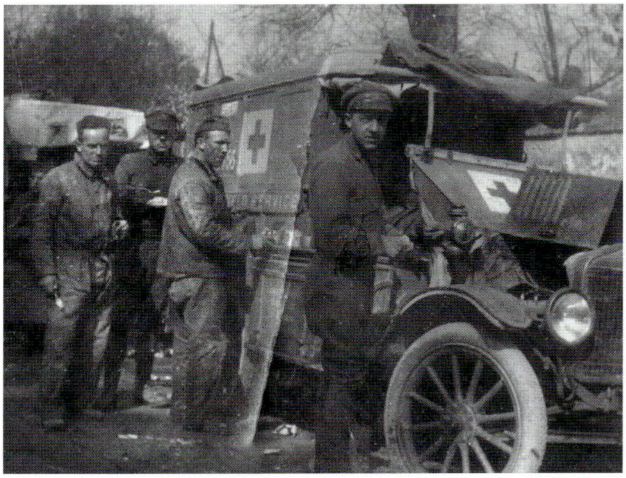

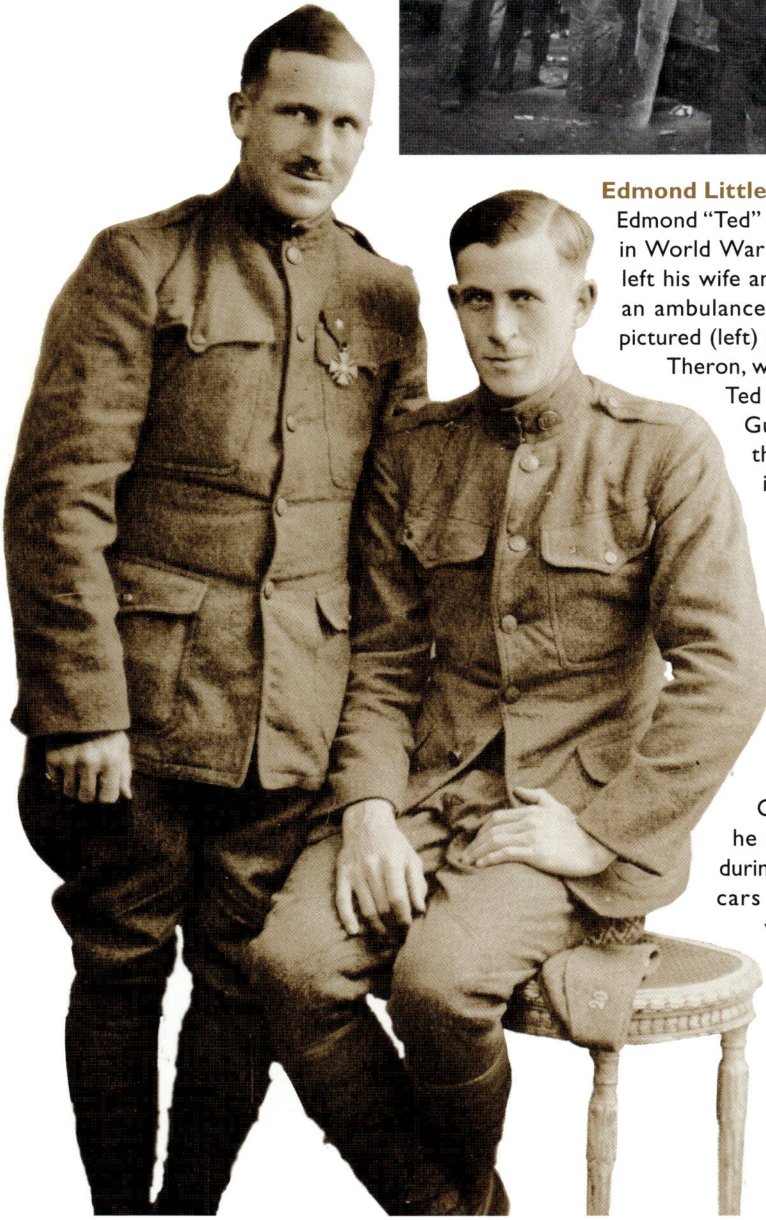

Edmond Littlefield

Edmond "Ted" Littlefield decided to fight in World War I in September 1917. He left his wife and young son to serve as an ambulance driver in France. He is pictured (left) standing with his brother Theron, who also served in the war. Ted was awarded the Croix de Guerre for heroic conduct three times during his time in the service. He was the first soldier from Ogden to receive this high honor. Above, Littlefield is pictured with fellow soldiers, from left to right, Charles Love, Don Murphy, Littlefield, and Pal Palamountain along with their ambulances. Littlefield's third Croix de Guerre was received after he crossed the Alsne River during a battle and put together cars to help transport the wounded back to safety in 1918. Littlefield and his brother, Theron, were welcomed home to fanfare in 1919.

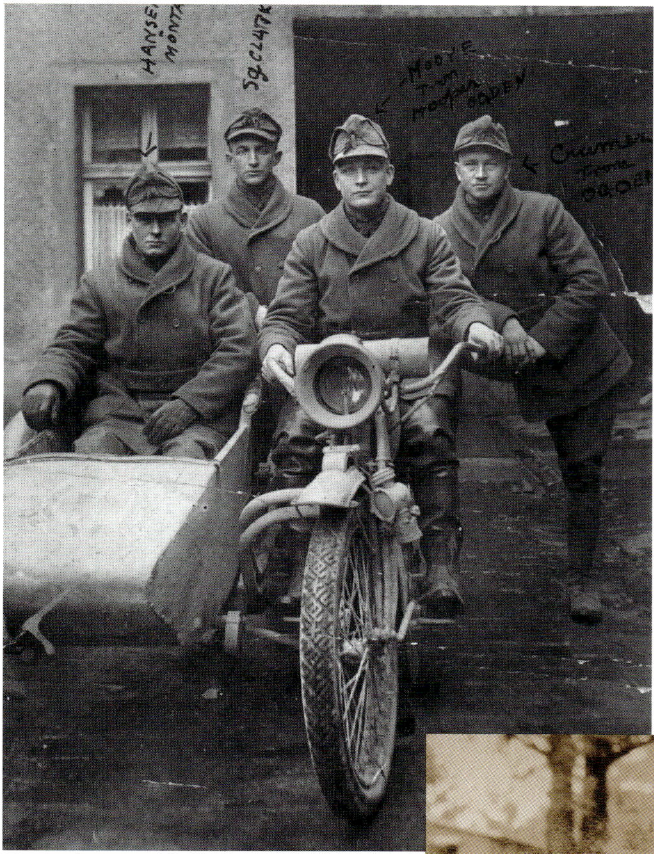

Henry Kramer
Serving in World War I was a duty felt by many of the men from Ogden and the surrounding area. Pictured here are, from left to right, Hansen from Montana, Sgt. Clark, Joseph O. Moore from Hooper, and Henry Kramer from Ogden. Kramer enlisted in September 1917 in the 347th Machine Gun Battalion. He was killed on September 29, 1918, on the ridge overlooking the town of Genes, France.

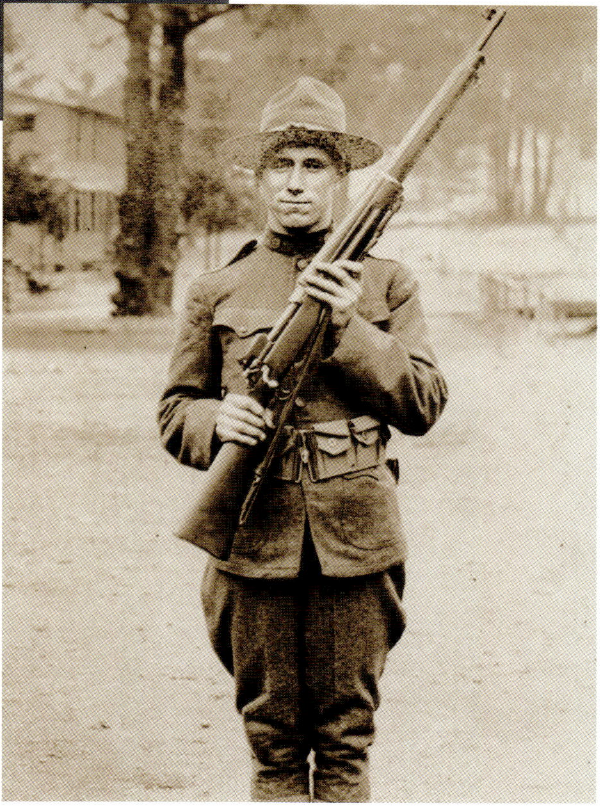

Stanley Purrington
Stanley Purrington joined the United States Army in February 1918 from Ogden. He was sent to Camp Fremont in California and then to France. In France, he served at Camp Pontanezen as part of the occupying forces. He was a battalion sergeant major in the 8th Infantry. He returned home from war on August 30, 1919. He died in Northern Utah on June 1, 1971.

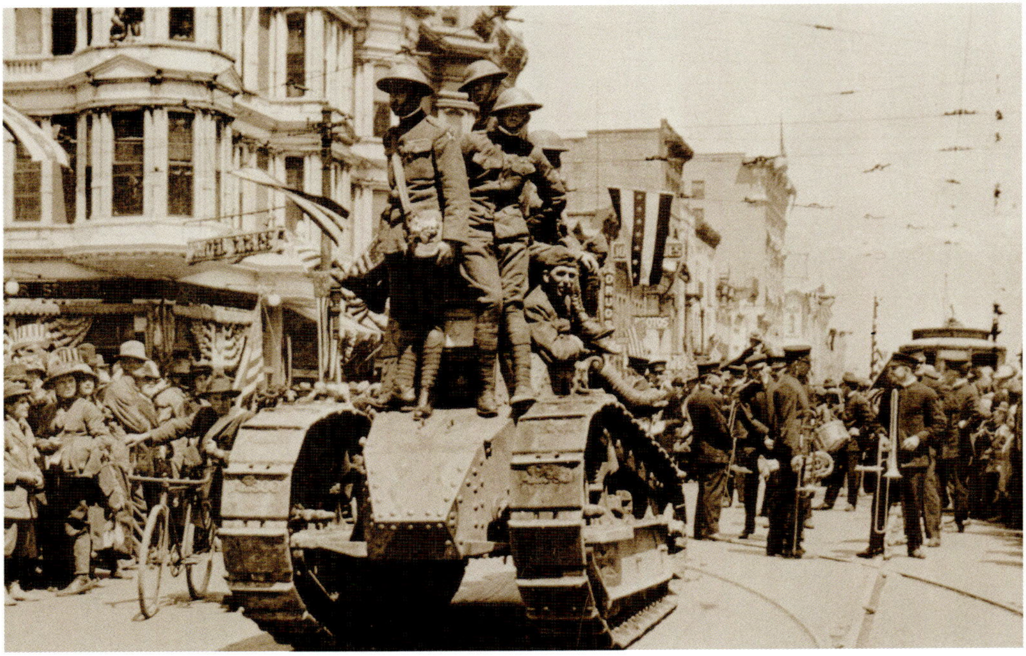

World War I Veterans in Parade
When World War I ended, the returning troops were often greeted with fanfare and parades in their honor. During 1919, Ogden held several parades showcasing the returning soldiers. On January 17, 1919, the 145th Field Artillery was the first to be greeted as they paraded down the business streets. In May 1919, Ogden celebrated the 50th anniversary of the Golden Spike, and soldiers, sailors, and marines were honored. A special division, under the direction of Capt. J.R. Ward of the 145th Field Artillery, marched along with the floats, and a fireworks display was set off that night. Airplanes from Mather Field in Sacramento also arrived after following the Southern Pacific route to Ogden.

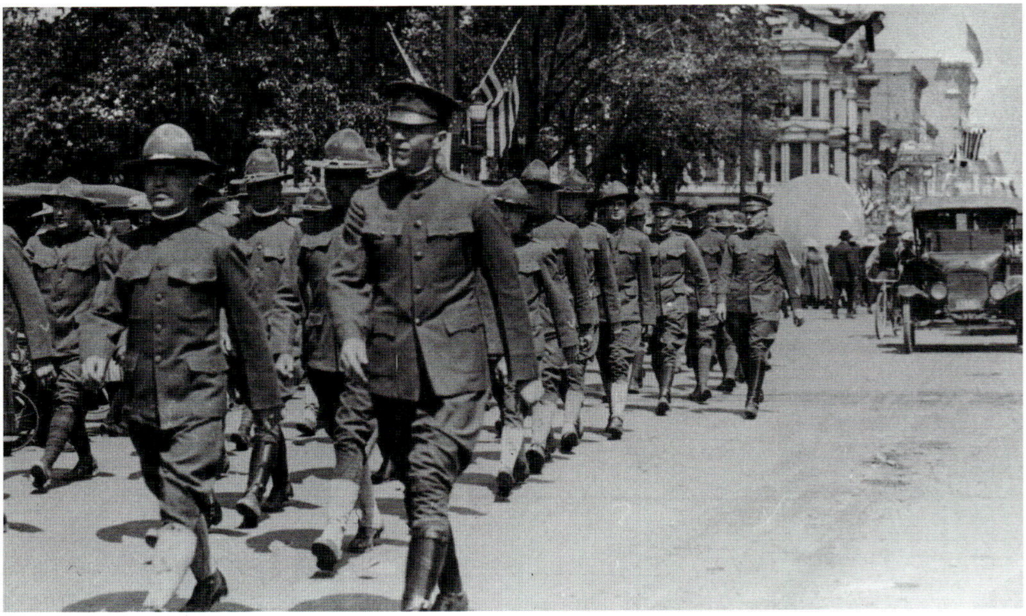

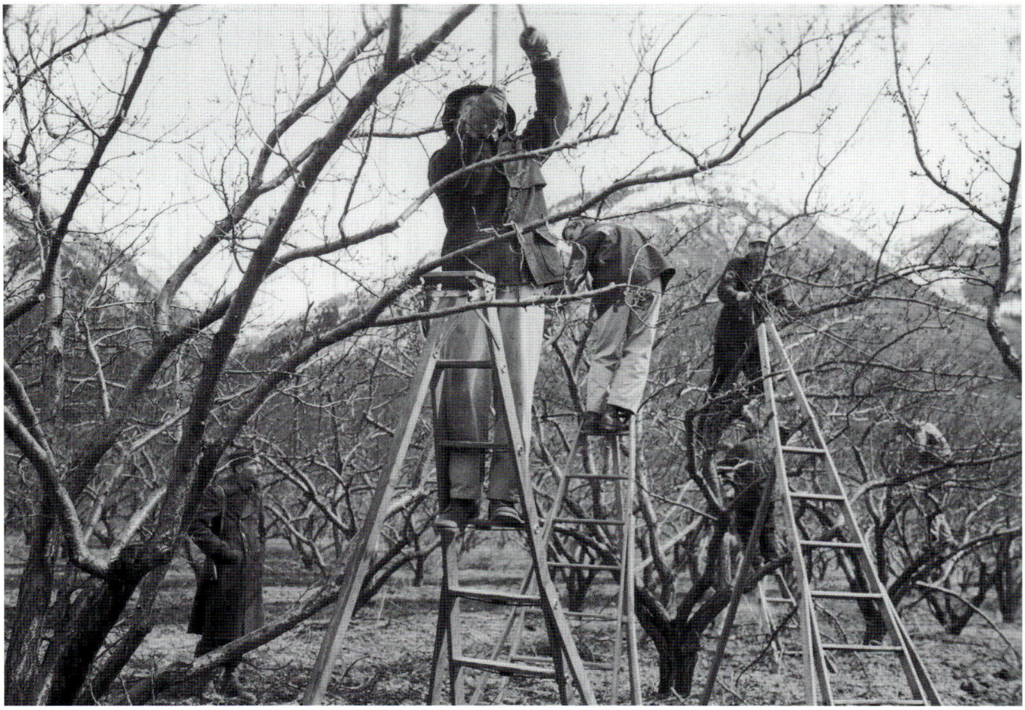

Prisoners of War

From 1943 to 1946, a prisoner of war camp was operated at Defense Depot Ogden and held 7,000 Italian and German soldiers. Due to a shortage in manual labor around Weber County, the prisoners were allowed to work for 80¢ a day at local farms and orchards. Pictured above is a group of prisoners picking apples at a quota of 50 bushels of apples a day. After they made the quota, they were taken down to a store and allowed to buy what they needed. The prisoners were also responsible for the care and repair of their clothing and shoes. From April to July 1943, seven cobblers (below) repaired about 1,200 pairs of shoes by hand. When they were trained in the use of modern shoe-repairing machinery they repaired 3,000 pairs a month.

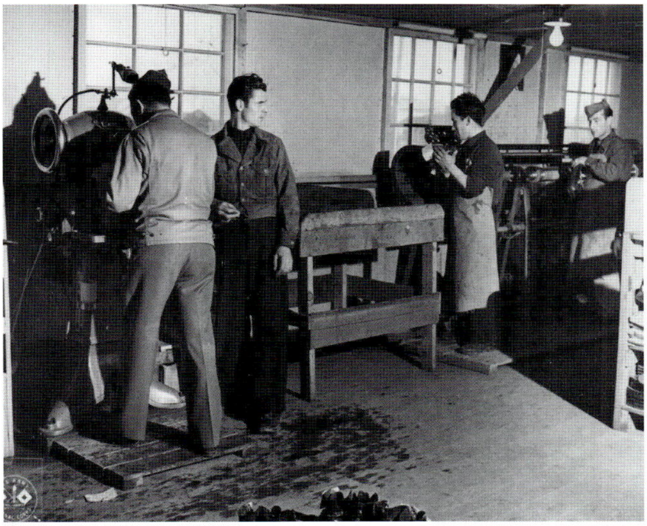

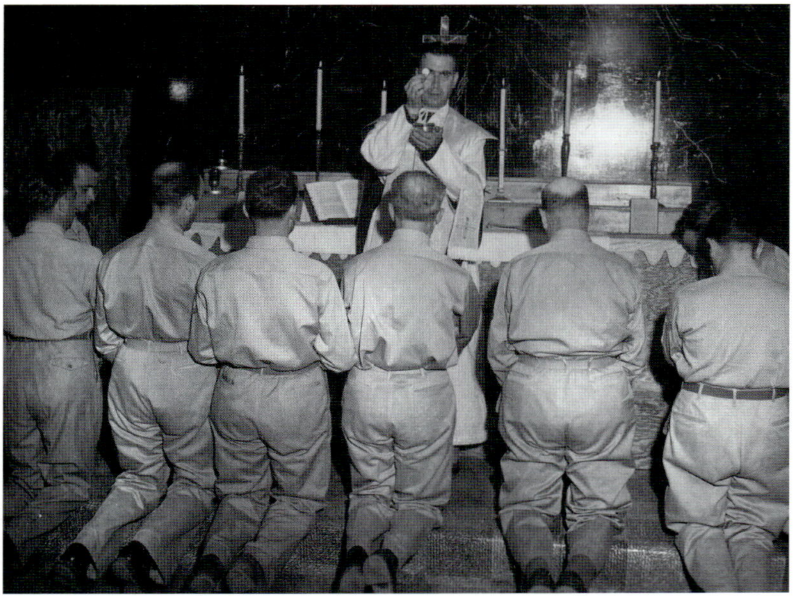

Chaplain Raphael Monteleone

Chaplain Raphael Monteleone was the post chaplain for the Utah Army services. From 1943 to 1945, he conducted Catholic services at the Italian Service Unit camp and prisoner of war camp. In early 1945, he even signed for two Italian POWs to take brides in their native Italy. He often organized dances at St. Joseph's Catholic Church between the Italians and local Catholic girls. He was transferred back East in 1945.

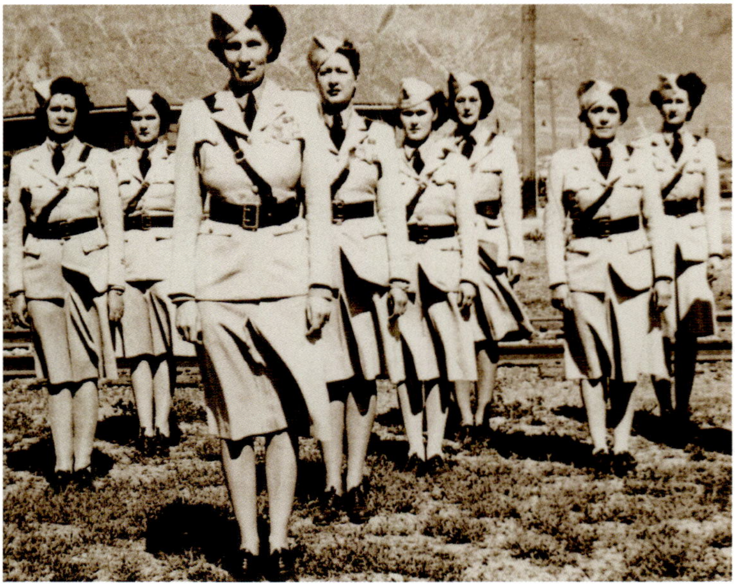

Women's Army Corps

The Women's Army Corps was established in 1942 as a branch of the US Army. About 150,000 women served in the WACs during World War II. Most served stateside such as this group of women who were stationed at Defense Depot Ogden where they were guards or served in other positions. The WACs were disbanded in 1978.

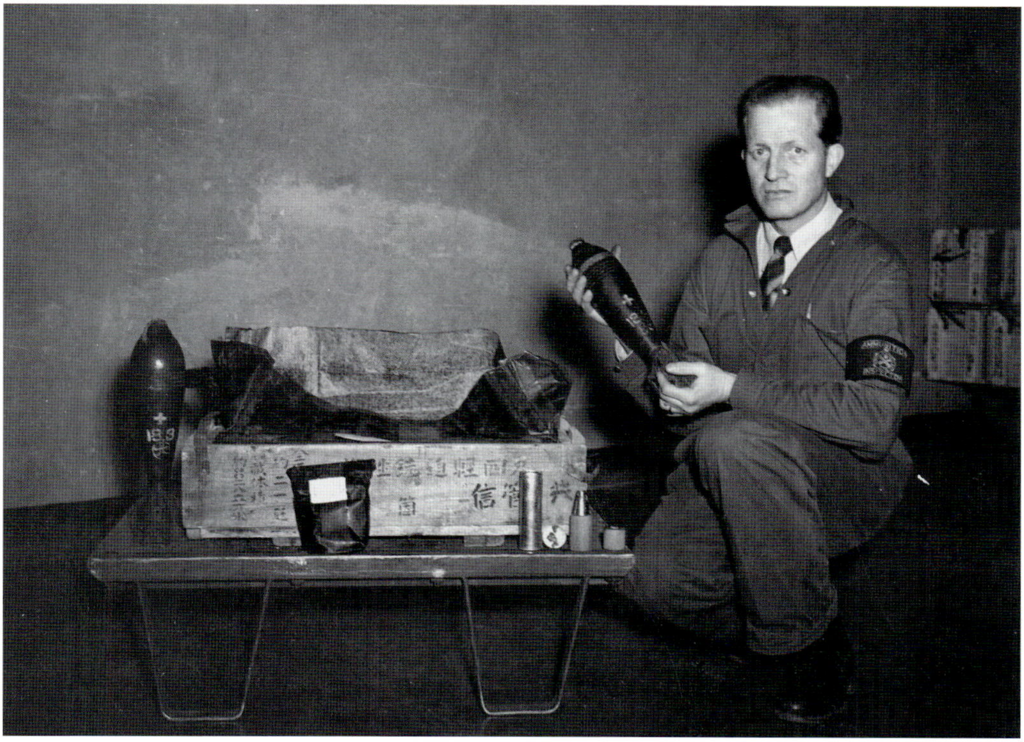

Lyle Richins

The Ogden Arsenal was built in Ogden following World War I. It was to provide a suitable site to store munitions for the US Army Ordnance Department. The facilities included storage igloos, a bomb-loading plant, and railroad facilities. It was in use from World War II through the Korean War. Pictured here is Lyle Richins, an ammunition inspector, holding Japanese motor shells at the arsenal.

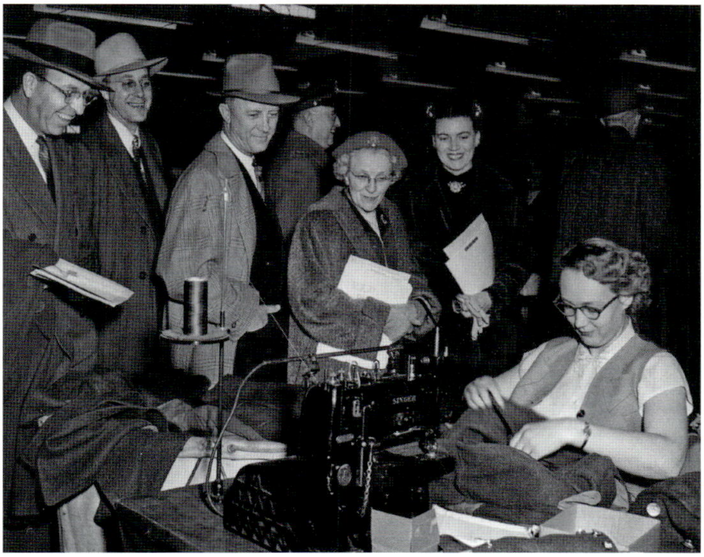

Ogden City Council at Defense Depot Ogden

The Defense Depot Ogden was established during World War II as a key supply point for the Sixth Army, Alaska, and Pacific Area. On March 6, 1952, the Ogden City Council was invited to visit the depot. Pictured here are, from left to right, E.J. Allison, Charles Stark, Mayor George T. Frost, Athleen Fisburn, and Elizabeth Tillotson. The tour included the new engineer maintenance shop and the crane to unload shipments.

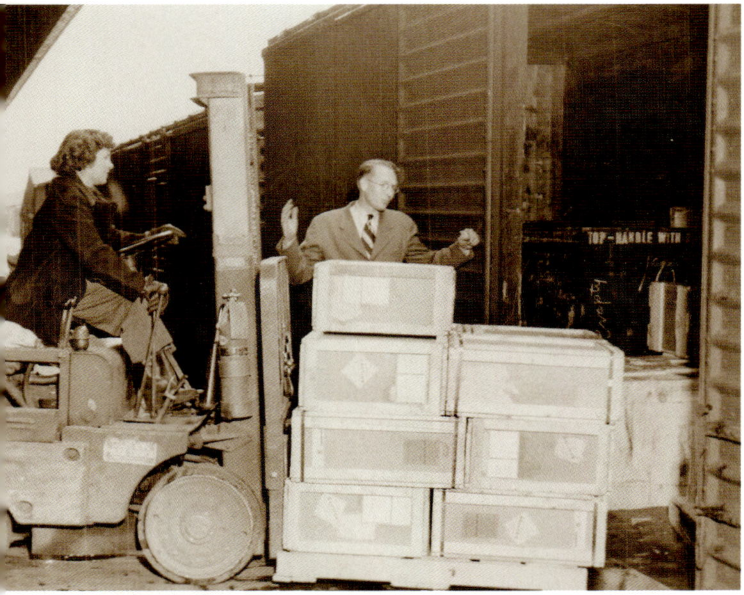

Elma Compton and H.H. Kipp

With the outbreak of World War II, local businesses suffered from a labor shortage as young men were shipped overseas. This was apparent in even the civil positions at military installations such as the Ogden Arsenal, where typically male jobs were performed by women. Here is Elma Compton driving a forklift as H.H. Kipp, the warehouse supervisor, guides her in January 1944.

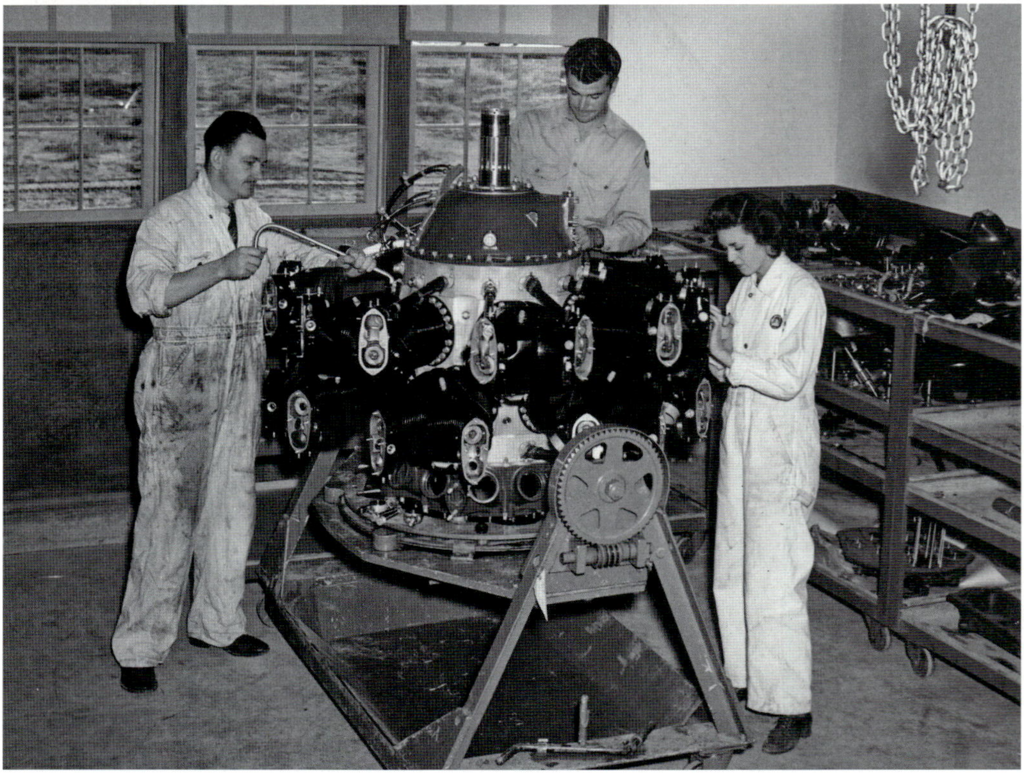

Hill Field Workers

Military and civilian personnel at the four major war bases in the Ogden area observed Armistice Day in 1942 by pressing forward with their duties. Shown here is a typical scene at Ogden Air Depot, Hill Field, where a group is working on Allison liquid-cooled, in-line plane engines. In the photograph, from left to right, are Donald P. Ransomer, Pvt. Jack Hyde, and Jean Gilles.

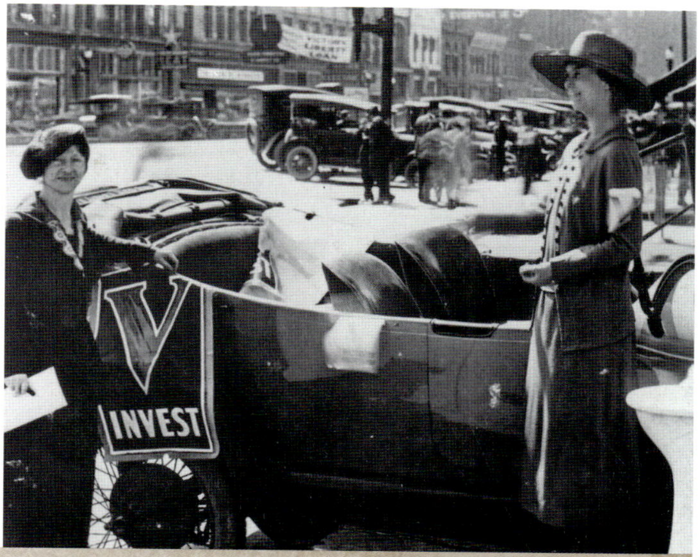

Gene and Carie Browning

The outbreak of World War I affected Ogden on all fronts. With the men going off to war, women at home did what they could to support the war effort. Most of the women's clubs volunteered at the Red Cross and campaigned for war bonds. During one of their drives, Ogden women brought in more than $2,400 in one day. Pictured here are Gene and Carie Browning, daughters of Matt and John Browning, selling war bonds.

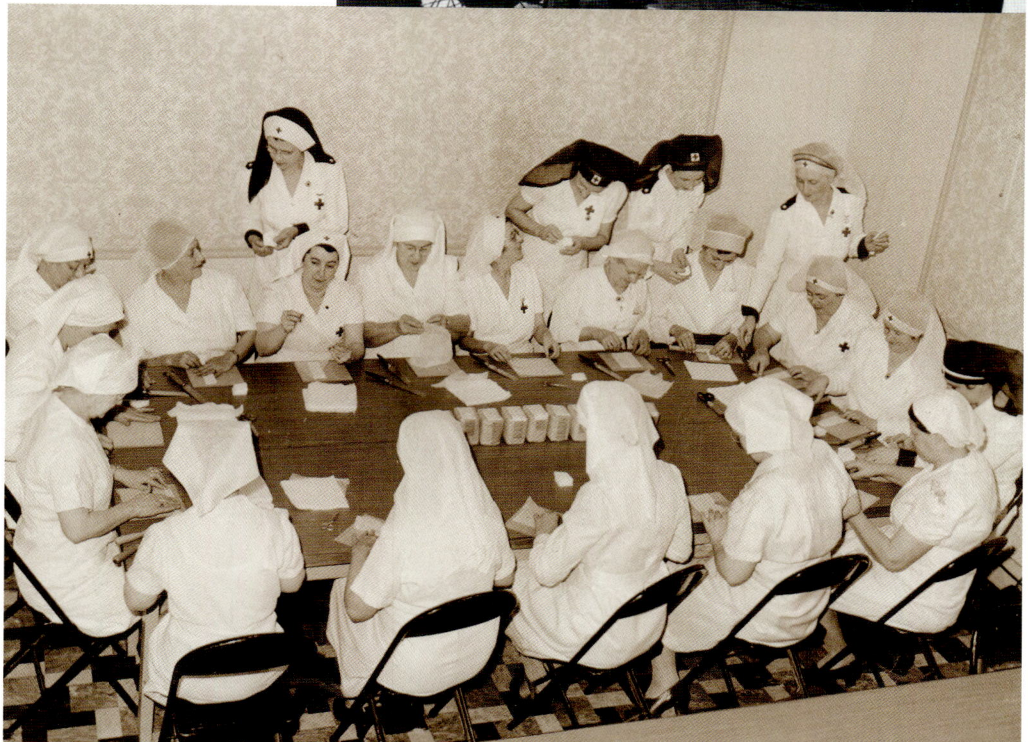

Ogden's Red Cross Volunteers

Early in November 1942, Ogden's women were asked to help the Red Cross make surgical dressings to be shipped overseas. By the end of November, work had begun in the Utah Power & Light Company auditorium and within two days 1,600 bandages were made. Women volunteered to work in the center from 10:00 a.m. to 3:00 p.m. at least one day a week. A year-and-a-half later, it was reported that a million dressings had been made nationwide.

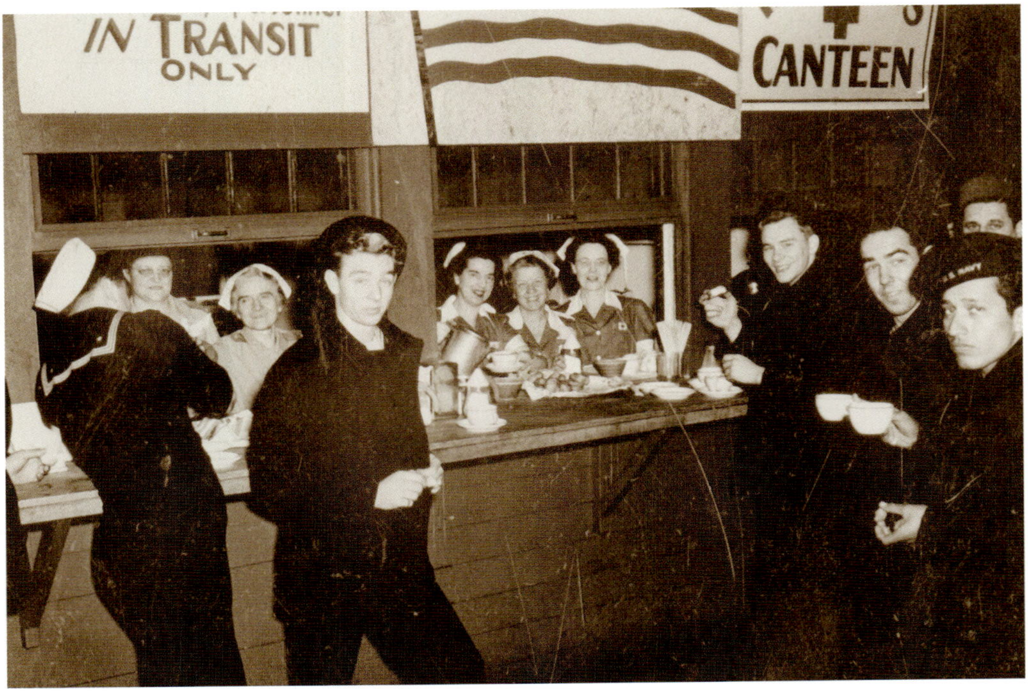

Red Cross Canteen

On March 25, 1942, the American Red Cross opened a canteen at the Union Station to feed sandwiches, coffee, and baked goods to members of the US Armed Forces in transit. Open from 7:30 a.m. until 10:30 p.m., seven days a week, the canteen was staffed by local women who logged over 107,000 hours of service and fed over 1.6 million servicemen until the canteen's closing on January 3, 1946. Sgt. Frank Dubek later wrote to the women who had served him: "Want to thank you all for what you have contributed during my stop in your city. Will never forget the day and hope to visit your city again."

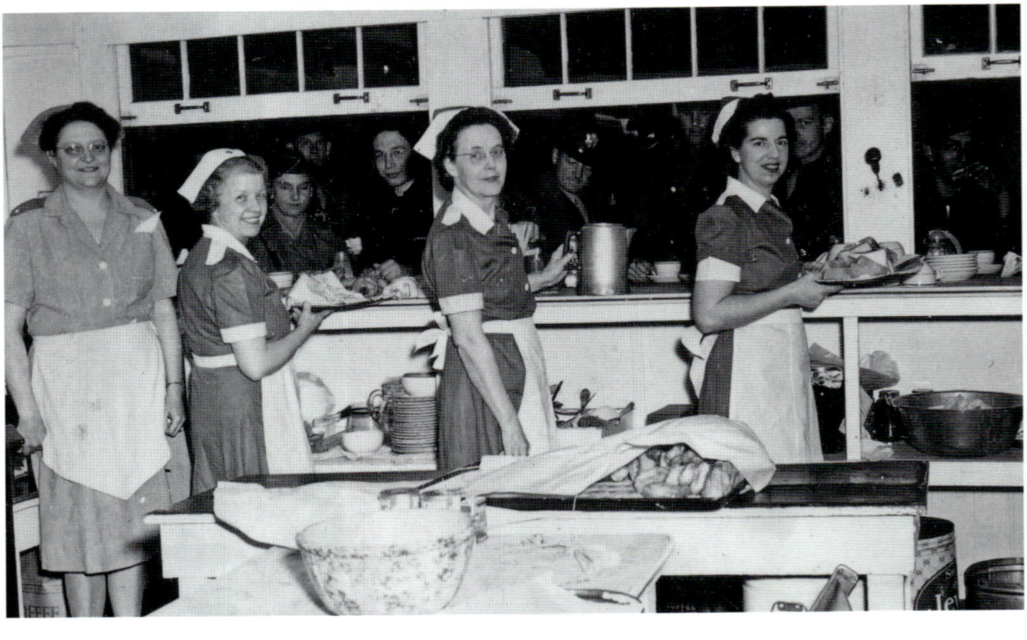

CHAPTER SIX

Voices of the People

Local and National Leaders

Ogden's involvement in politics has varied from the local to the national stage. The first mayor of Ogden was Lorin Farr who served in that capacity for over 20 years without pay. In 1889, Fred J. Kiesel became the first non-Mormon mayor of Ogden. Kiesel took it upon himself to try and advance Ogden. This included changing the street names to the names of US presidents and moving the city's northern boundary. He also served two terms in the state senate. Other mayors that impacted Ogden City were Harman Peery, who brought national attention to Ogden through the Pioneer Days celebrations in the 1930s and 1940s, and Raymond Wright who started the sister-city relationship with Hof, Germany, and created a new fire station and water treatment plant to Ogden.

In 1951, Ogden City accepted a new charter form of government with a city council in charge. That same year, six men and one woman were elected to city council, including G. Stanley Brewer, George T. Frost, Mary Woolley, Raymond S. Wright, Thorstein Larsen, and C. Austin Seager. This form of government stood until 1992, when the city transitioned to a mayor-council form. As time passed in Ogden, women became more involved in politics with several women serving on city council and serving in the legislature. Some of these pioneering women were Sarah Anderson (1897–1899), Mary Coulter (1903–1905), Jane Manning (1913–1915), Rosanne King (1977–1983), and Gaye Littleton (1983–1987).

Another side of political activity is the work done in precincts, state and national committees, and Utah legislature. Ogden had several people who have worked in these fields, including Richard Richards, Myrene Brewer, Elizabeth Vance, and Alex Hurtado. They were involved with both political parties on a national level. Ogden was home for congressional delegates, including Henry Aldous Dixon and Laurence Burton. Olene Walker served four terms in the Utah House of Representatives before she became the first woman to be elected as lieutenant governor and then governor of Utah.

Frederick Johann Kiesel

Born in 1841 in Ludwigsburg, Germany, to a shoe manufacturer, Frederick Johann Kiesel eventually became one of Ogden, Utah's, most important business and political leaders. Kiesel grew in success and prominence while in Ogden. In 1879, the local newspaper called his company "A mammoth institution of Ogden." On February 11, 1889, Kiesel became Ogden's first non-Mormon mayor. His campaign was based on his opposition to the blending of church and state, which he saw developing in Ogden. Kiesel continued as a public servant, serving at the state constitutional convention, and two terms as a state senator. Though originally considered an outsider, Kiesel found his place in the Ogden community, and by the time he died in April 1919, he had forever changed its landscape.

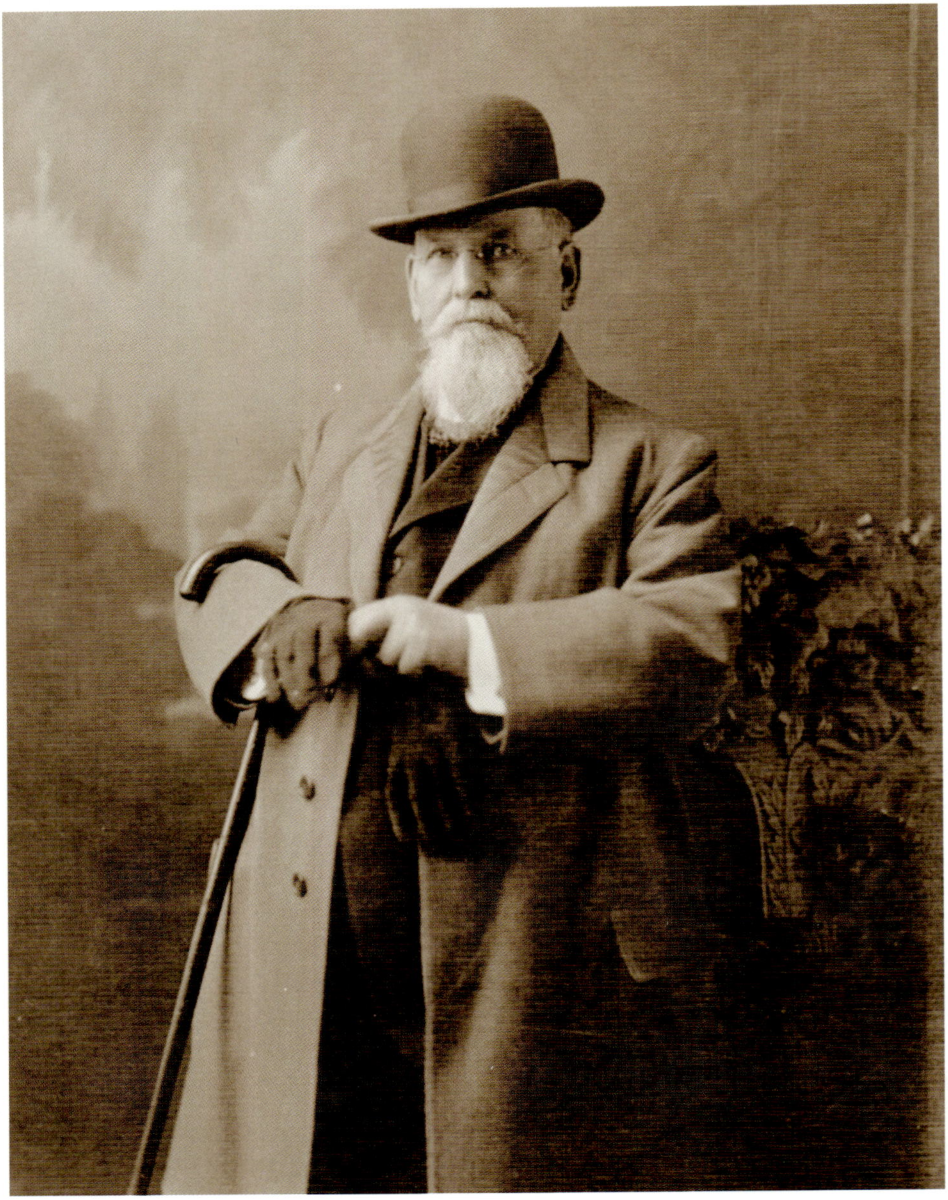

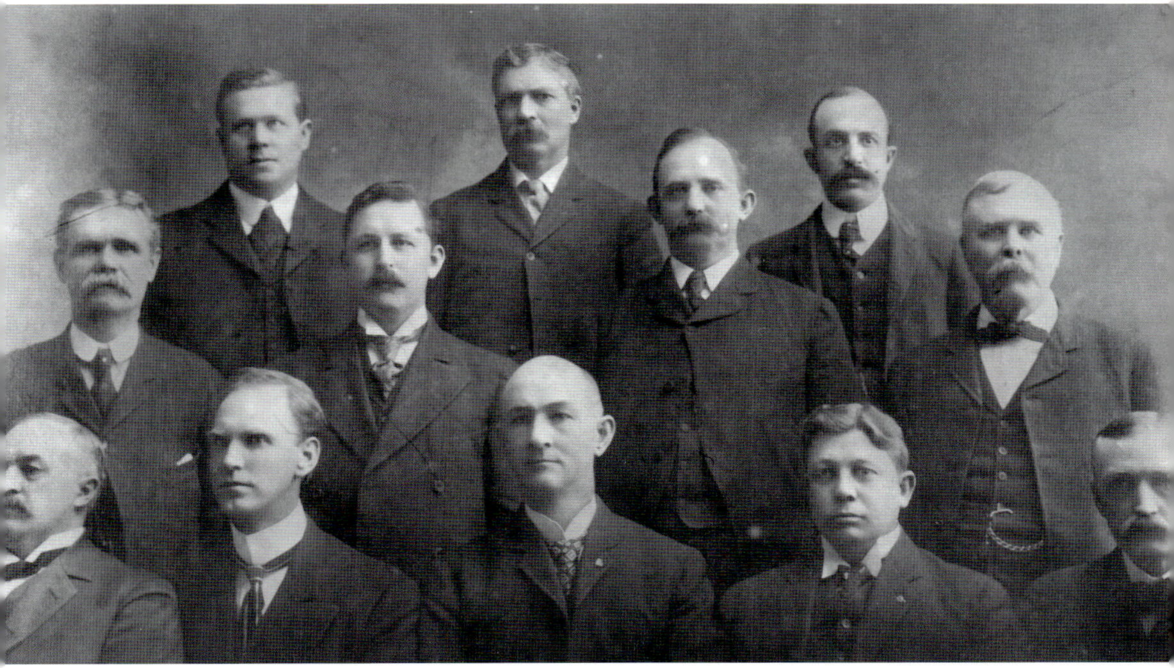

Ogden City Council

The Ogden City Council was established in 1851, consisting of a mayor, four alderman, and nine councilors. It was created to direct the affairs of the city and given jurisdiction over the water and timber within city limits. The council had the authority to levy and collect taxes. The first city council was also responsible for the establishment of schools and hospitals and the construction of water and lighting systems and public buildings.

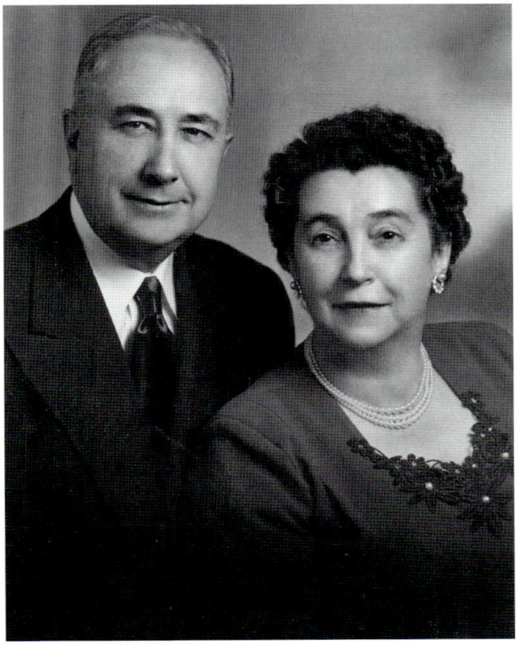

Raymond Wright

Raymond S. Wright was born in Ogden Valley in 1894. Wright worked for Southern Pacific Railroad for 46 years, retiring in 1959 as office manager. In 1951, he was elected to the Ogden City Council. Wright was then elected Ogden city mayor in 1953 and served until 1959. During his time as mayor, he started the sister city program with Hof, Germany. He is pictured here with wife, Florence.

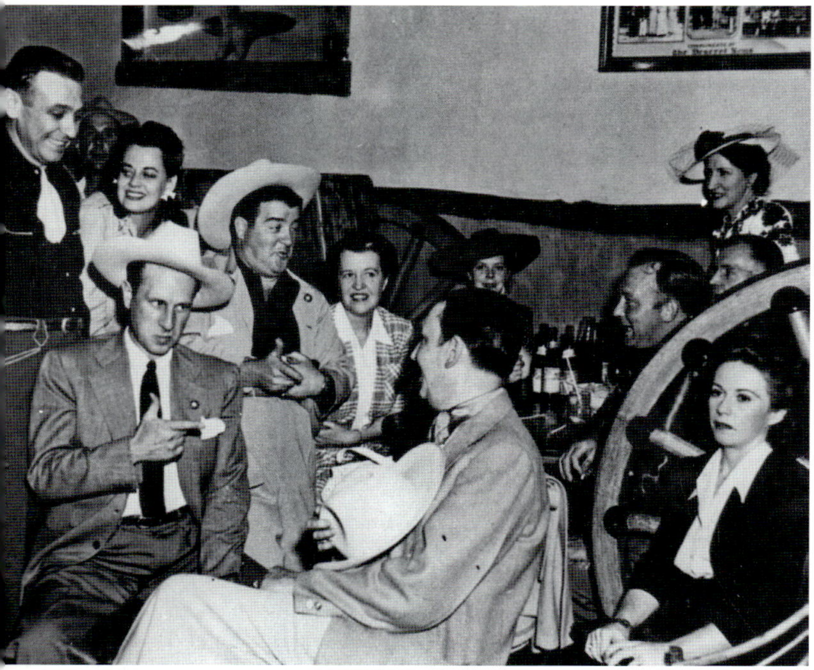

Harman Peery

Harman Peery was elected mayor of Ogden for three terms from 1934 to 1939, 1942 to 1943, and 1948 to 1949. During his time in office he ran with the philosophy of Ogden as a "wide open city." He felt it was better to tax vices than to control them. He started the Ogden Pioneer Days in 1934, which he tried to make a national event by bringing in famous people, such as Abbot and Costello, whom he is pictured with in the front.

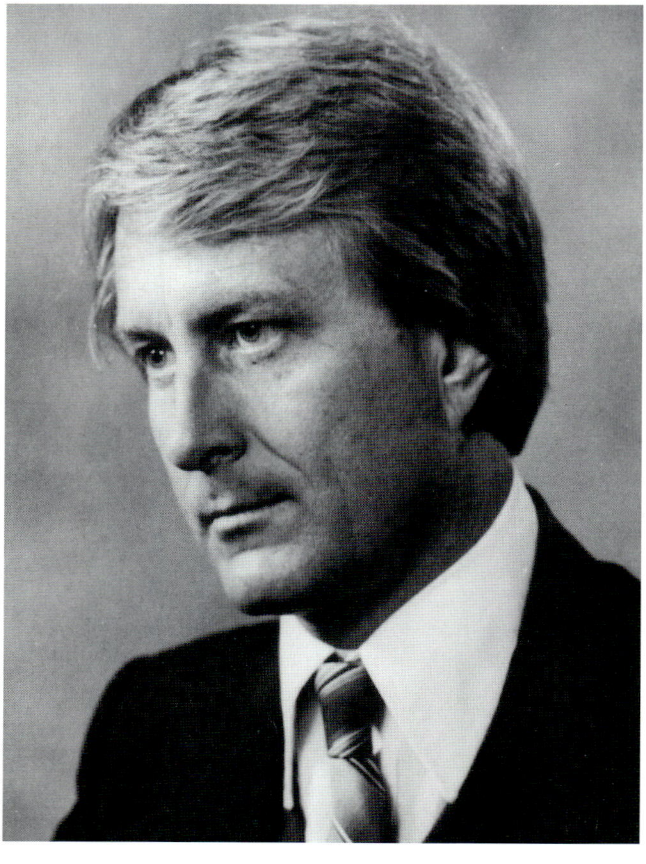

A. Stephen Dirks

A. Stephen Dirks served as mayor of Ogden from 1973 to 1983. Prior to Mayor Mathew Godfrey, Dirks was the longest mayor in office in modern times. Dirks was responsible for converting the Union Station into the Union Station Museum to help keep the history of the railroad in Ogden alive. He ran for Congress in 1982 unsuccessfully against Jim Hansen.

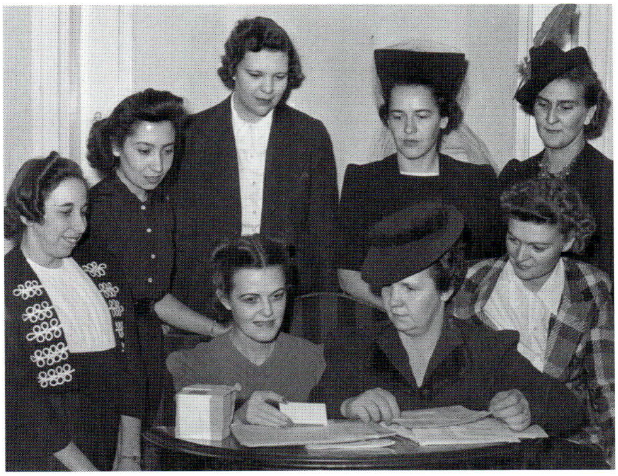

Elizabeth A. Vance

Elizabeth A. Vance (above, pictured first row, right, wearing hat) was born on October 15, 1905, to Charles W. and Mary Christensen Averett. Vance married John M. Vance on December 31, 1927. Vance got involved with Democratic Party politics when she was appointed to the office of Deputy Weber County Recorder in the early 1930s. She served as National Committeewoman, Utah president, Utah chairwoman, and Weber County chairwoman for the Utah Young Democrats. From 1933 to 1950, Vance worked as a member of the Executive Council of the Utah Democratic Central Committee. In 1951, Vance became the first woman in 42 years to win election to the Utah House of Representatives from Weber County. Vance held the position of Utah legislator for seven consecutive terms and was head of every major House Committee, earning her the nickname "Mrs. Democrat."

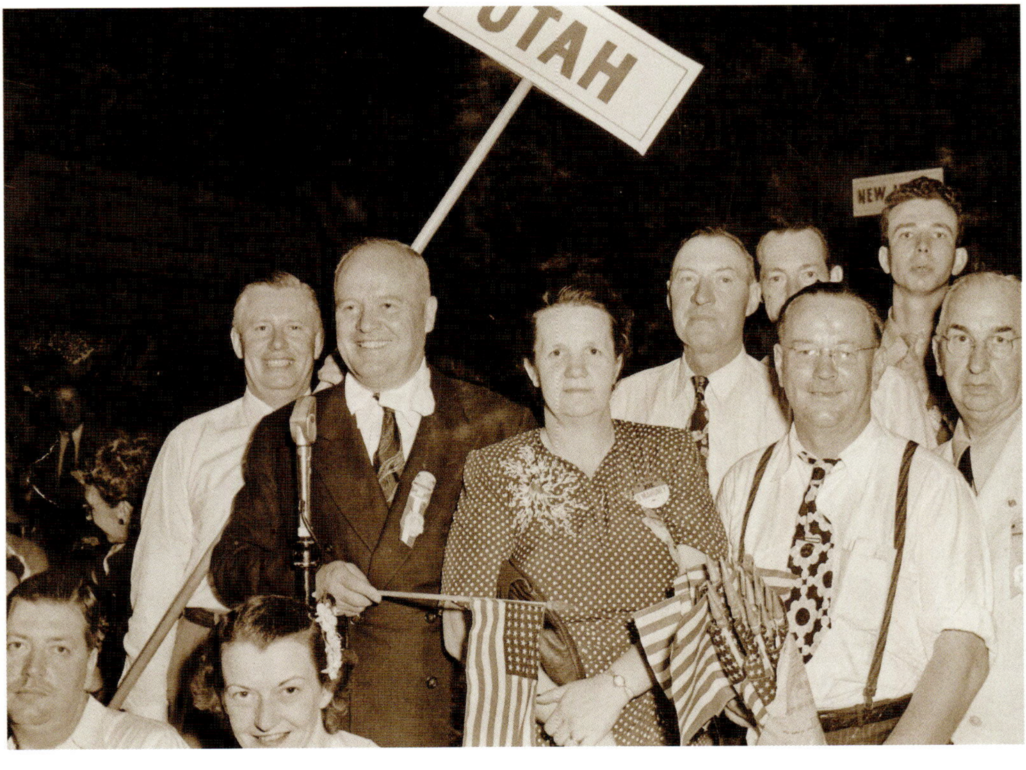

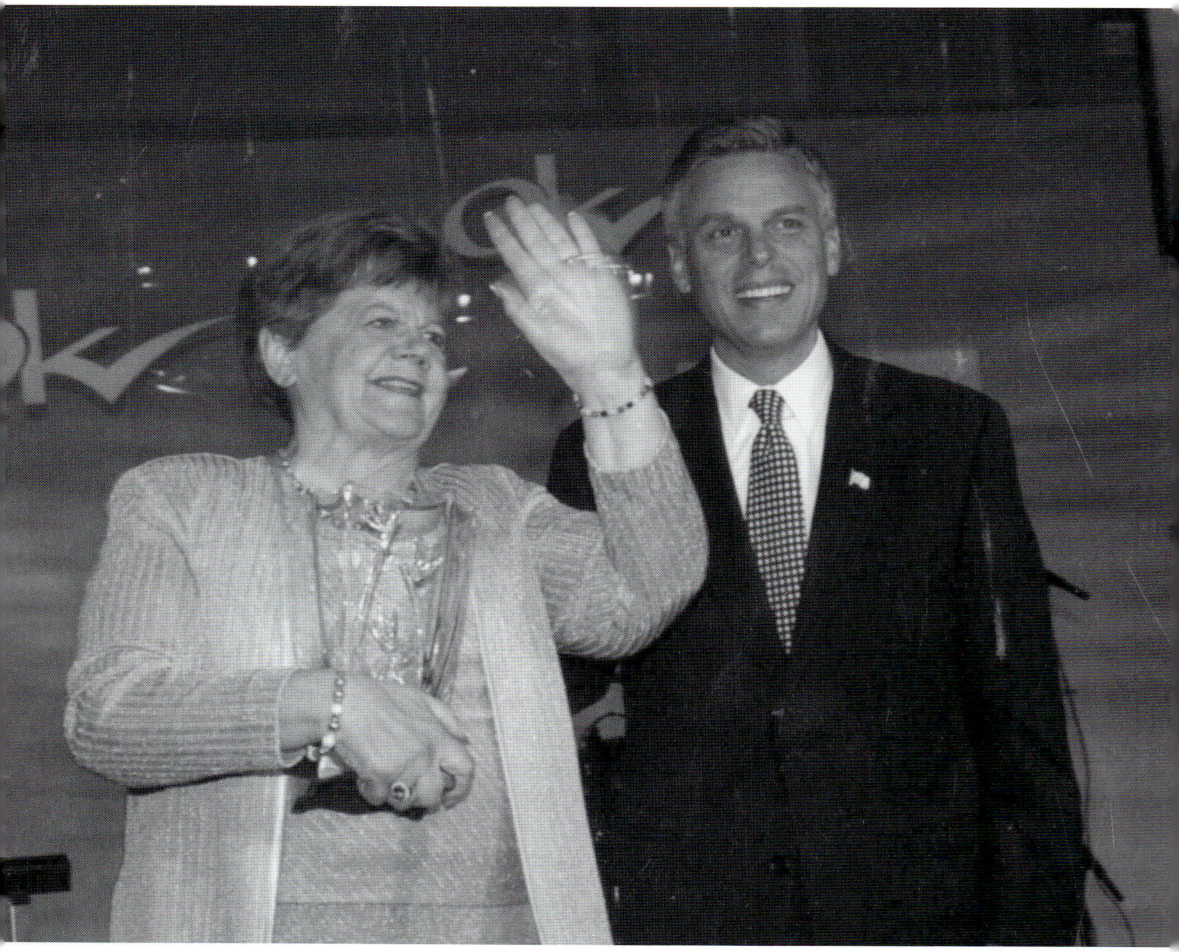

Olene Walker
Olene Walker was born on November 15, 1930. Walker spent eight years in the Utah State Legislature including a term as majority whip. While serving as Utah's first woman lieutenant governor for 10 years, Walker spearheaded many important initiatives, including education programs, budget security measures, health care reform, and workforce development. She led the Healthcare Reform Task Force that resulted in the establishment of the Children's Health Insurance Program (CHIP), ensuring affordable health care for Utah's children. Walker also served as chair of the Workforce Task Force, resulting in the development of the Department of Workforce Services. In 2003, Walker assumed the office of Utah State Governor after former governor Mike Leavitt was nominated to lead the Environmental Protection Agency. She was the first female governor in the state of Utah. Walker served as governor until the end of Leavitt's term in 2005. In the photograph, she is standing with her successor, John Huntsman Jr.

Henry Aldous Dixon

Henry Aldous Dixon was born on June 29, 1890. He became an instructor at Weber College in 1914, and by 1919, he was serving as president of the college. He served as president again from 1937 to 1953. He was known for his knowledge of vocational education and started the technical education program at Weber. From 1955 to 1961, he was served in the US House of Representatives, as he is pictured at right. He died in Ogden in 1967.

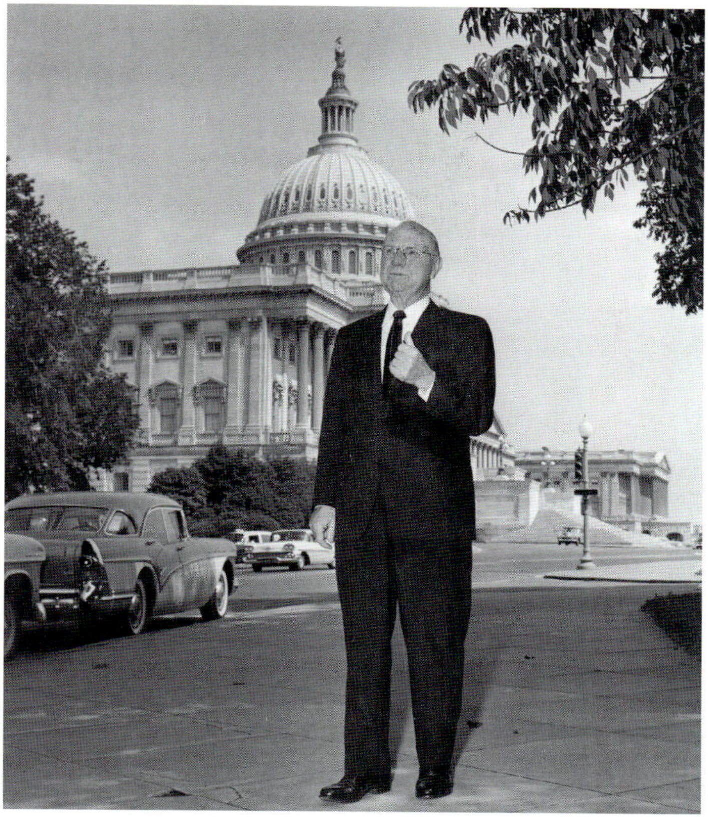

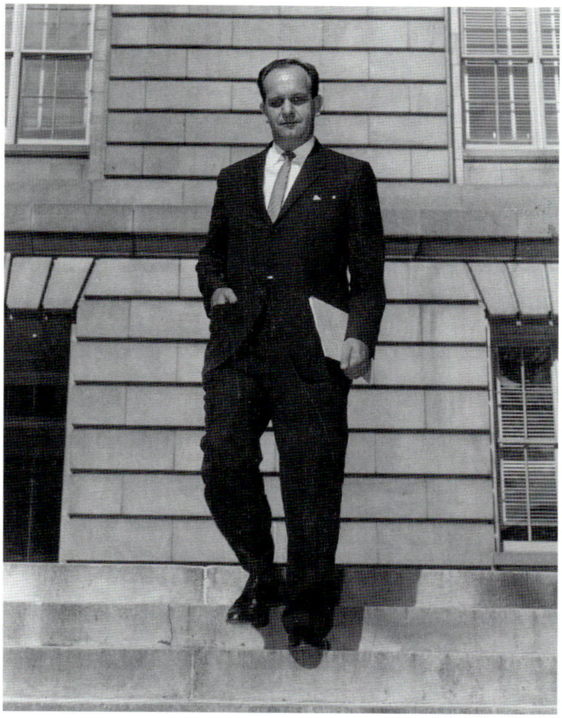

Laurence J. Burton

Laurence J. Burton was born on October 30, 1926. He served as the legislative assistant to US Rep. Henry Aldous Dixon in 1957 and 1958. Burton was also the administrative assistant to Utah Gov. George Dewey Clyde from 1960 to 1962, and served as a delegate at the Republican National Convention in 1969. He was elected to the US House of Representatives in 1962 and served four successive terms until 1970.

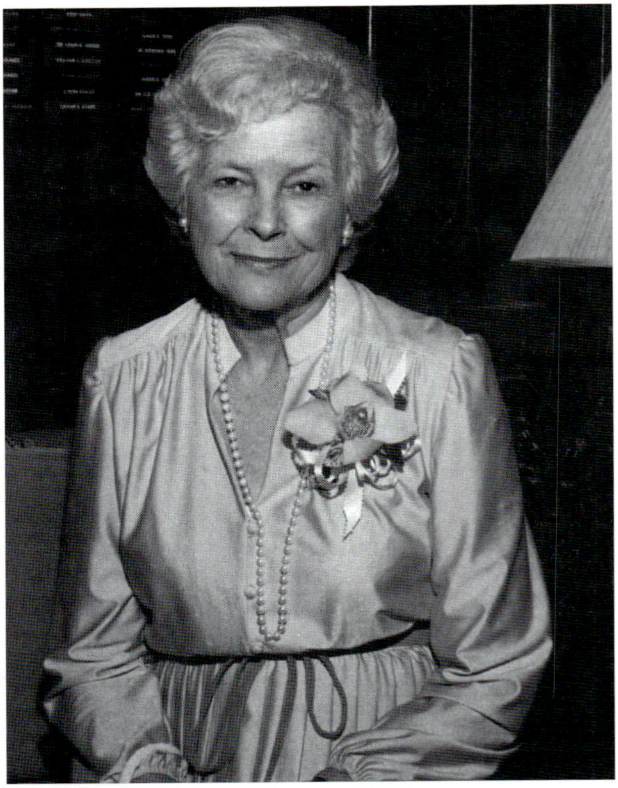

Myrene Brewer

Myrene Rich Brewer was born in 1906. She was very active in civic projects, including the League for Better Government in Ogden and the American Red Cross program. She was also an active participant in the Republican Party, serving in numerous capacities including the Republican State Board and as the National Committee Woman for Utah. She was a delegate to the national conventions in 1968 and 1972.

Alex Hurtado

Alex Hurtado served as an Ogden City Councilman from 1971 to 1981. He became the director of National Hispanic Affairs in Ronald Reagan's presidency. In 1981, he was the director of Political Affairs of the Republican National Committee, becoming the first minority to be appointed to this position. Here, he is pictured flanked by Ronald Reagan and George Bush.

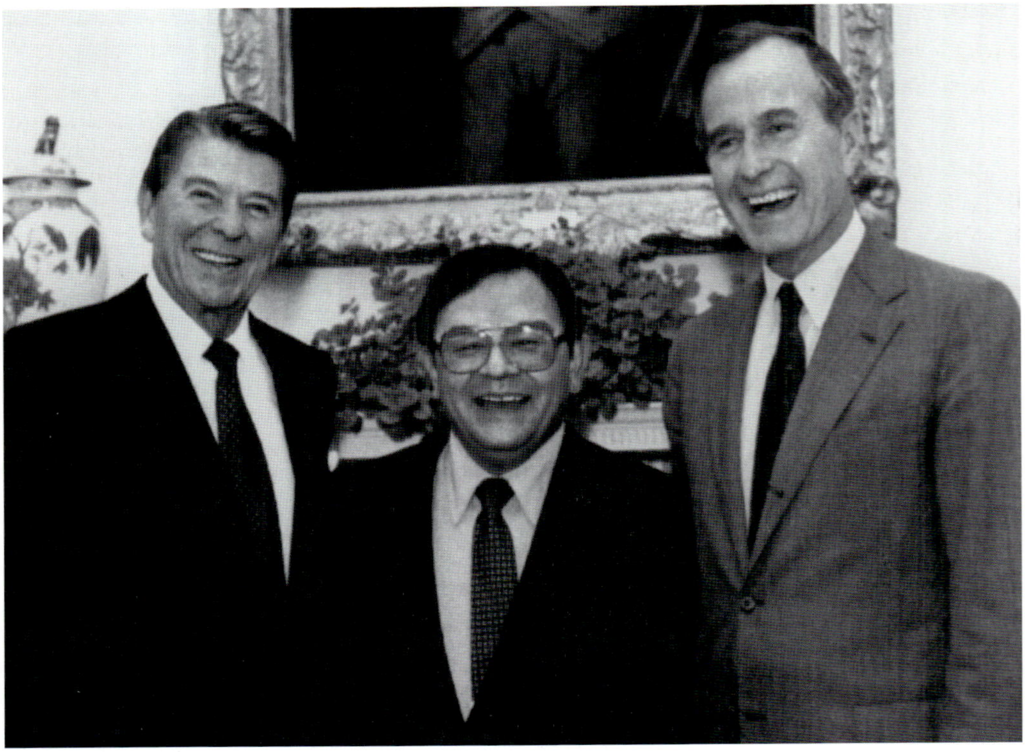

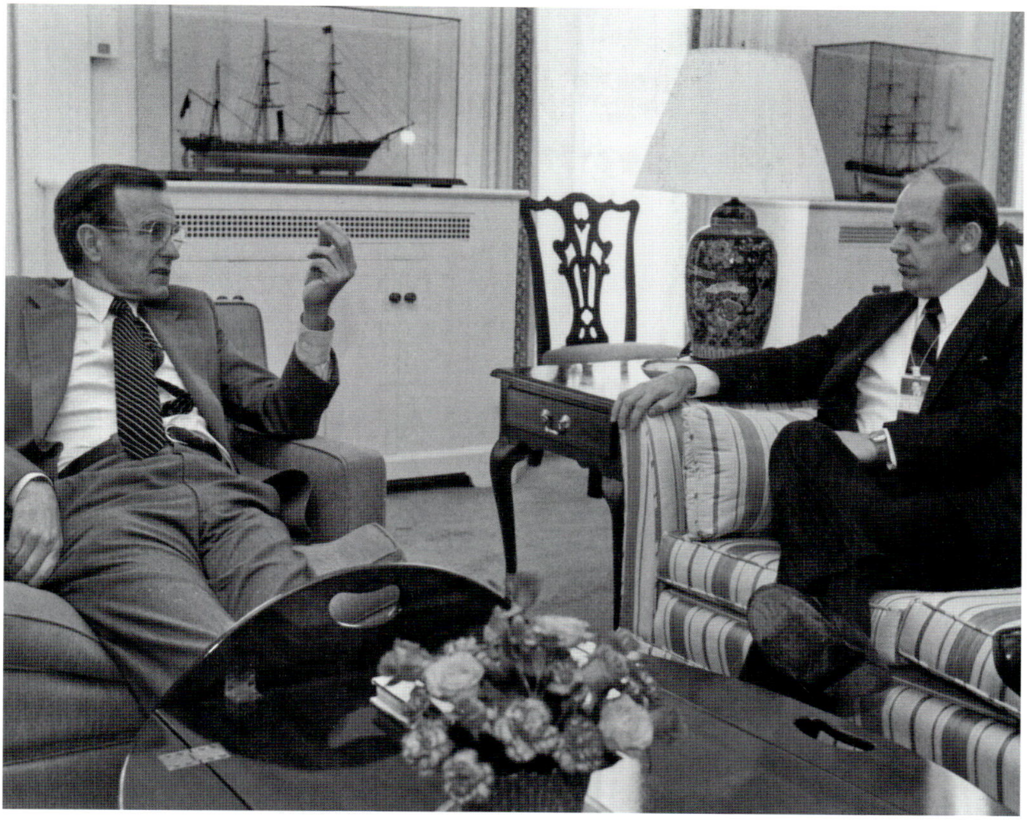

Richard Richards
Richard Richards was born in Ogden on May 14, 1932. He attended his first two years of college at Weber College where he started the "College Republicans" to participate in various political campaigns. While in law school at the University of Utah, he helped in H. Aldous Dixon's and Laurence Burton's congressional campaigns. Burton asked him to come to Washington, DC, to run his office. While there, he made national political connections. He was elected as chairman of the Republic National Committee from 1981 to 1983 and was an essential part of Ronald Reagan's presidential campaign in 1980. Later, Richards became the campaign advisor for Pres. George H. W. Bush. The Richard Richards Institute at Weber State University is named in honor of him.

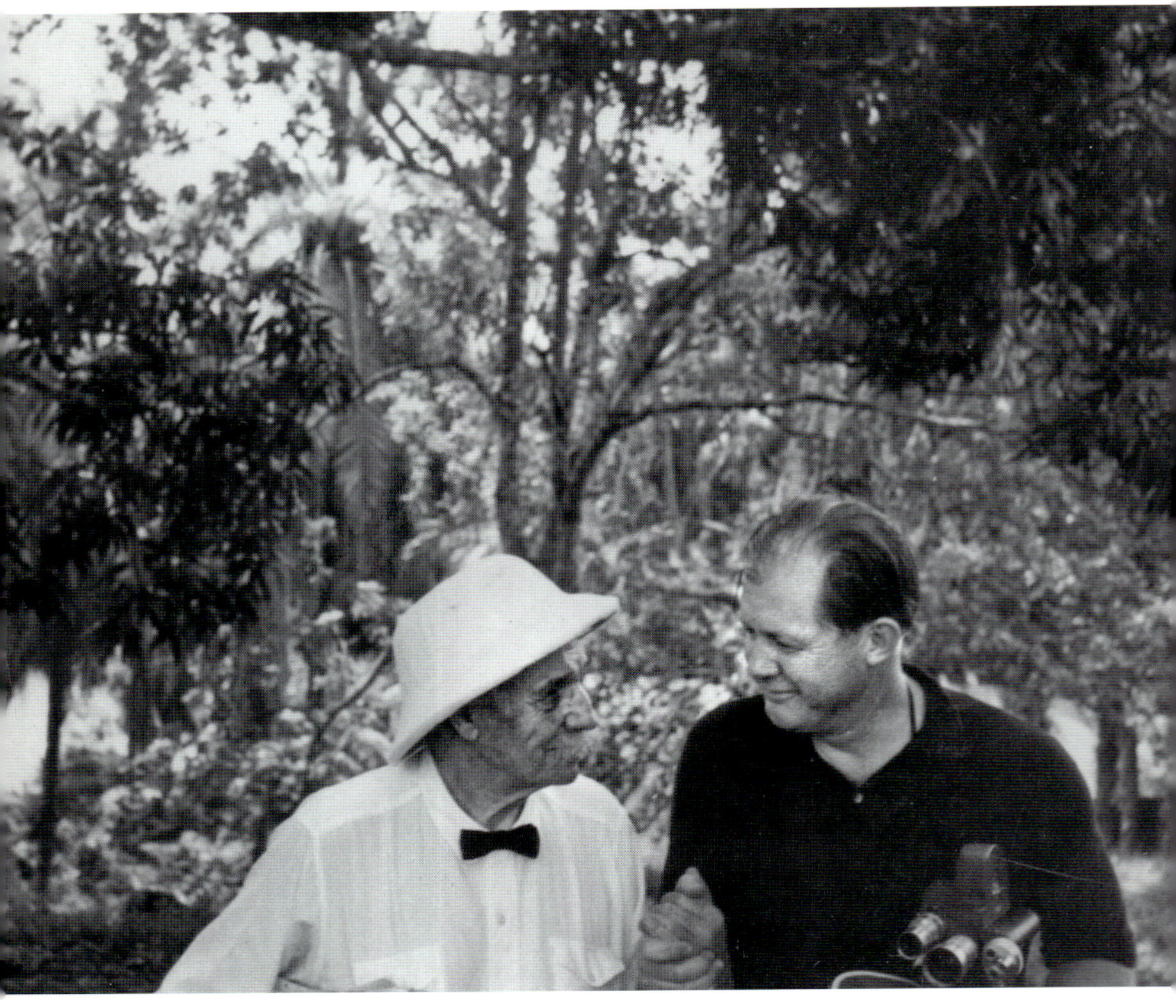

Mark Evans Austad

Mark Evans Austad (right) had a versatile career as a broadcaster, journalist, and ambassador. He began his career at KSL radio in 1941, after Earl J. Glad heard him speak at a Rotary Club meeting and offered Austad a job. Shortly after beginning that job, Austad was drafted into the Army and sent to the Walter Reed Hospital due to an earlier injury. While there he worked on the staff of the hospital radio station, and later became staff sergeant in charge of operations, moderating a weekly program featuring political personalities, such as Eleanor Roosevelt. Austad continued in the broadcasting business for more than 30 years, becoming vice president of public affairs for Metromedia, and filming several documentaries, including his 1961 film *The Light That Shines from Lambarene*. This film took Austad to the jungle of Africa where he met with and interviewed Dr. Albert Schweitzer (left), an experience that would have a lasting impression upon him. In 1969, Austad was asked to serve on Nixon's inaugural committee. He served on two more inaugural committees, including Reagan's in 1981. Austad also served as a delegate to the United Nations in 1973, and in 1974, he was appointed ambassador to Finland. After serving as ambassador until 1977, Austad became the first US diplomat to receive the White Rose and the Order of the Lion—the highest honorary awards of the Finnish government. In 1981, he was appointed ambassador to Norway, the native land of both his parents. Austad died of a heart attack at his home in Arizona in 1988.

CHAPTER SEVEN

Service and Sisterhood

Women's Organizations

Dr. Jane Skolfield, first female doctor in Utah and cofounder of the Child Culture Club, once said, "Women can become mighty factors in every cause. It is her hand that can rule the world if she will." While Ogden's club women may not have sought to rule the world, they have certainly influenced every worthy cause in the community.

Organized in 1898, the Child Culture Club was the first civic organization for women in Ogden, but over the years many other clubs were formed. While these clubs all had a social component, allowing the women to build friendships with one another, the clubs also provided opportunities for valuable service, particularly to the children of Ogden. Over and over again, Ogden's club women saw needs in the community and proactively worked to solve problems. They became advocates, lobbied legislatures, demanded accountability from leaders, and managed large financial holdings.

In 1913, the Martha Society opened a day nursery to support working mothers who would otherwise have to leave their children at home. They also cared for orphans and abandoned children until state agencies could make other arrangements for the children. In the late 1940s, as polio epidemics swept the nation, a group of Ogden mothers went to work, volunteering at hospitals, and relieving overtaxed medical staff. In the 1980s, the Junior League women started a Guardian Ad Litem program to advocate for abused children. Ogden women have organized fundraisers and food drives, sold war bonds, supported libraries and college students, and encouraged art programs in the community. They have also worked to strengthen women in their individual lives. Whether through books clubs and other programs that encouraged learning, or through professional organizations for working women, Ogden's women sought to build solidarity and support for one another.

With their remarkable dedication and generosity, these club women have left behind a legacy of civic-mindedness and sisterhood for generations to come. While most of the clubs have since disbanded, some, like the Junior League, continue to serve the community. But whether or not they are members of a club, Ogden's women continue to make a significant impact to the causes of the day.

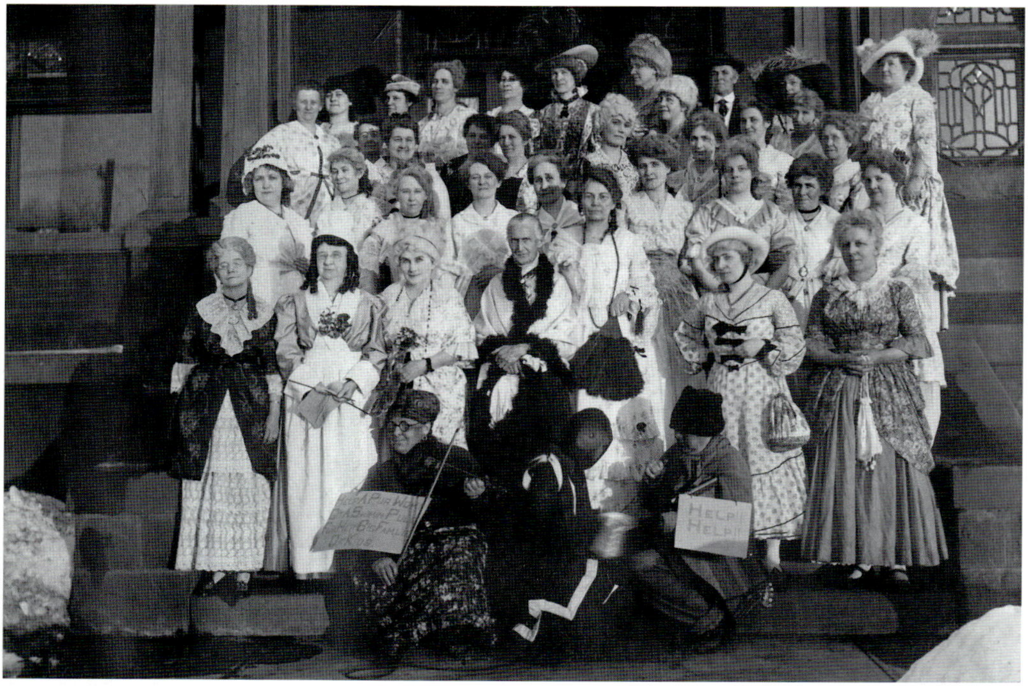

Child Culture Club
Organized in 1898 to help Ogden mothers improve their parenting skills through education, the Child Culture Club went on to become one of the leading civic organizations in Ogden. Early club women, including Dr. Jane Skolfield and Annie Taylor Dee, (second row, second from left) worked to end child labor, improve education, and fund Ogden's first blood bank.

General Federated Women's Clubs
In the summer of 1921, the Federation of Women's Clubs held their annual convention in Salt Lake City. At the end of the week, Ogden's chapter played host to the federation's general council, touring Ogden Canyon and stopping for lunch at the Hermitage Resort. The federation was founded in New York City in 1890, and club members took on the social issues of the day, including child labor, prison reform, and public health.

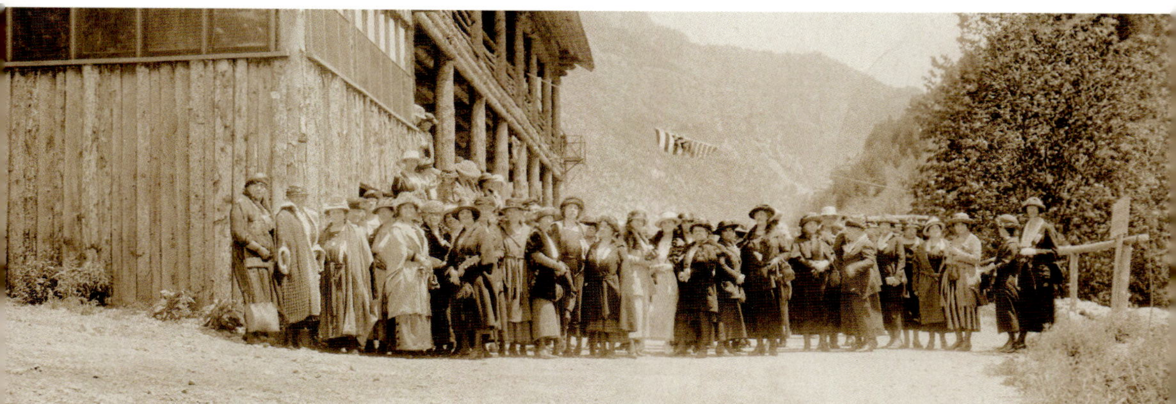

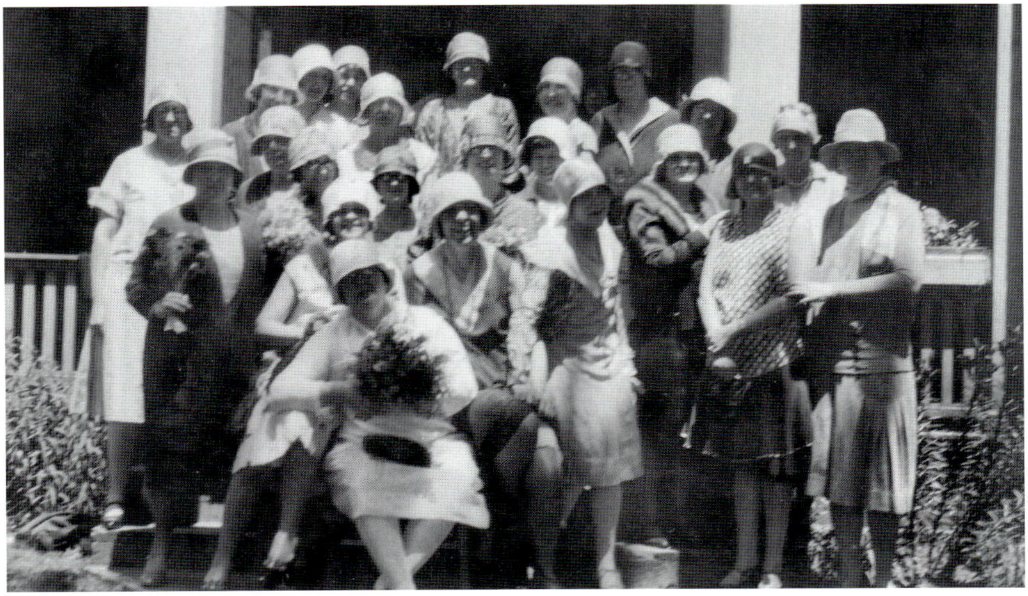

Professional and Business Women Club

The Ogden chapter of the Professional and Business Women Club was organized in 1922 with the goal of raising education standards for business women and providing scholarships for those seeking training. When the Depression hit, both the local and national chapters worked especially hard to ensure a "Better Business Woman for a Better Business World" by continuing its financial aid and breaking down barriers for women in the workplace.

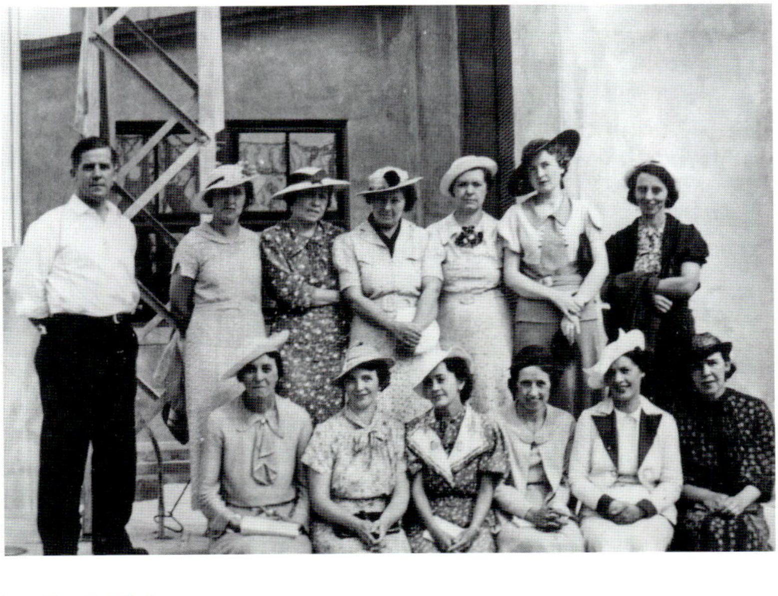

North Ogden Book Club

Founded in 1935 by a group of friends, the North Ogden Book Club was organized "to read and review the latest published books." In 1938, the group also traveled to Idaho to tour power plants. Elsie Bailey (front row, far left) provided entertainment on the trip by telling fortunes to the driver and guides. The men were so impressed with the accuracy of their fortunes they didn't charge the group for the trip.

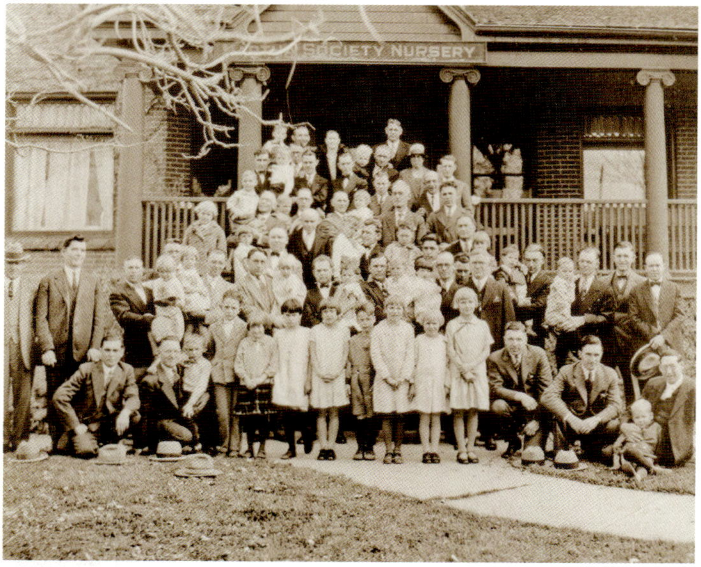

Martha Society Nursery

In 1913, the Martha Society, an organization dedicated to community service, opened a day nursery to provide childcare for Ogden's working mothers. When the nursery opened, only three children were registered, but four years later, average daily attendance grew to 55 children. One-third of the nursery's costs were covered by parents, but the Martha Society covered all other expenses. Shown here are the nursery children with Ogden barbers who donated free haircuts.

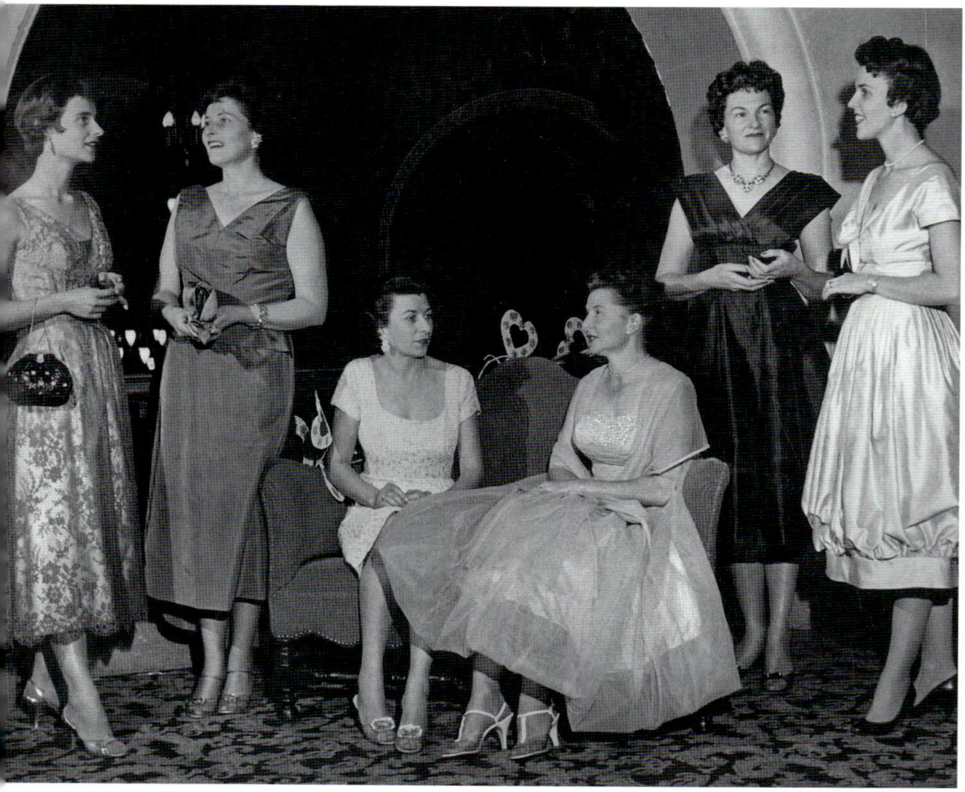

Junior League of Ogden

In 1947, the day nursery, renamed the Martha Home, was turned over to the Welfare League, which eventually became the Junior League of Ogden. For 12 years, the league operated the home, helping an estimated 900 children. The league also organized an annual charity ball to raise funds for the home; shown here is a group of club members at the 1958 ball, held at the Hotel Ben Lomond.

Guardian Ad Litem Program

In 1982, the Junior League of Ogden developed a Guardian Ad Litem program for Weber County. League members served as volunteer advocates for abused or neglected children going through the court system. The league lobbied the Utah State Legislature for and received $10,000 to support the project, which was supervised by attorney Jane Marquardt. (shown on the left).

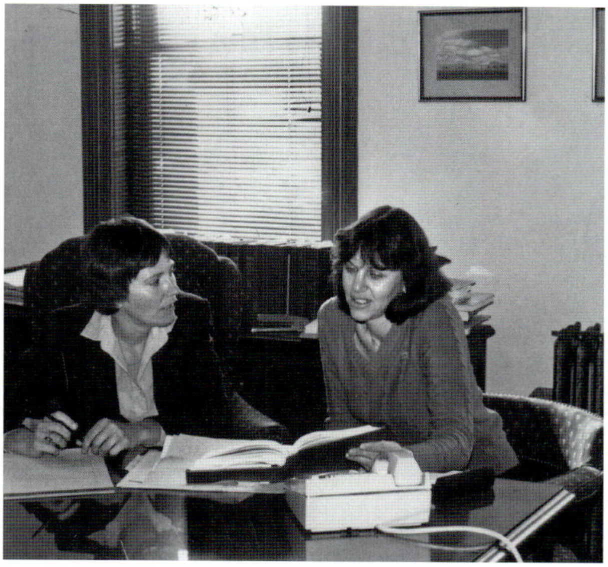

Red Cross Headquarters

Red Cross volunteers have served Ogden and Weber County for nearly 100 years. In 1952, Jamie Corn was traveling with her three children to meet her husband stationed in Washington when she was injured in a car accident. The Red Cross stepped in to care for her children and to arrange transportation; they even found a veterinarian to care for the family dog. This kind of service has marked the Red Cross for generations.

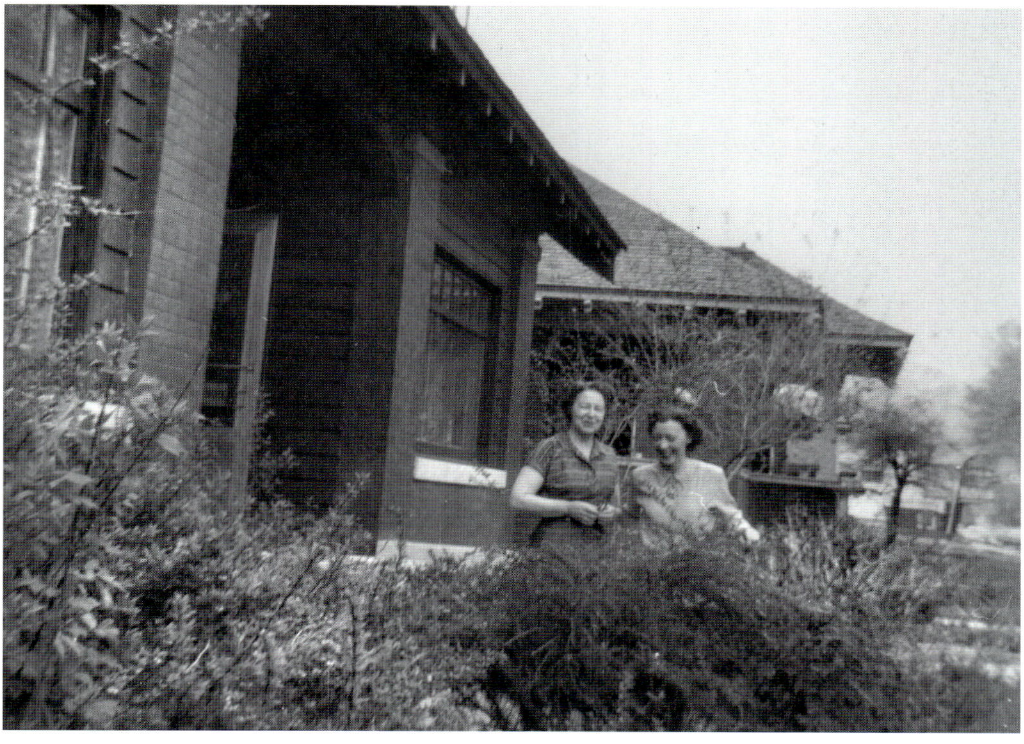

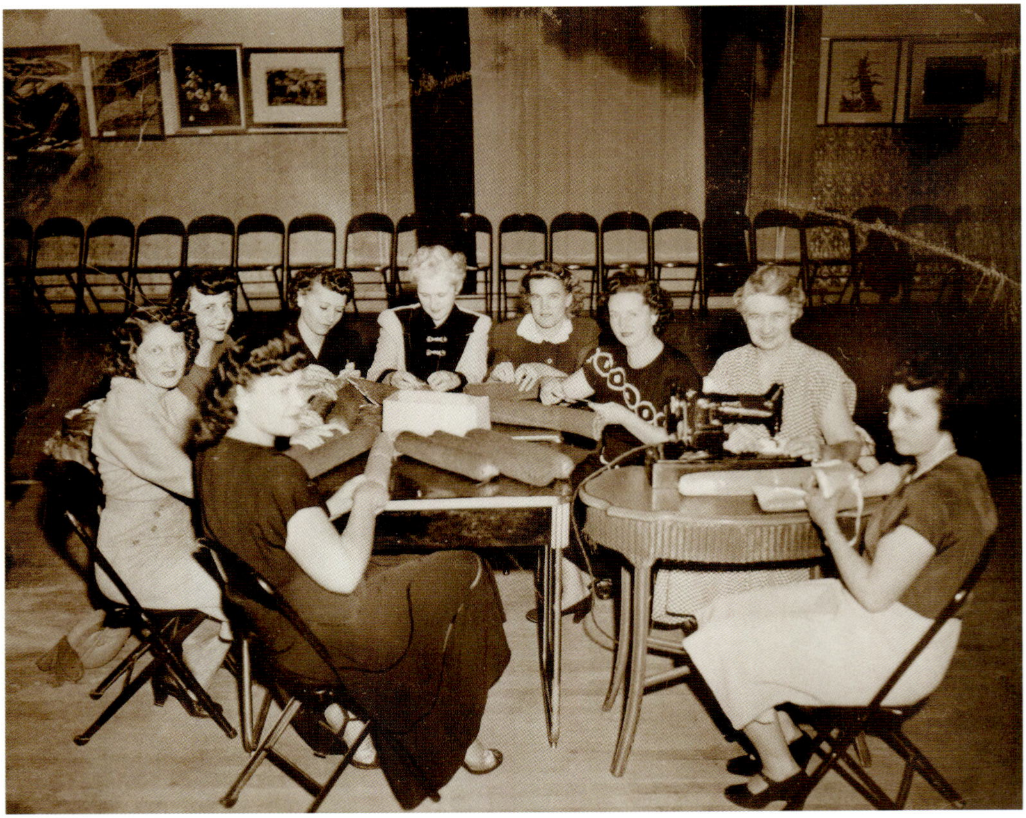

Polio Emergency Volunteers Club

When Jane Ballingham and Mabel Poulson (far right) met in 1946, both were traveling from Ogden to Salt Lake City to visit their sons who were being treated for polio. They quickly learned of the hospital's desperate need for volunteers to care for the patients, many of whom were young, frightened children. Ballingham and Poulson decided to organize a club to coordinate volunteer efforts, especially in case of an epidemic. The Polio Emergency Volunteers Club was the first such club organized in the state of Utah, and its members worked in polio wards feeding patients, changing beds and diapers, and entertaining the children. The women also spent time making the bandages and sandbags necessary for treatments, gathering other supplies, and organizing fundraisers to purchase needed equipment. Sister Mary Margaret, supervisor of St. Benedict's Hospital in Ogden, said of the volunteers, "I can't even think what we would have done without them." But for the volunteers, many of whom were in similar situations to Ballingham and Poulson, it was a chance to be near their children in the hospital and feel useful. When Poulson asked her son the best time to visit he told her that bedtime, when the lights were turned out, was hardest for him. So every night for three months she went to the ward to read stories until the children fell asleep. It was this kind of tender, personal care that the children needed so desperately, and that the volunteers dedicated themselves to providing. When the Salk vaccine was released in 1955, the Polio Emergency Volunteers, who had already given so much, continued to volunteer their time educating the community about the vaccine and assisting schools in the vaccination process.

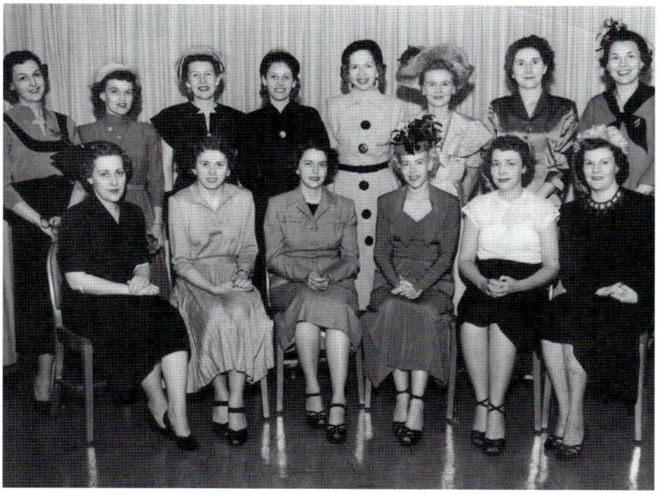

Chareya Club Founders
The Chareya Club was founded as a junior branch of the Aglaia Club in 1951. The 15 charter members (shown here) began volunteering in various capacities and raising funds for projects, such as playground and athletic equipment for the State Industrial School, clothing for students at the Indian School in Brigham City, and food drives for families in need.

Weber County's Singing Mothers
The year 1942 marked the 100th anniversary of the founding of the LDS Relief Society. Celebrations were organized around the state, including a performance by Weber County's Singing Mothers. The concert, held in the Ogden Tabernacle, included a special cantata written for the occasion. Only a few weeks later, all other centennial celebrations were canceled due to wartime restrictions, but the Singing Mothers would continue to perform in Weber County for many more years.

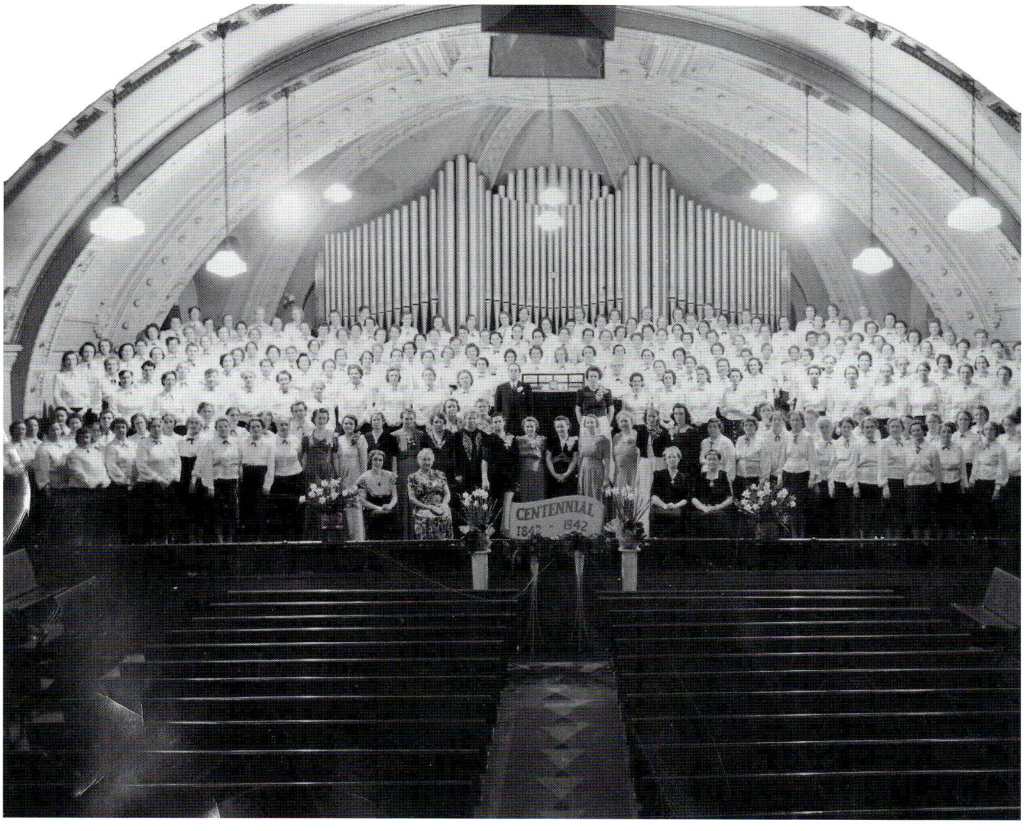

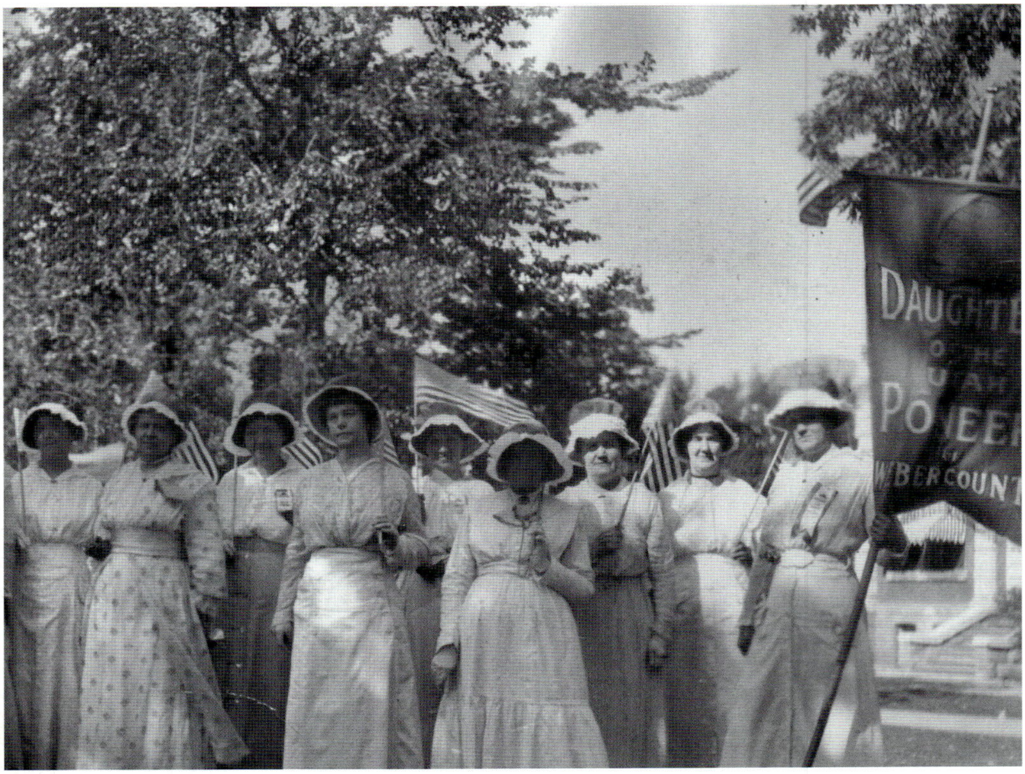

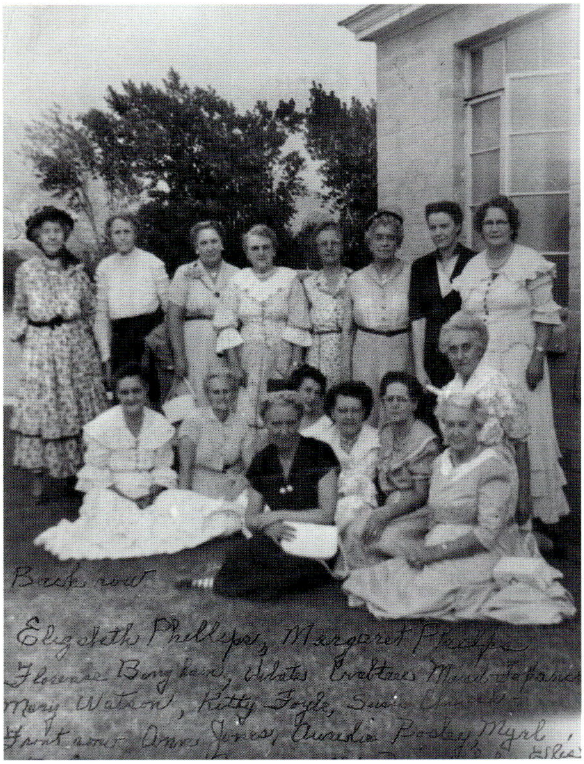

Daughters of Utah Pioneers
The Daughters of Utah Pioneers was founded in 1901 in Salt Lake City in order to honor the men and women who settled the state prior to 1869; membership is made up of direct descendants of these pioneers. The Weber DUP was founded in 1912 and organized into seven camps. In 1916, a special celebration (above) was held to honor Weber County's pioneers, which included a parade, games, and fireworks. Surviving pioneers were also invited to a special banquet in Ogden Canyon, a tradition that was continued for many years. Weber County DUP members have also spent considerable time and effort preserving historic landmarks, and volunteering in the community. The women also get together for socials, such as this one (left) in 1954.

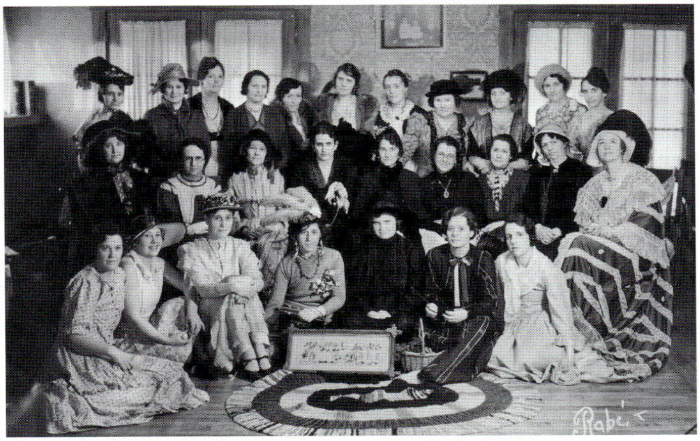

Altruist Club

The Altruist Club was organized in 1924 as the junior branch of the Child Culture Club. Most of its work involved child development and education issues. The women gathered food and clothing for needy families, taught music and craft lessons at the State Industrial School, and contributed to scholarship funds. For many years, they also made and sold Christmas puddings—as many as 400 all made in one day—to raise money for local cerebral palsy patients. They also liked to have fun together, celebrating their founder's day (above) or holding "hobo lunches" in Ogden Canyon (below).

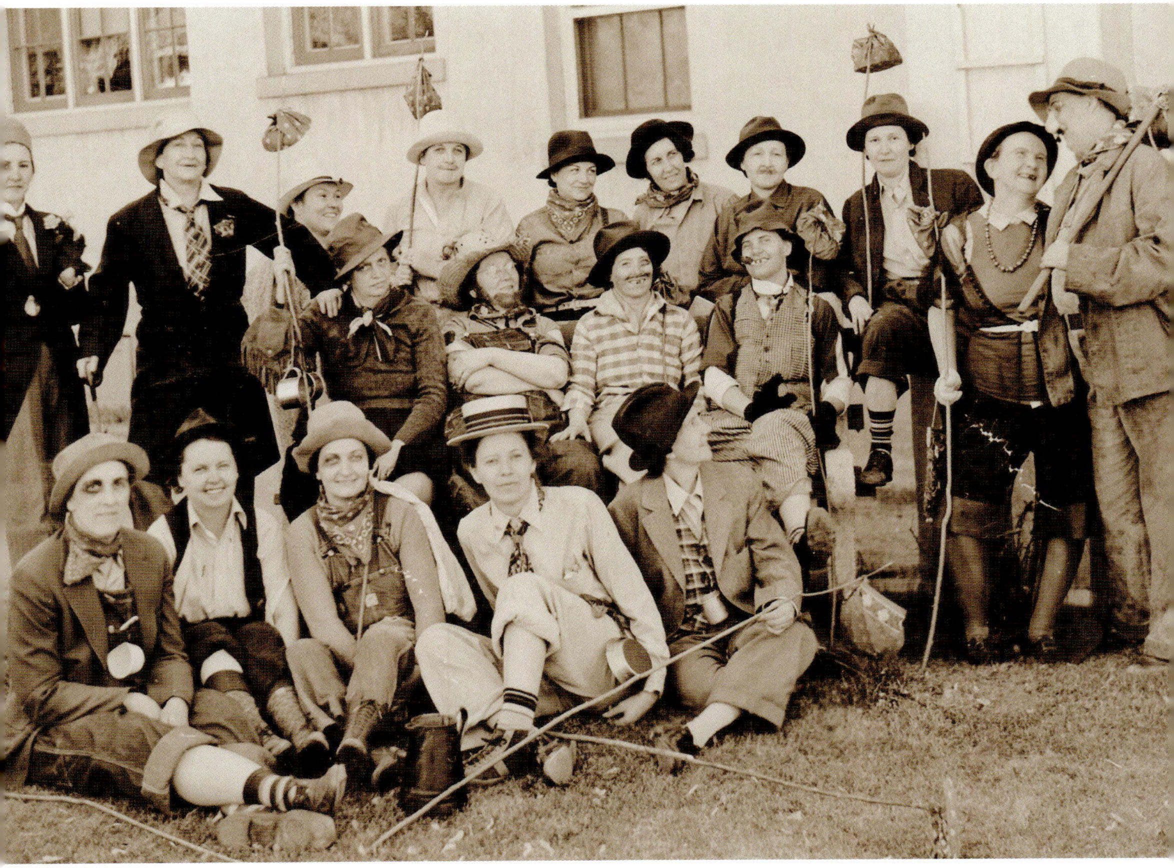

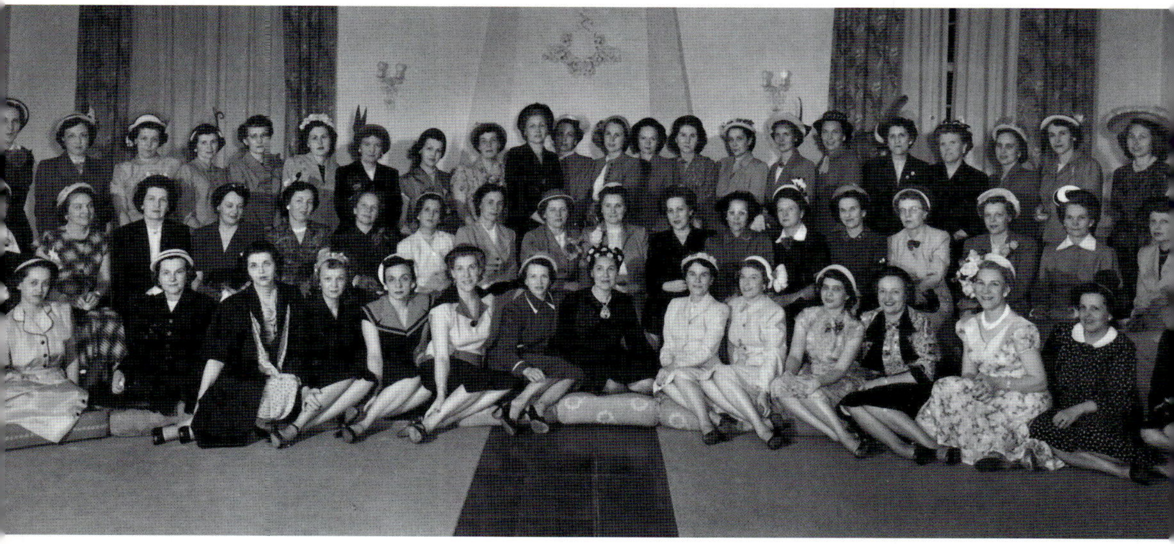

Aglaia Club

Founded in 1939, Aglaia Club members were quickly swept up in the community's home front efforts during World War II. Members volunteered for the state's canning and food campaign, gathered almost 152,000 pounds of clothing, sold war bonds, wrapped presents for soldiers, and sponsored a USO recreation room. Later, the club would go on to raise money for scholarships and local hospitals through its annual fashion show.

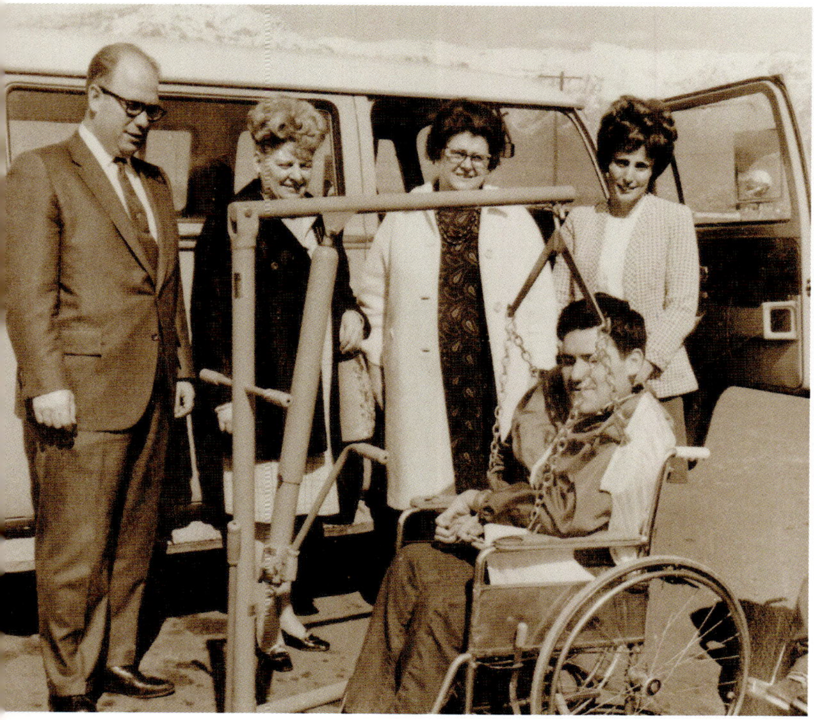

Altrusa Club

One of several hundred chapters, the Ogden Altrusa Club was organized in 1954. Guided by the club's motto—Patriotism, Efficiency, Service—the Altrusa women committed themselves to engaging in their community. In 1970, a committee was formed to raise funds for a hydraulic lift for students with cerebral palsy at Wahlquist Junior High. According to Hazel Barker, physical handicap director at the school, the lift made it possible for the students to continue their education.

CHAPTER EIGHT

Out and About in Ogden

Culture and Recreation

Ogden has long been one of the most culturally diverse communities in the state of Utah. With the growth that came after the railroad arrived, Ogden became home to men and women of all backgrounds, religions, and ethnicities. Ogden has not been immune to the challenges of such a diverse community, and in the late 1800s, religious tensions in particular were high. Fortunately, Ogdenites have found much to unite them and much to celebrate together.

Ogdenites have long loved good music. The state's first brass band was organized in Ogden, and it performed around the region for decades. Since that time, Ogden has been home to many other musicians. Railroad companies and other businesses formed their own bands, like the Union Pacific Terminals Band, to perform at special functions. Shorty Ross and his band were popular performers at dance halls in the 1940s, and Glenn Hanson, a music educator, organized several groups that performed around the country.

In the 1930s, Mayor Harman Peery started Ogden's Pioneer Day celebrations, with parades, beard growing contests, and performances of *Roland Parry's All Faces West*, a musical about the early pioneers. Annual parties were held on Old Folks Day to honor Ogden's senior citizens, and every year Ogden celebrates the holiday season with Christmas Village.

Sports are also an important part of Ogden's culture. Baseball has been played in Ogden since its earliest days, and today it is still home to the Raptors, a farm team for the LA Dodgers. Ogden Canyon winter sportsmen have enjoyed skiing some of the best snow in the country and ski jumping at Snow Basin. Throughout the year, Ogdenites like to cheer for their favorite school teams, including the Weber State Wildcats.

In Ogden's early days there were often tensions between LDS and non-LDS denominations. As the community focused on other issues like education, these tensions eased, and today, the area is home to many denominations and two religious orders: the Mount Benedict Monastery and the Abbey of Our Lady of the Holy Trinity. Despite challenges in the past, Ogdenites continue to work and play towards their future.

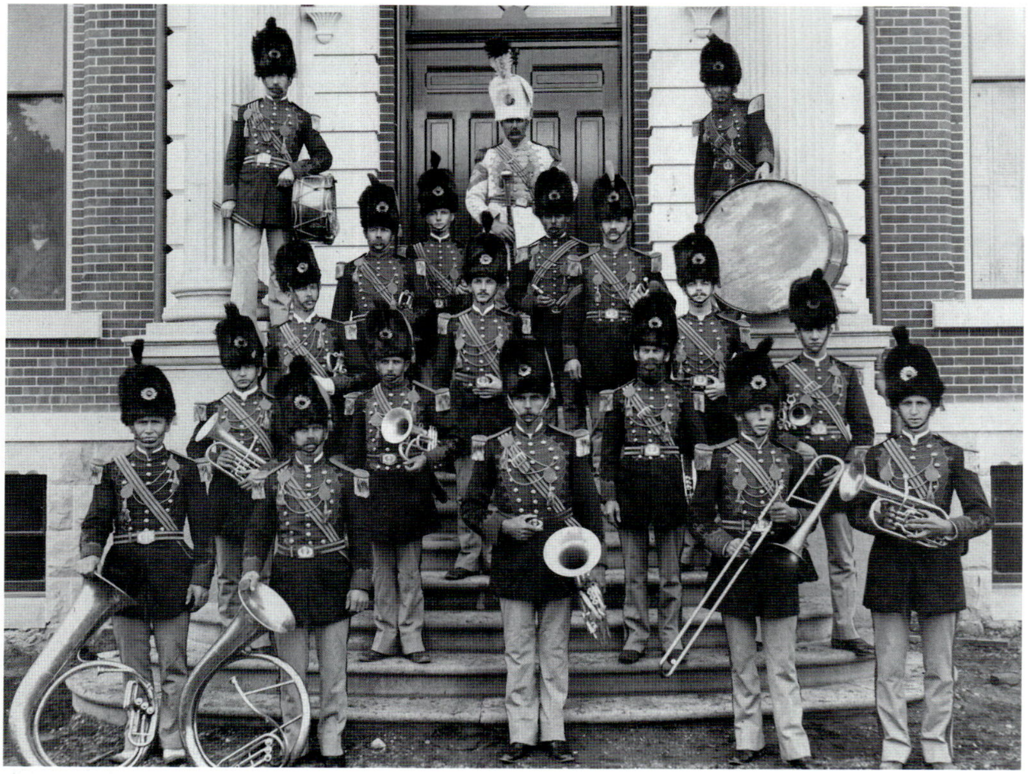

Ogden City Brass Band

The Ogden City Brass Band, thought to be the first such band organized in the Utah Territory, was founded in 1856. It performed at the driving of the Golden Spike in 1869, and gave other performances throughout the West. Although the group had several directors in its history, the drum major shown here is Charles E. Layne, who also served as sheriff of Weber County.

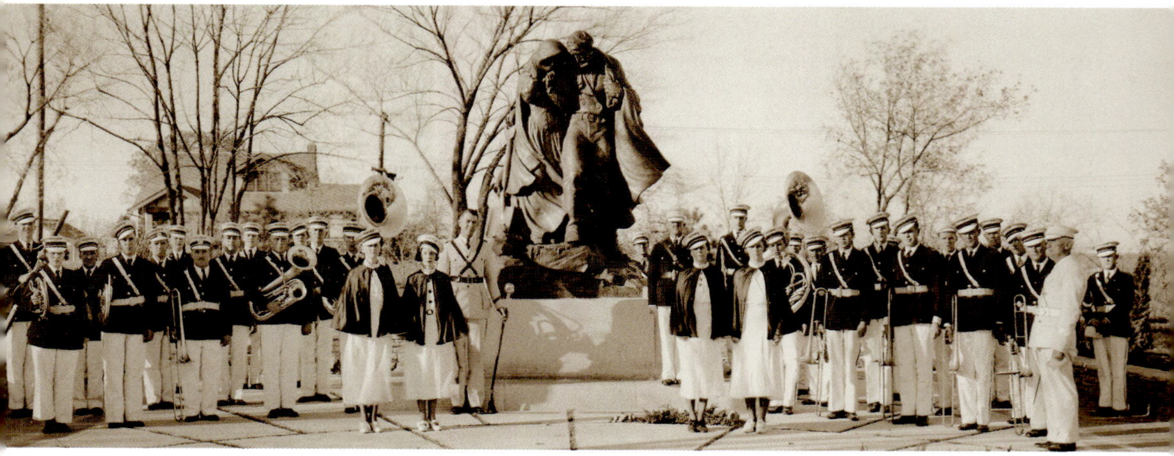

Union Pacific Terminals Band

The Ogden Union Pacific Terminals Band was made up of about 40 members, all railroad employees. Led by Henry Otte, the band performed around the US and gave concerts at the Union Depot during the summer. The band is shown here in Nebraska after leading a parade in Omaha.

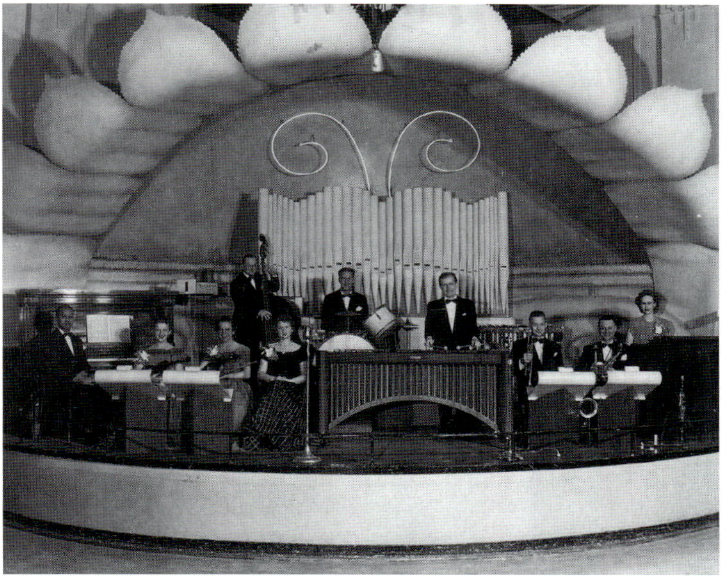

Shorty Ross Orchestra
In the 1950s and 1960s, the Shorty Ross Orchestra was one of the main bands that played in the dance halls around Ogden. Here, the band is pictured on the main stage of the Berthana that was located on Twenty-fourth Street and Grant Avenue. Ross is on the xylophone, Vern Harrop is on the trumpet, Ida Kyle is on the piano, Clyde Sparrow is on the bass fiddle, and Wayne Devereaux is on the organ.

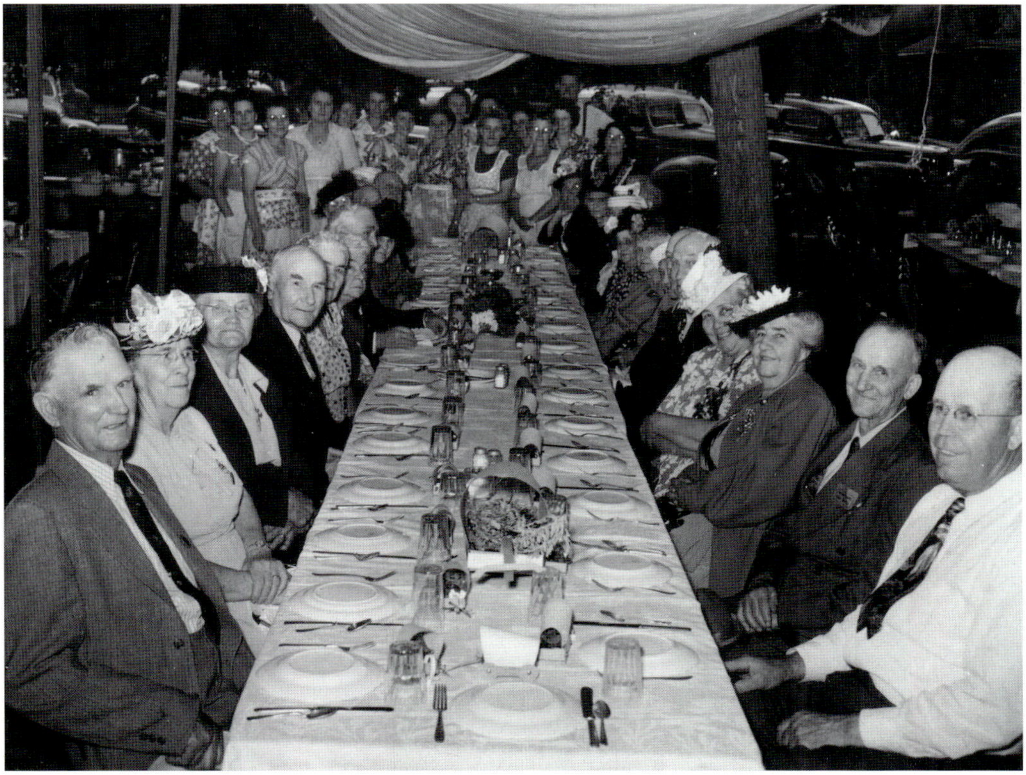

Old Folks Day
In 1875, Charles R. Savage approached Edward Hunter, the presiding bishop of the LDS church, about establishing Old Folks Day. This day was to honor and pay special attention to the older generations in the community. The people of Weber County entertained the aged people in their individual wards as well. Here is the celebration of the 10th Ward at Lorin Farr Park in the 1940s.

93

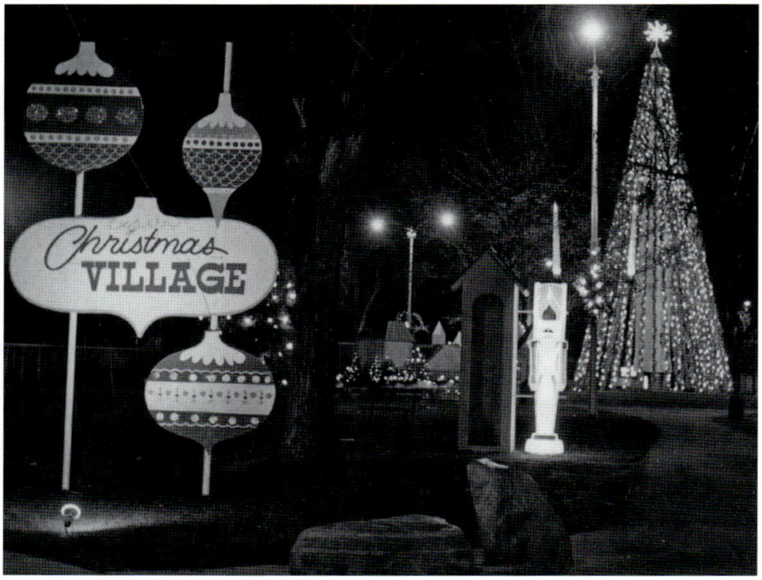

Christmas Village

In 1962, Jerry Green and the Retail Merchants Committee of the Ogden Chamber of Commerce started work on creating Christmas Village in downtown Ogden. The village opened in the West Municipal Park after Thanksgiving 1962. It started with a parade of floats and Santa Claus, followed by 10,000 spectators watching as all the lights in the park were switched on. Jerry Green billed it as "The most outstanding Christmas show in the intermountain country." The village was lit every night, including the missile tree in the center, throughout the holiday season. Santa Claus was in his castle each night for children of all ages to visit. Pictured above is the entrance to Christmas Village, and pictured below are (from left to right) Mayor Merle Allen, Jim Patterson, Dick Pizza, and Jerry Green preparing for Christmas Village.

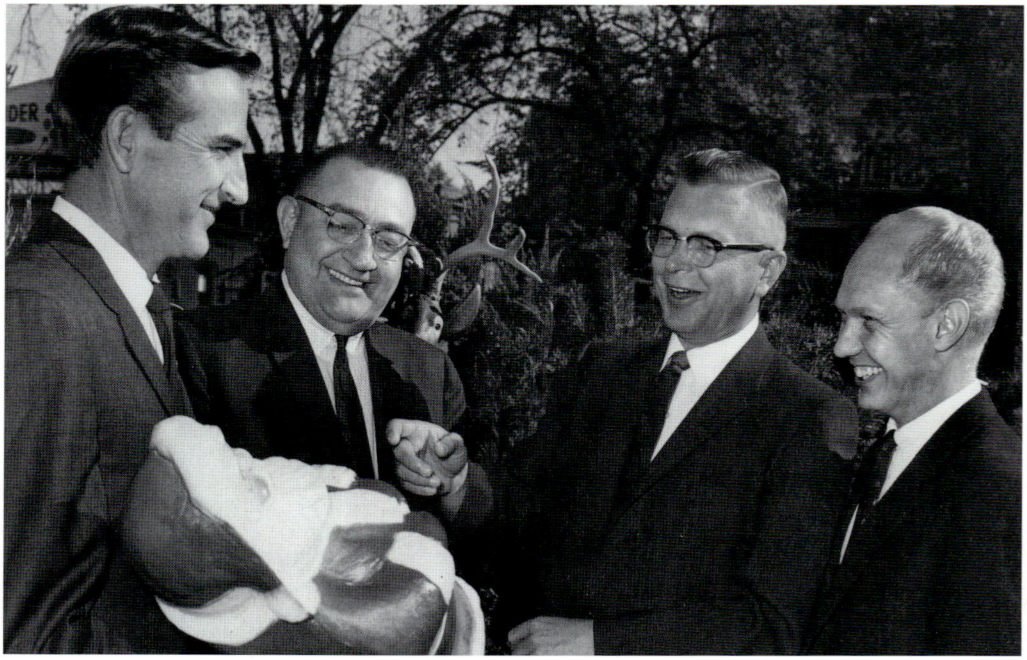

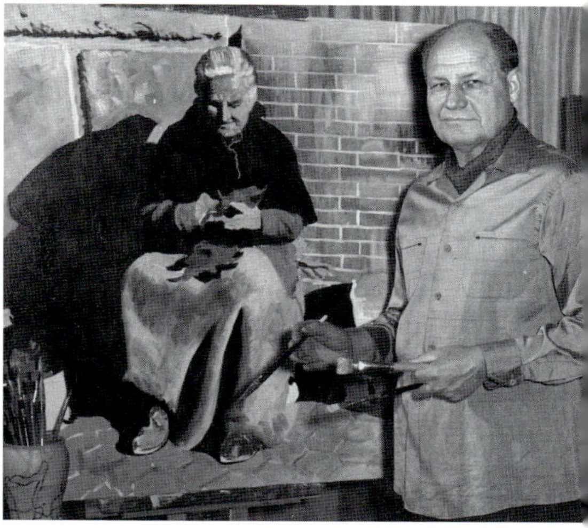

Farrell Collett

Farrell Collett was born in 1907. He began his professional career teaching art at Ogden High School. In 1939, he was offered a contract to head the art department at Weber College. He worked for Weber until he retired in 1976. During that time, he continued to work on his animal paintings. In 1982, the Collett Art Building at Weber College was named in his honor. Collett passed away in 2000.

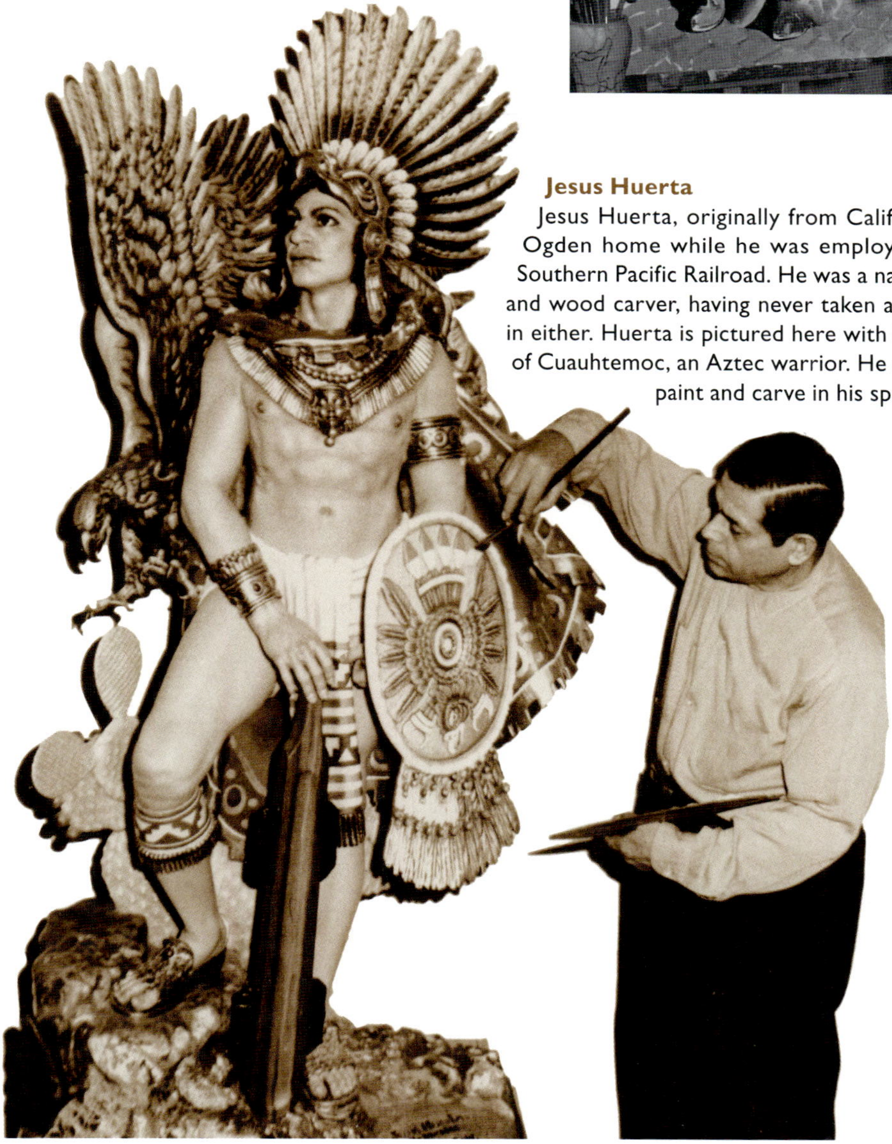

Jesus Huerta

Jesus Huerta, originally from California, called Ogden home while he was employed with the Southern Pacific Railroad. He was a natural painter and wood carver, having never taken a formal class in either. Huerta is pictured here with his sculpture of Cuauhtemoc, an Aztec warrior. He continued to paint and carve in his spare time.

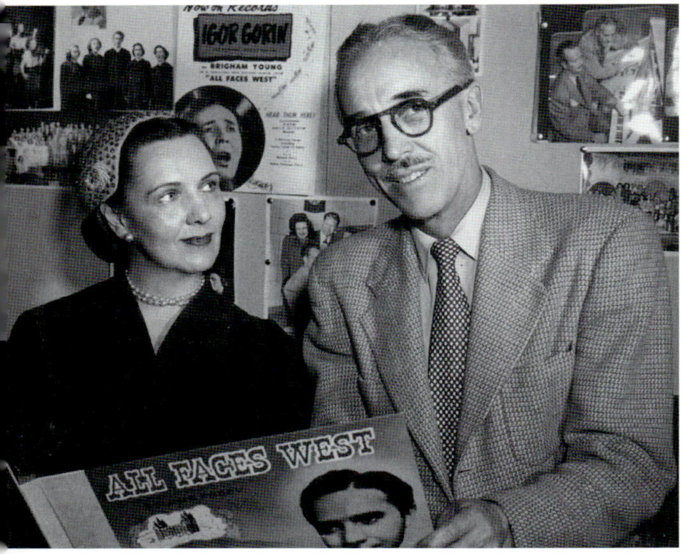

Roland and Helen Parry

When Roland Parry wrote *All Faces West* for a Pioneer Day celebration in 1955, he could hardly expect the international attention his work would receive or the lasting popularity of his musical about the Mormon pioneers. Famed baritone Igor Gorin (below, left) played the role of Brigham Young and sang the lyrics written by Parry's wife, Helen. A lasting friendship was formed between Gorin and the Parrys, and Gorin would repeat the role almost every year. Recordings of his performance were played around the country and in several other nations as well. Some of the songs were even broadcast into Soviet countries as part of the Voices of America broadcast. Roland and Helen continued to work together on other compositions, later settling in California.

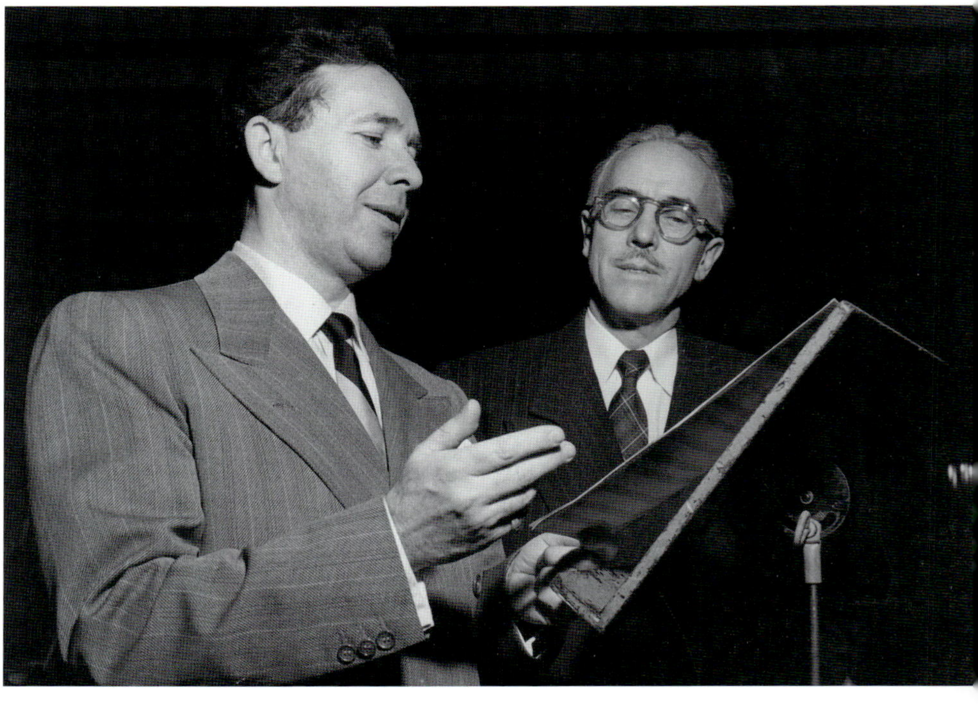

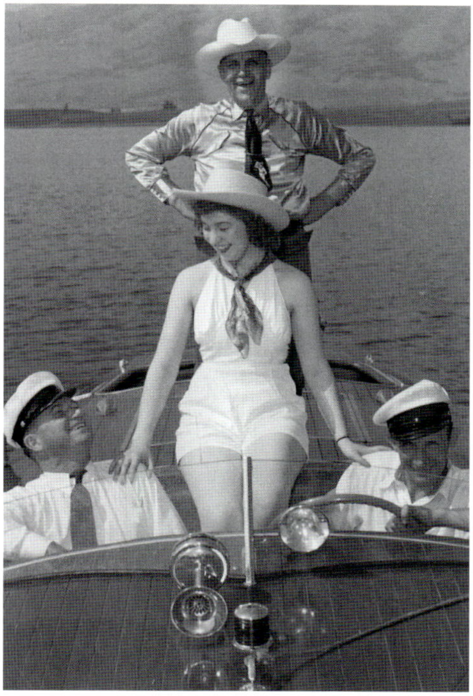

Ogden Pioneer Days

Ogden Pioneer Days was first celebrated in the summer of 1934 after Mayor Harman W. Peery (standing) organized a Western festival to boost the spirits of the locals and entice tourists to visit the city. Peery wanted Ogden Pioneer Days to become a national attraction that would continue for years to come. Here, Peery is pictured on a boat with a rodeo queen.

Del Adams

The first Ogden Pioneer Days in 1934 featured the Ogden Pioneer Pageant of Progress. Pictured here is Del Adams as Jim Bridger along with his fellow trappers and Indian guide. They are, from left to right, Del Adams, Chester Young, M.V. McIntyre, Sam Burch, Walter Prothero, and Mike Bennett in front of the Ben Lomond Hotel on Twenty-fifth Street and Washington Avenue. The men dressed in costume including provisions, rifles, and pelts.

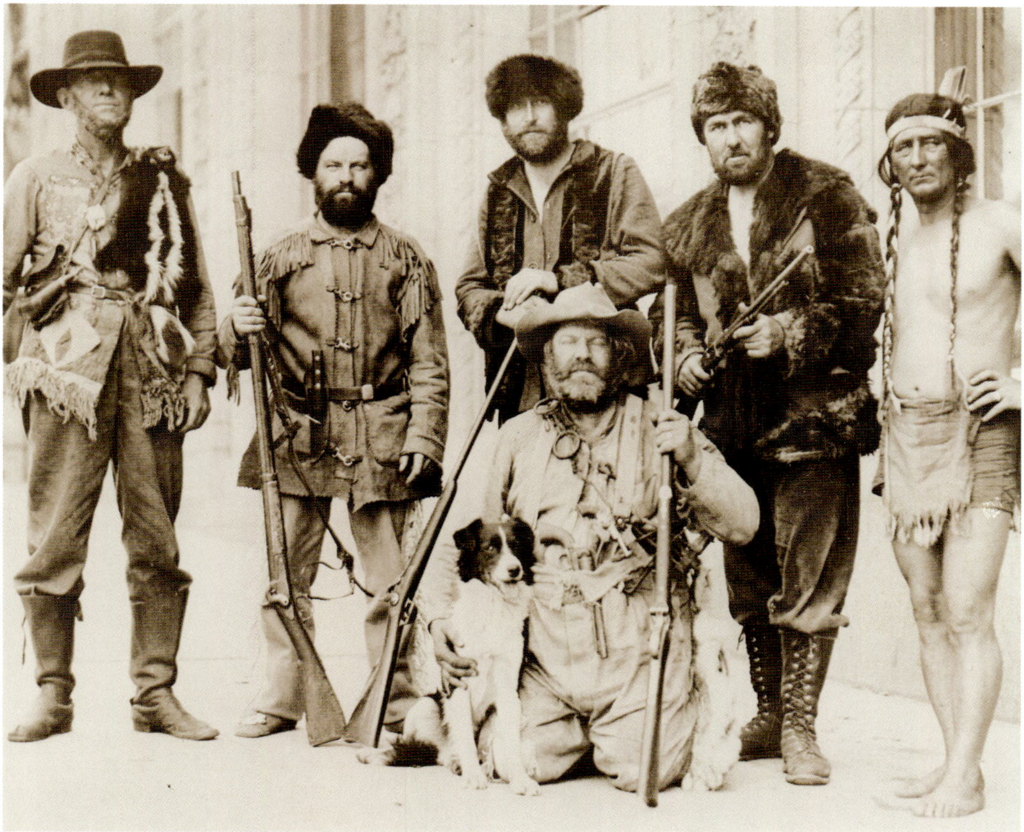

97

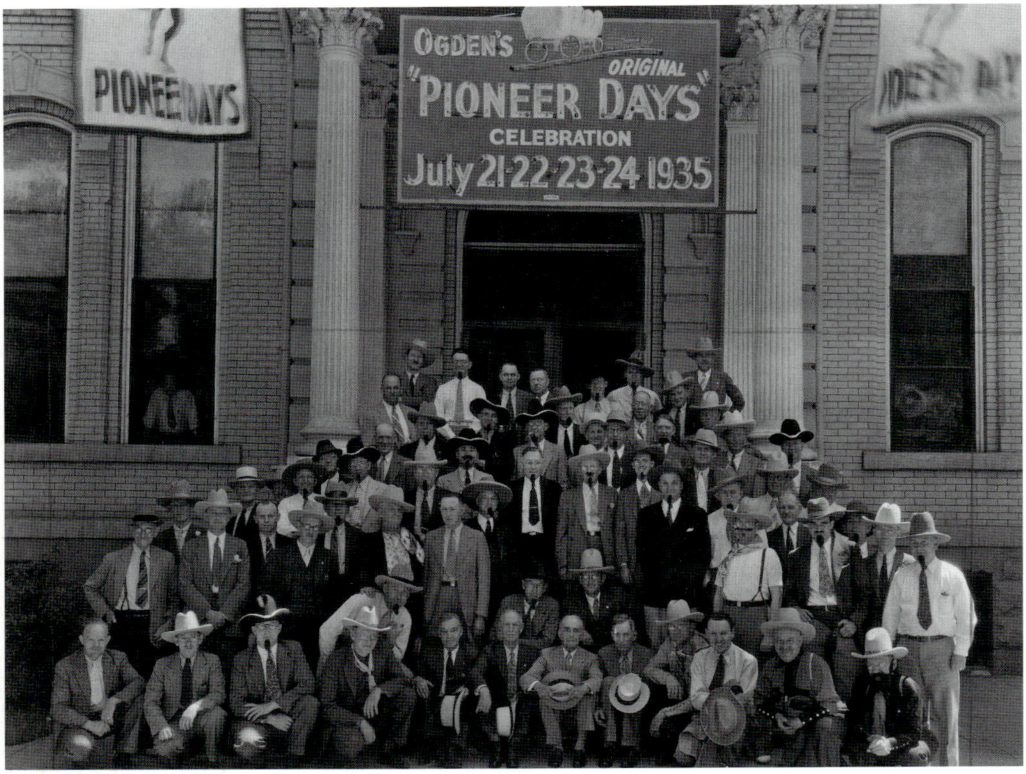

Beard Growing Contest

Part of the 1935 Pioneer Days celebration was a beard-growing contest, which was initiated by the local police wagering to see who would be itching to shave first. Pictured here are a group of the organizers, some with fake beards. Harman Peery is third from the right on the first row. The winner of the contest was chosen during the festivities.

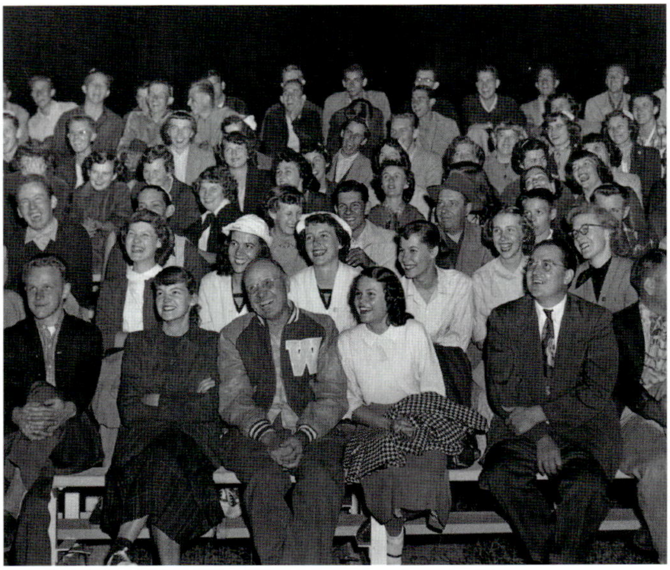

Henry Aldous Dixon

Henry Aldous Dixon (first row, center), during his presidency at Weber College, was one of the staunchest supporters of sports at the school. He was always a spectator at home football, basketball, and baseball games, and on many occasions accompanied the teams on road trips. His efforts brought about the new stadium on the new Weber College campus. Dixon also initiated steps for a new field house. Here he is cheering on the football team in 1952.

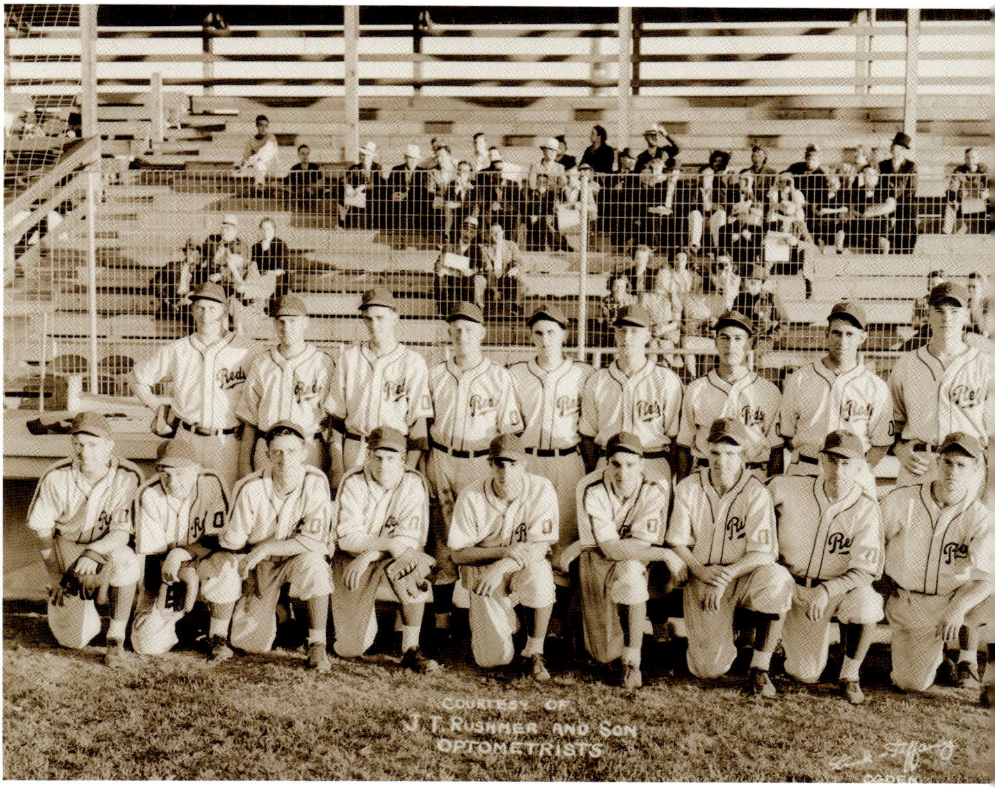

Ogden Reds
Ogden was a founding member of the Pioneer League in 1939. By 1940, the Ogden Reds baseball team (pictured) was the Pioneer League champions. With manager Bill McCorry, the team played to win at John Affleck Park. Included in the winning team was Bobby Adams (first from left on bottom row). Adams went on to play with Joe DiMaggio during World War II at Santa Ana and in the Pacific.

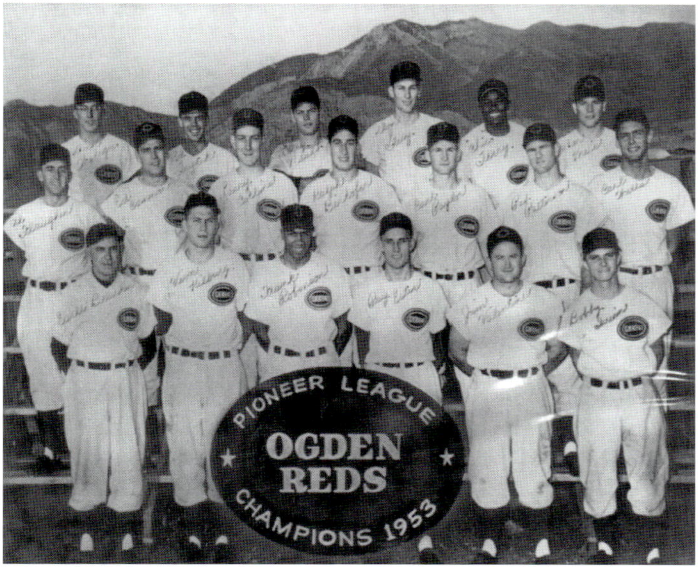

Ogden Reds
In 1939, the Ogden Reds were also designated as a farm league for the Cincinnati Redlegs. The Ogden Reds operated from 1939 to 1942 and 1946 to 1955. In 1953, the team was again crowned the Pioneer League champions. On the championship team was future hall-of-famer Frank Robinson, who joined the team right out of high school. The team was honored with a program and gifts for winning.

99

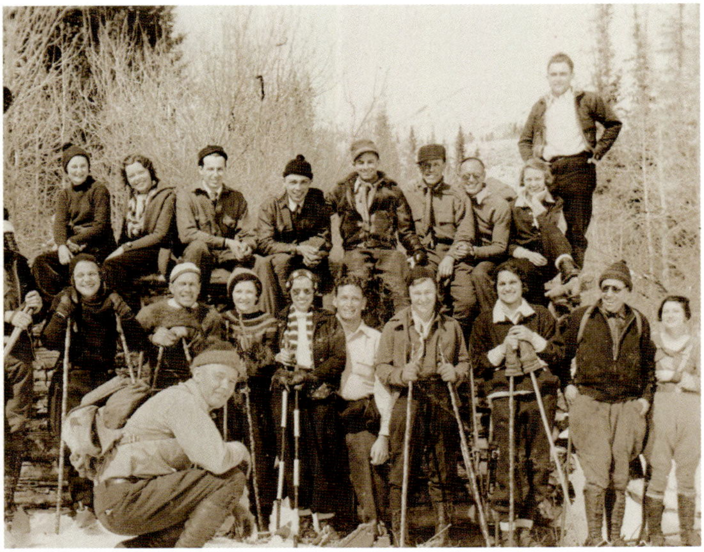

Ralph Johnston and Friends
Although Ralph Johnston (seated, center) was born in Arizona and had never seen snow until he was 17, he became an avid skier and collector of ski memorabilia. He was also involved in the early days of the Snow Basin Ski Patrol, founded in the 1940s. Patrol members cleared rocks and brush on the slopes, then took turns patrolling them in case of injuries. Johnson died in 2002 at the age of 97.

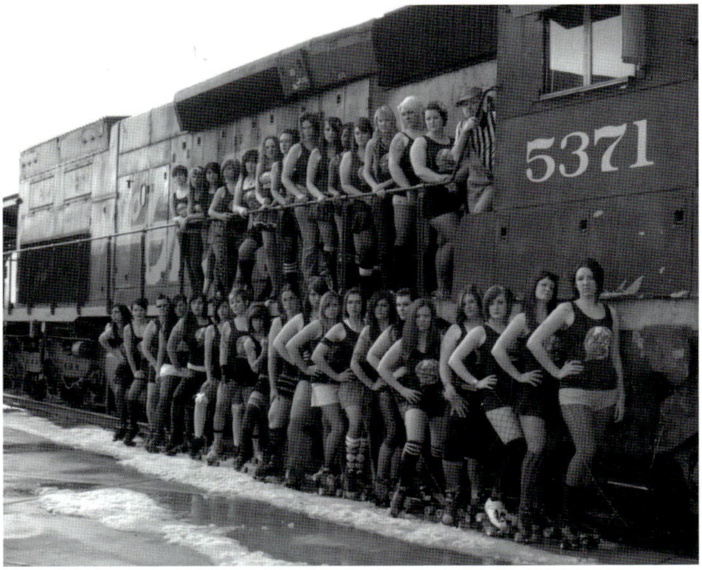

Junction City Roller Dolls
In 2008, the Junction City Roller Dolls were established in Ogden by four dedicated skaters and their friends. The mission was to build a league that would revive the love for roller derby in the local area. They wanted a place where women of all shapes and sizes could compete and feel confident. In 2011, the team was accepted as members of the Women's Flat Track Derby Association. (Photograph courtesy of Junction City Roller Dolls.)

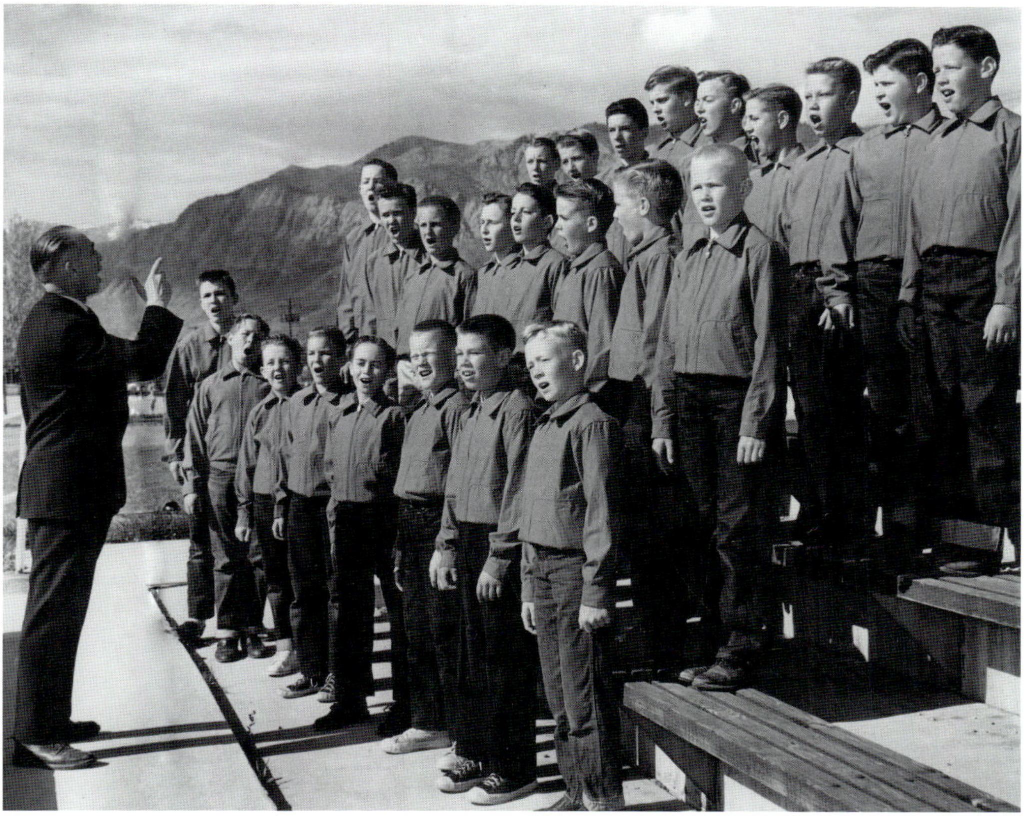

Glenn Hanson

Glenn Hanson was a longtime music educator in Ogden, and with his wife, Faye, he founded several musical groups. Picture above, Hanson conducts the Ogden Utah Boys Chorus and Trumpet Choir. The group of 66 boys traveled to Wyoming, Nebraska, Washington, DC, and Colorado. The choir was started in 1954 as a nonsectarian group with the idea of developing musical talent and an attitude of cooperation through music. Hansen also founded the Ogden-Weber Symphonic choir (below), which performed at the Seattle World's Fair in 1962. Hanson died in 1964, but is remembered for his love of music, summed up in a message he gave choir members: "Music gives to the performer and to the listener the rare and wonderful experience of feeling vibrantly alive, and sharing that feeling with others . . . Just before we sing think of Goethe's advice—'Remember to live.'"

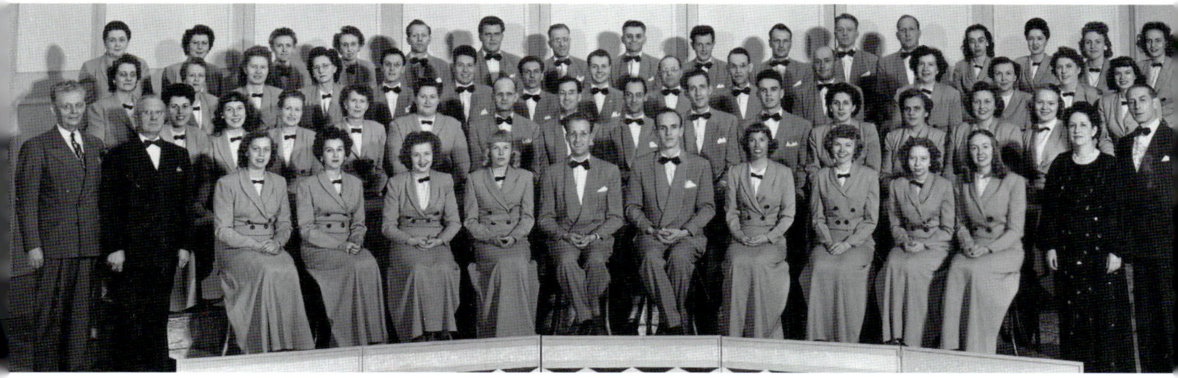

101

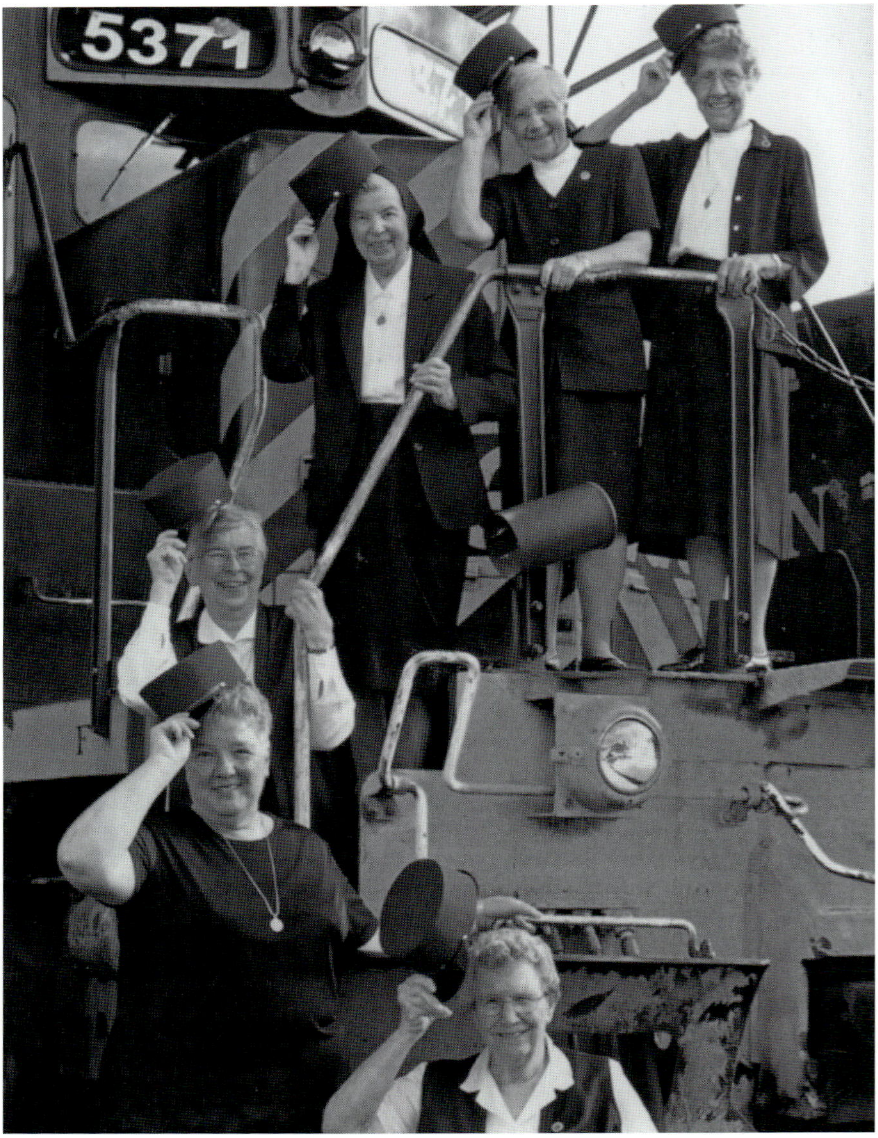

Sisters of St. Benedict

In 1944, the Sisters of St. Benedict came to Utah from Minnesota in response to a request from city and county officials to build and operate St. Benedict's Hospital. Over the years, the sisters' work has expanded to include education, parish ministry, and retreat work. The sisters' courage to lead and grow while serving the community's health care needs brought many changes to the hospital, including a new facility in Washington Terrace in 1977. Today, the sisters still serve the local community through the hospital and St. Benedict's Foundation. They were honored in 2012 with the Lieutenant Governor's Lifetime Achievement Award for 66 years of involvement. Pictured here are, from bottom to top, Sr. Jean Gibson, Sr. Iris Beckwith, Sr. Mary Zenzen, Sr. Luke Hoschette, Sr. Danile Knight, and Sr. Stephanie Mongeon. (Photograph courtesy of St. Benedict's Foundation.)

Abbey of Our Lady of the Holy Trinity

The Abbey of Our Lady of the Holy Trinity was founded in May 1947 in Ogden Valley by 35 monks from the Order of the Cistercians of the Strict Observance. The monks came to Utah from Gethsemani in Kentucky. The monks live in Quonset huts that were former military barracks. The monastery had a large farmland and raised bees for the honey. They also used to run beef cattle and sell eggs, bread, and cereal that they produced themselves. The monastery is being affected by the worldwide shortage of priests and clergy. No new monks have joined Holy Trinity Abbey in several years. The current abbot is Fr. David Altman.

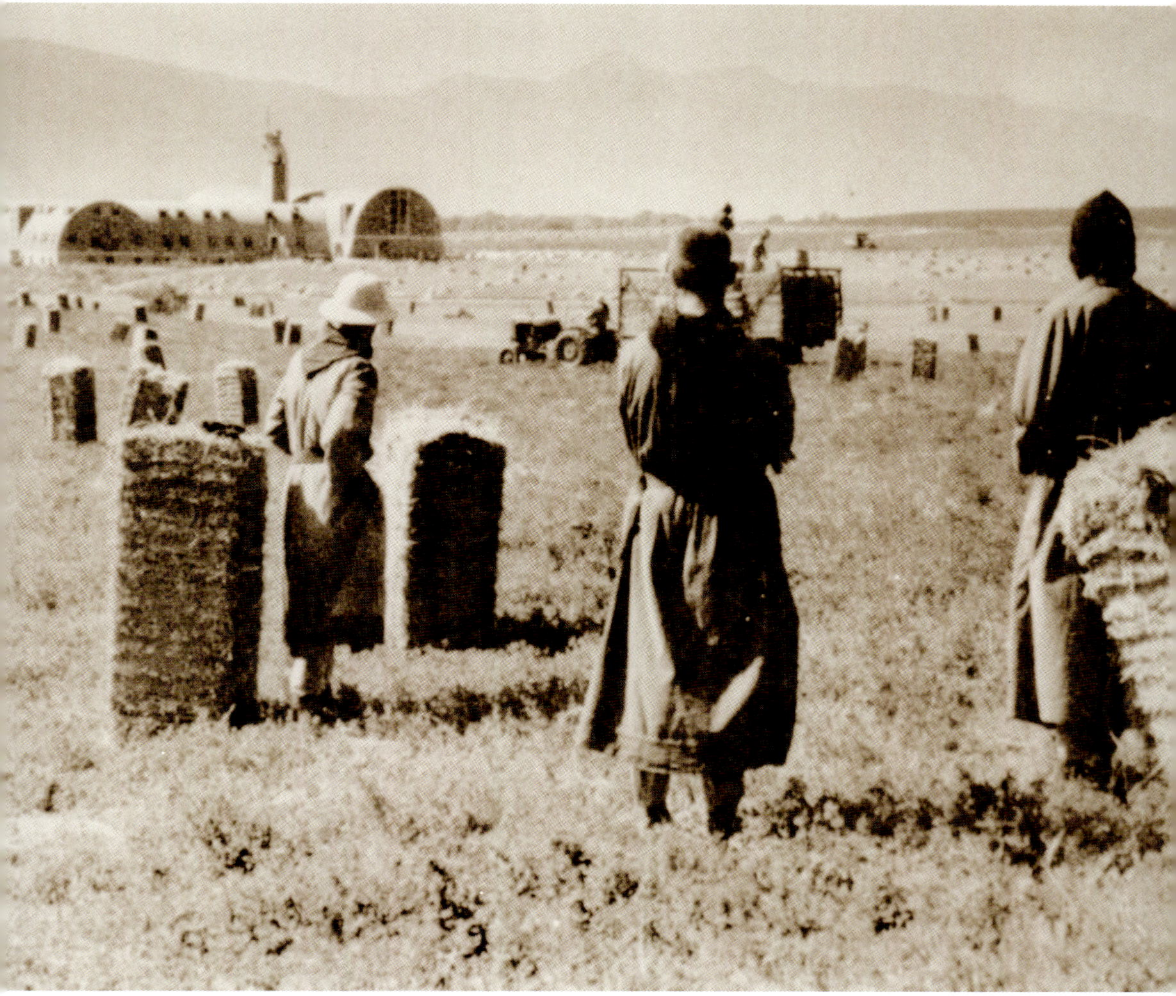

103

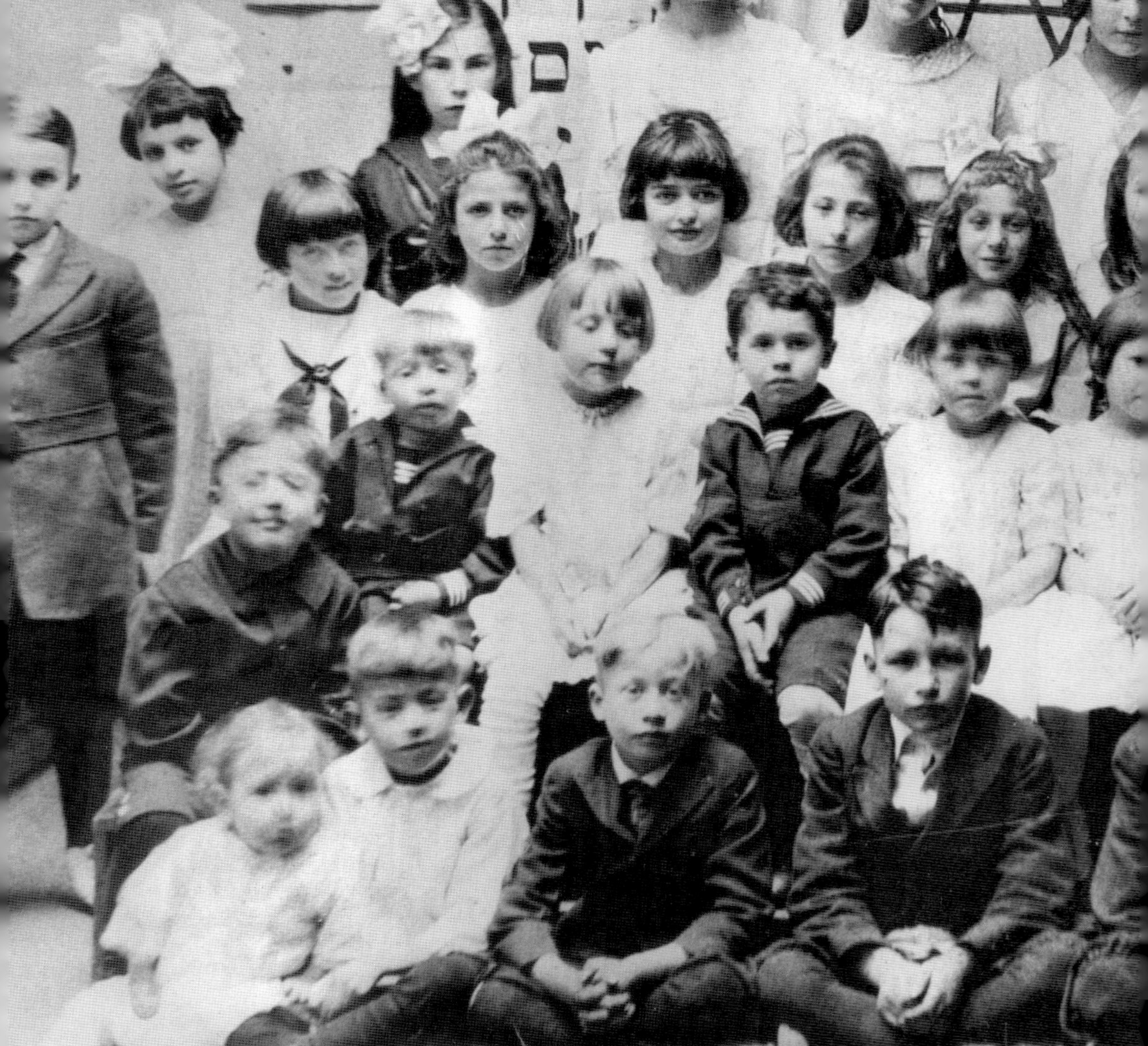
בגדה

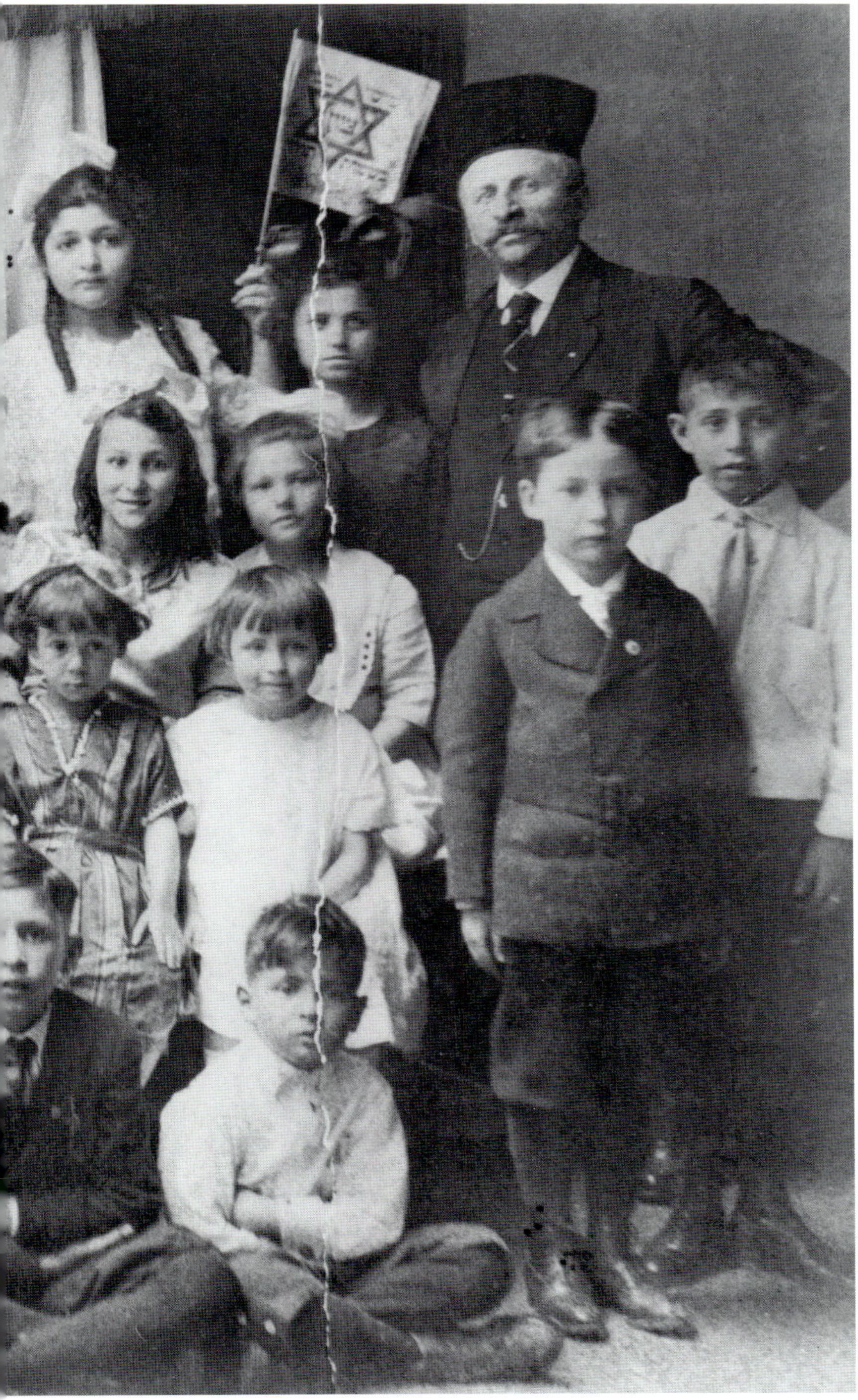

Rabbi Lazarus Lehrer

When Pres. Abraham Siner of the B'Rith Sholem congregation died in 1919, Rabbi Lazarus Lehrer (back, far right) was sent from Salt Lake City to lead the congregation. Although Rabbi Lehrer only remained in Ogden for three years, he did a great deal for the Jewish community. He contributed to several articles in the *Standard Examiner* explaining Jewish holidays and religious services, taught a children's class (shown here), and raised funds for a synagogue. In 1921, that synagogue was completed, and when Lehrer left in 1922 for a new post in Maryland, his congregation had doubled in size.

105

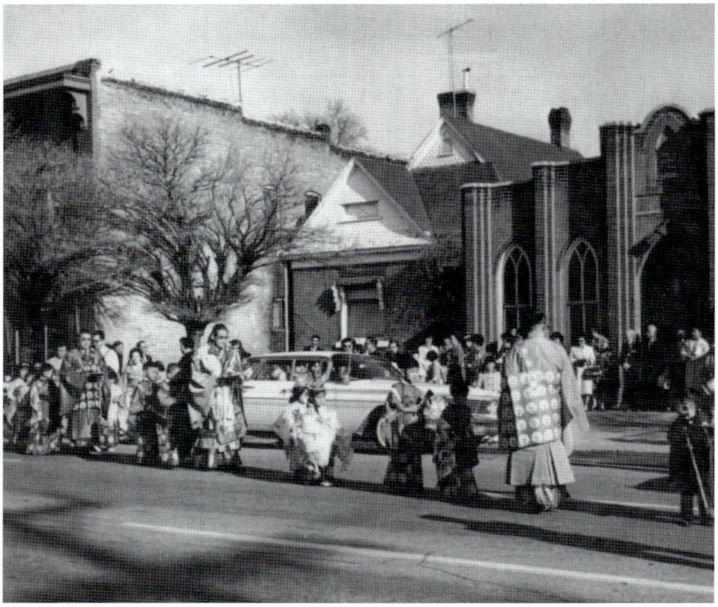

Ogden Buddhist Church

Weber County has a large Japanese American population with a rich history. In 1913, the first Buddhist temple was built in Ogden, and in 1918, a women's group was formed to help Japanese women adjust to life in America. After World War II, the Japanese population increased as many of the Camp Topaz internees remained in the state. The Buddhist congregation held parades such as this one to mark the birthday of Buddha.

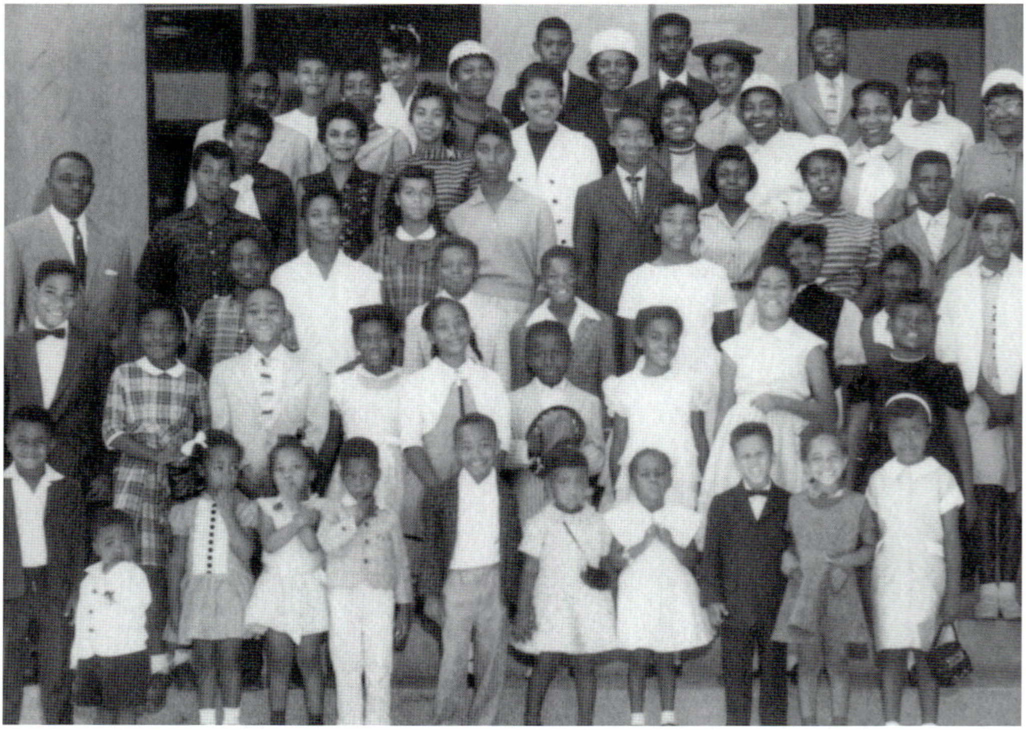

New Zion Baptist Church

The first Baptist congregation was organized in Ogden in 1881, with Dwight Spencer as minister. In 1918, the Wall Avenue Baptist Church was built, but 40 years later, after a period of rapid growth, the congregation outgrew its building. Rev. Benjamin J. Washington oversaw construction of the new building, and in 1956, the New Zion Baptist Church began holding services. The church stands today and continues to serve the community.

CHAPTER NINE

What a Contrast

Famous and Infamous

Ogden has been home to some of the nation's most famous names in the world of entertainment, sports and music. It even has its own homegrown celebrities who have changed the landscape and culture of the city. Some of the most popular known names from Ogden include jazz musician Red Nichols and singers the Osmond family. Several Ogdenites have graced the silver screen, including Moroni Olsen, Hal Ashby, Robert Walker, and Gedde Wantanabe. Authors including Bernard DeVoto and Fawn McKay Brodie have called Ogden home during their early lives. The Browning brothers first began designing and manufacturing guns in Ogden. They were heavily involved in the local trap shooting clubs.

Along with those on the national stage, Ogden has seen its share of locals that have influenced the city through their accomplishments: Isaac Goeckeritz, a local filmmaker whose documentaries on the local area have won Utah Best In State awards; local newspaper writer Charles Trentleman, who looks at national trends but also the history of Ogden and the historical impact on the city today; Anna Belle Weakley, who ran the Porters and Waiters Club and provided a musical outlet for jazz and African Americans before the Civil Rights movement; and Betty Stewart Moore, who worked to help the race relations between soldiers and civilians at Hill Air Force Base.

With the famous come the infamous citizens who left their mark on Ogden. Ogden was known as a rough town with the railroad and Twenty-fifth Street providing every vice known to man within the city blocks. During the early years in Ogden, a fair share of criminals walked the streets and served their time in Ogden. With Ogden being the home for the State Industrial School, juvenile delinquents from throughout the West made their way to Ogden. This included career criminal Jack Abbott, who spent his youth at the school. With the vices, prostitution was a norm in downtown Ogden. Several madams enjoyed a healthy business before the 1950s, including Belle London and Rose Davies. These stories help build the sorted history of Ogden.

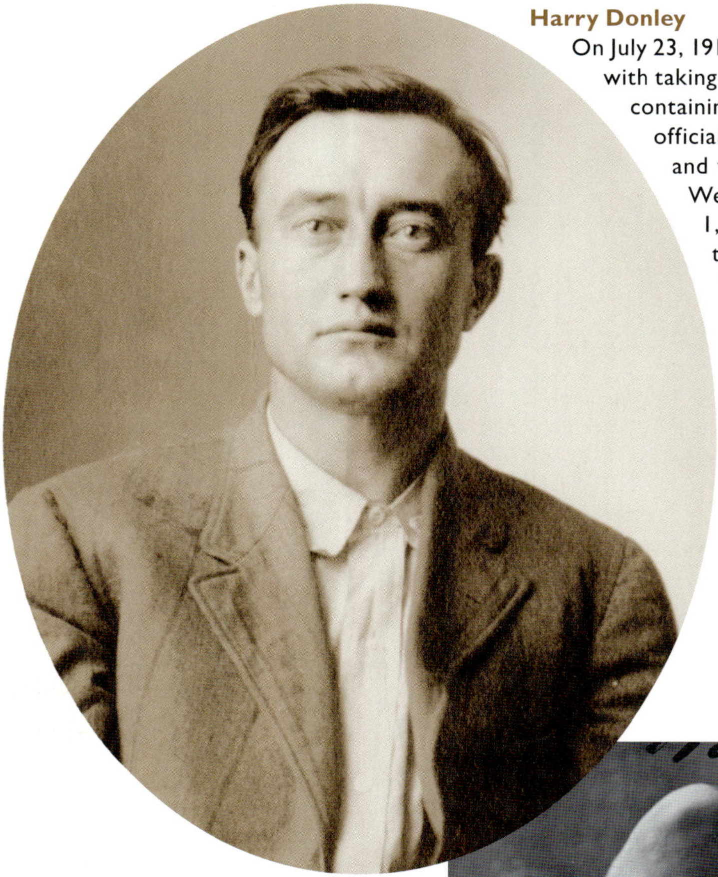

Harry Donley

On July 23, 1913, Harry Donley was charged with taking a purse from Thomas Nelson containing $8. In August 1913, he was officially charged with grand larceny and was held awaiting trial in the Weber County Jail. On October 1, 1913, Donley, along with two other prisoners, escaped from jail by enlarging the holes where the steam pipes entered the building.

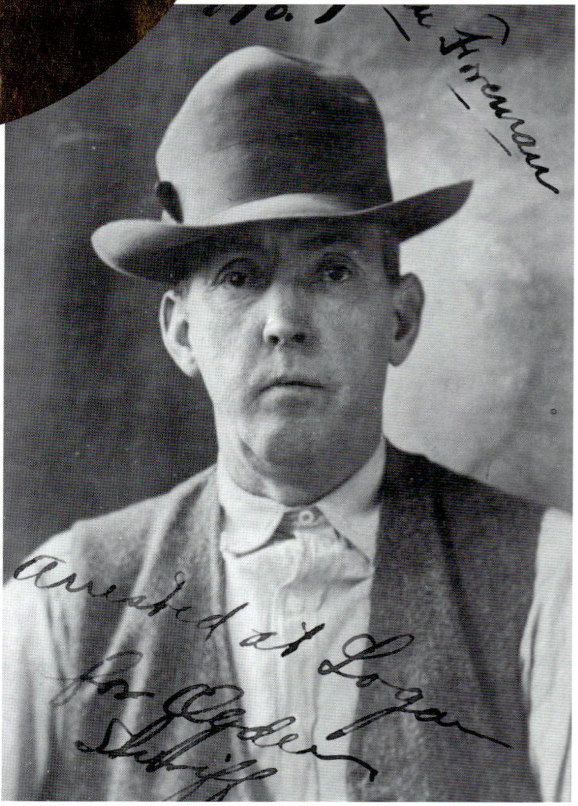

Ben Foreman

Ben Foreman was arrested in November 1913, and charged with stealing a horse-and-buggy from William Pierce and a man named Anderson. He was convicted of theft following a second trial on April 17, 1914. When facing his fourth term at the Utah State Penitentiary, he attempted suicide as he was walking into the prison on April 24, 1914. He was committed to the state mental hospital.

John M. Browning

John M. Browning was born in Ogden in January 1855. Browning designed many varieties of military and civilian firearms, cartridges, and gun mechanisms. He made his first firearm at age 13 in his father's gun shop, and was awarded his first patent on October 7, 1879. John is credited with 128 gun patents. From 1883, Browning worked in partnership with Winchester and designed a series of rifles and shotguns. In 1927, Browning founded Browning Arms Company, which was to market sporting designs rather than military. Besides Winchester-Colt, Remington, Fabrique Nationale de Herstal of Belgium, and Miroku have manufactured John Browning's designs. Browning died on November 26, 1926.

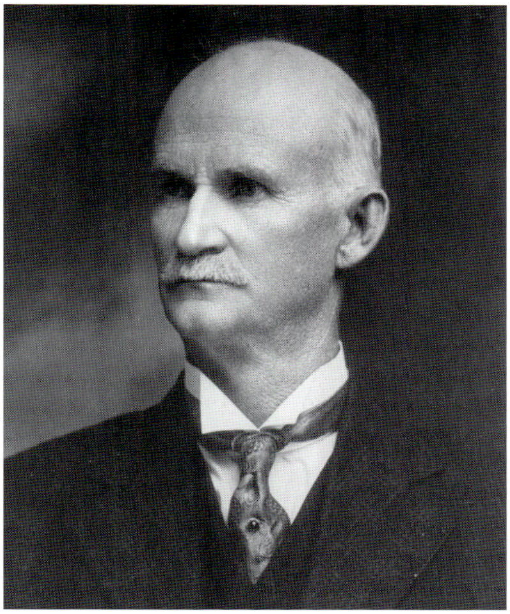

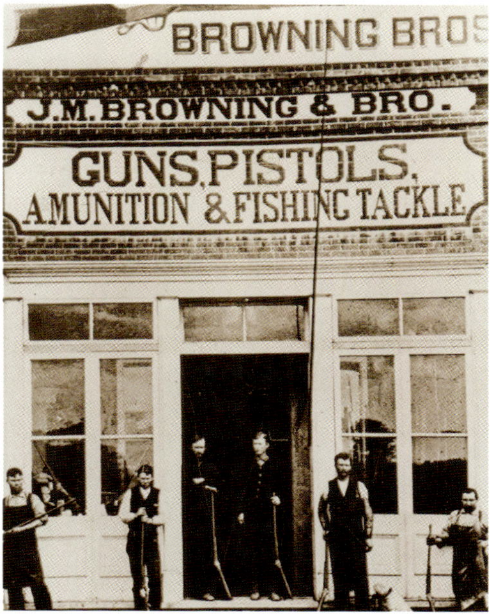

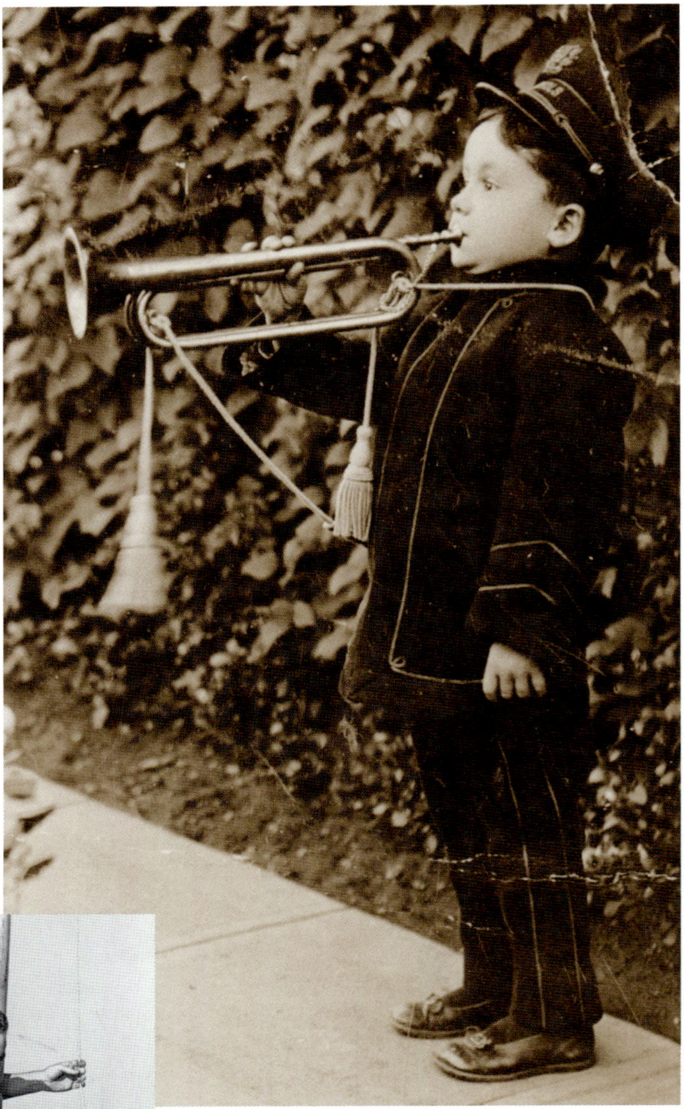

Red Nichols

Ernest Loring "Red" Nichols was born in Ogden on May 8, 1905. By the age of 12, Nichols was already playing difficult set pieces for his father's brass band. Nichols came to be an accomplished cornettist during the 1920s Jazz Age. He was in several bands, including Red Nichols and His Five Pennies, recording 10 to a dozen records a week. Nichols led Bob Hope's orchestra for a short period before leaving the music business to work in the wartime shipyards. Soon after the war ended, Nichols formed a new Five Pennies band, which became very popular in a short time. The 1959 Hollywood film *The Five Pennies*, was loosely based on Nichols's career and received four Academy Award nominations. On June 28, 1965, Nichols died in Las Vegas before a scheduled show at the Mint Hotel.

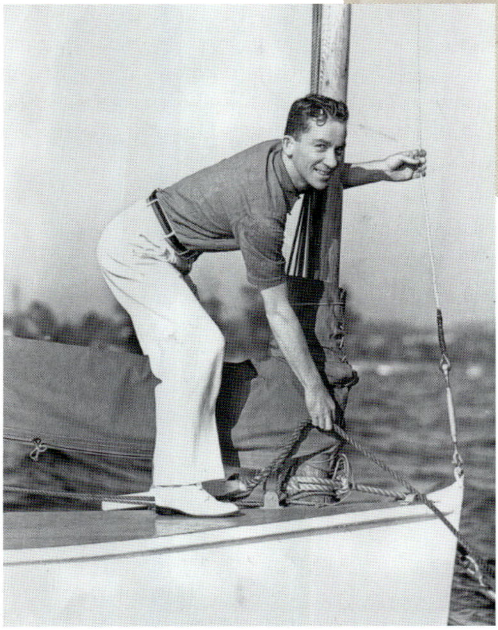

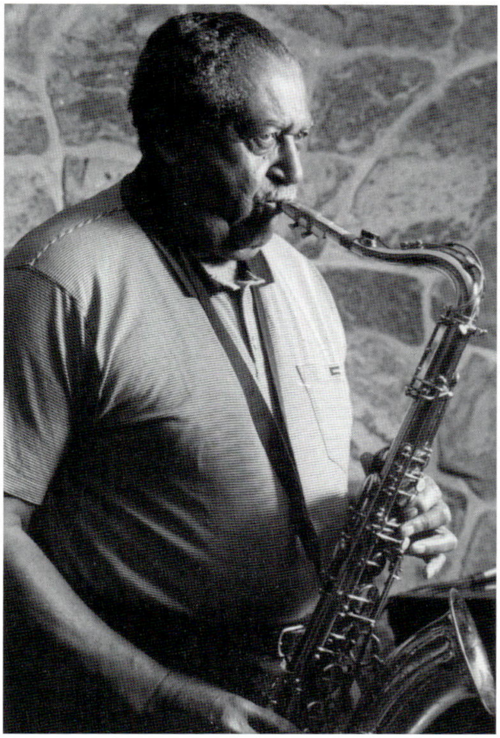

Joe McQueen
Joe McQueen was born in Dallas, Texas, in 1919. McQueen began playing professional jazz at the age of 16. In 1945, McQueen and his wife, Thelma, moved to Ogden. During his early years in Ogden, McQueen worked and played at the Porters and Waiters Club during a time when few venues were open to African Americans. He was the first African American in Utah to play at previously white-only establishments and to have a mixed race band. (Photograph courtesy of *Ogden Standard Examiner*.)

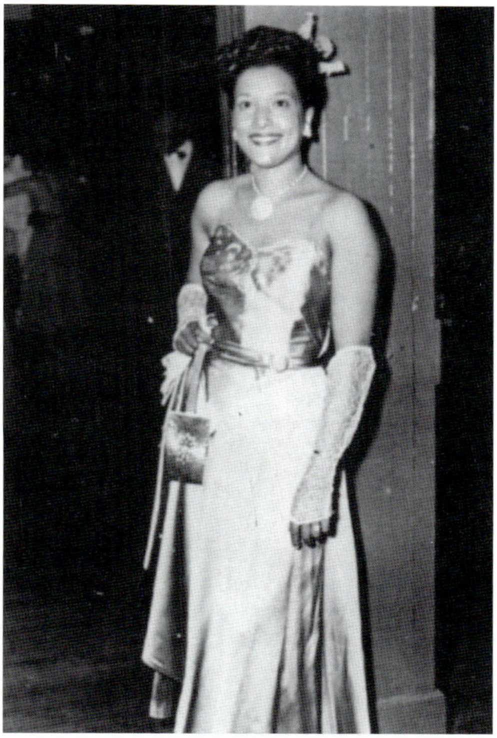

Anna Belle Weakley
Anna Belle Weakley moved to Ogden from Alabama in the 1930s and ran the Porters and Waiters Club and Hotel until 1960. It was the only diner and hotel that was open to African Americans in the Ogden area. Weakley and her husband would also feed black college students and military men. She also served on various boards including the YWCA, the Legal Aid Society, and the Governor's Black Advisory Council. (Photograph courtesy of Issac Goeckeritz.)

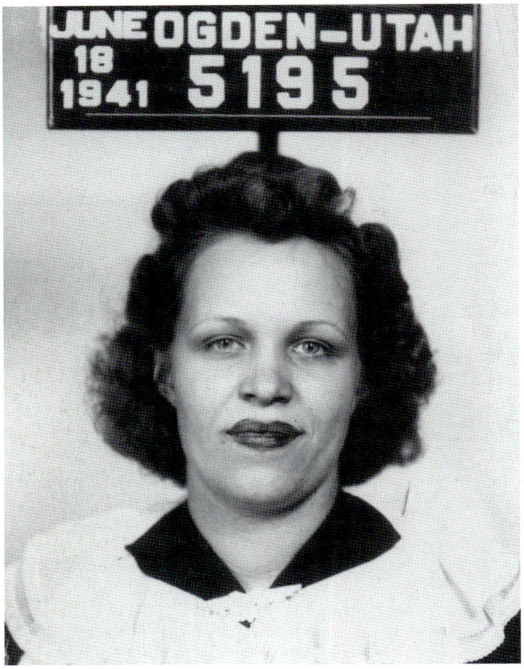

Peggy Wagner

Prostitution in Ogden has had a long history back to the early 1900s with Belle London. The profession was at a high again during World War II as many soldiers passed through Ogden on the trains. When arrested, girls like Peggy Wagner were charged with vagrancy, tested for venereal disease, and released if negative. If positive, they were treated and then shipped out of town.

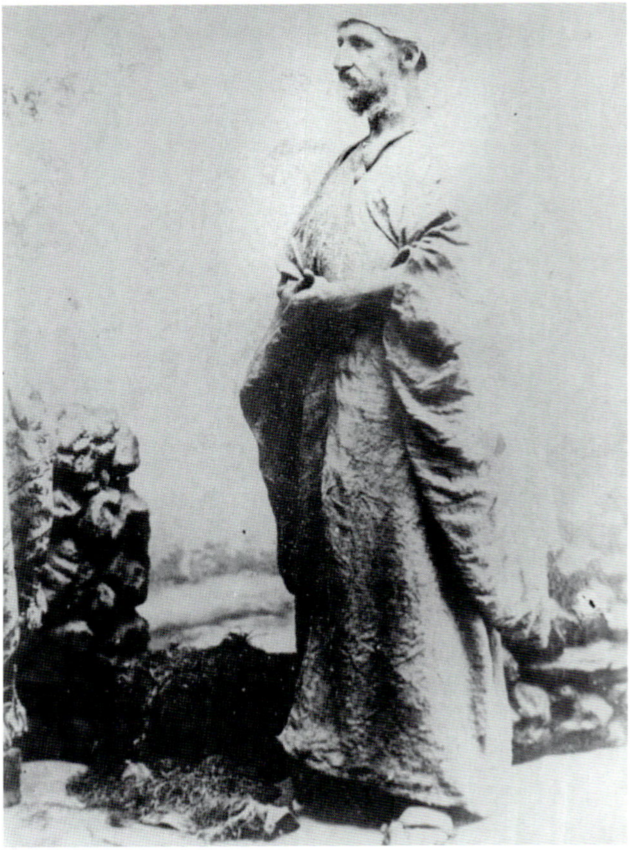

Louis the Carpenter

During the early 20th century, Ogden was full of interesting characters. Louis the carpenter was just one of them. Louis lived in a tent on an irrigation ditch at Twenty-fifth Street and Lincoln Avenue. He worked as a carpenter by day and wandered the streets as a preacher by night. He wore robes, which were made of gunny sacking and bathed in the irrigation ditch year-round.

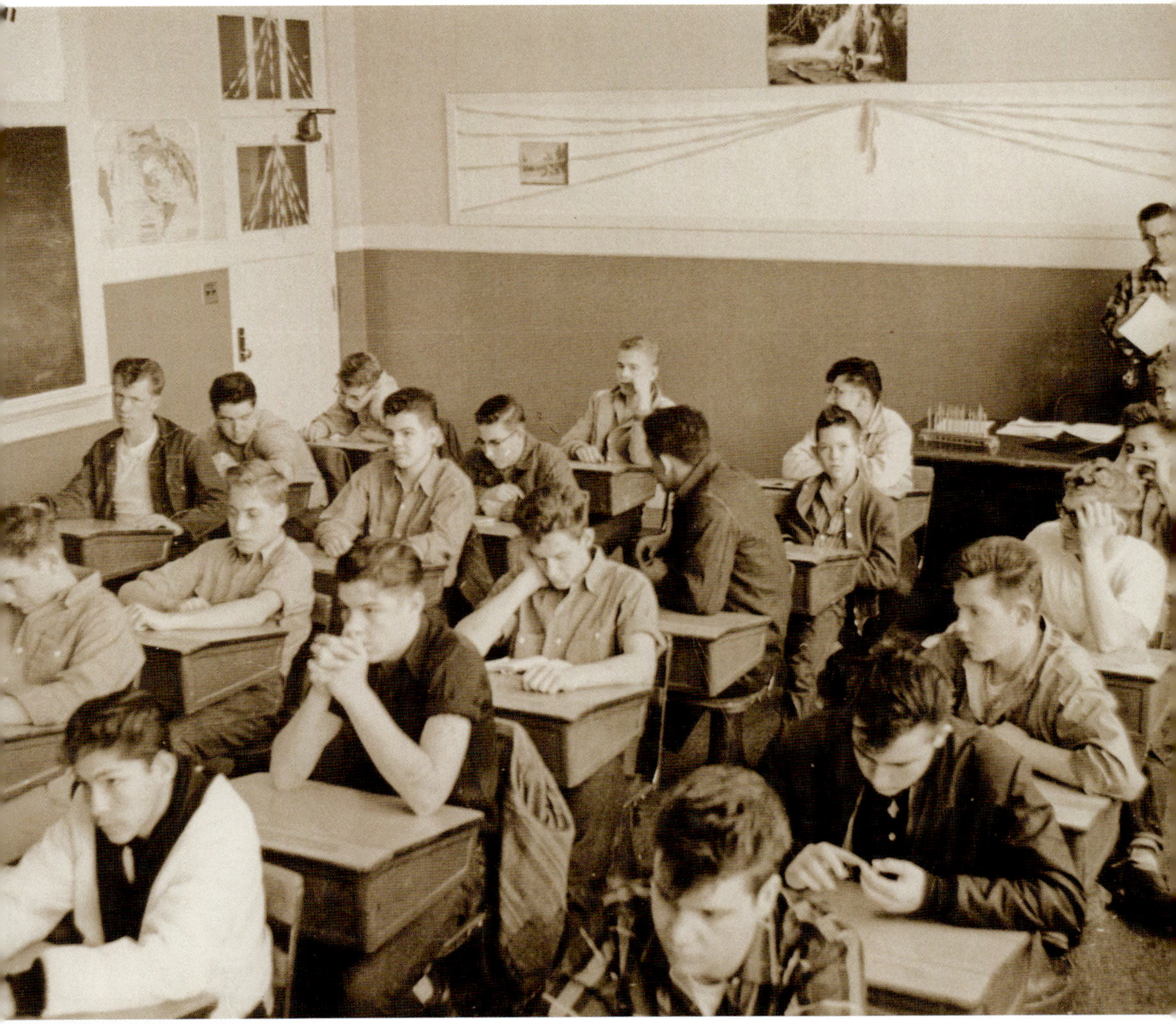

Jack Henry Abbott

Jack Henry Abbott was born in Oscoda, Michigan, in 1944. By the age of 12, he was sent to the State Industrial School in Ogden, Utah, where this photograph was taken. He is in the second row, fifth back. He stayed there until he was released at the age of 18. Abbott ended up spending most of his life in prison and authored the book *In the Belly of the Beast*. He was released from prison in 1981 after gaining praise for his writing and being lauded by many, including author Norman Mailer. Six weeks after his release, he fatally stabbed a man during a fight and was convicted of manslaughter. He committed suicide in prison in 2002.

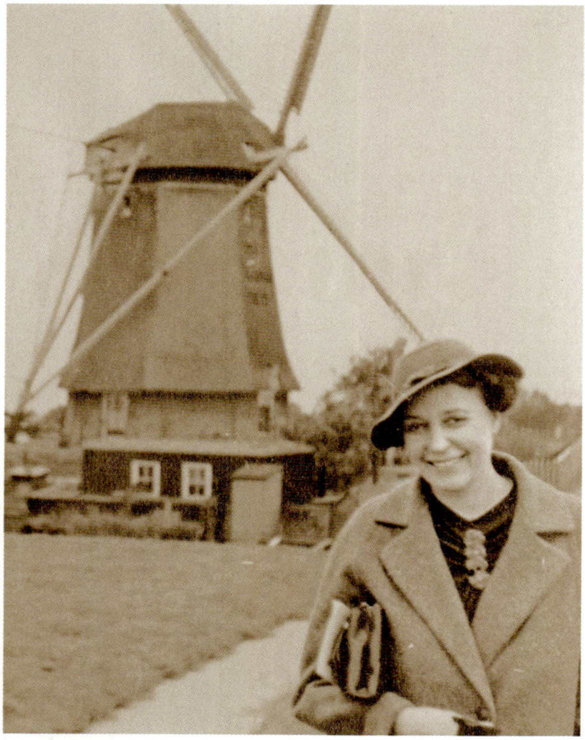

Cora Kasius

A prominent social worker from Ogden, Cora Kasius moved to New York in 1928. By 1945, she served on the faculties of New York University, Columbia University, and New York School of Social Work. Kasius was appointed welfare liaison officer to aid in the rehabilitation of Holland after its destruction during World War II. In 1964, she was honored by the National Conference on Social Welfare for her leadership role in social work.

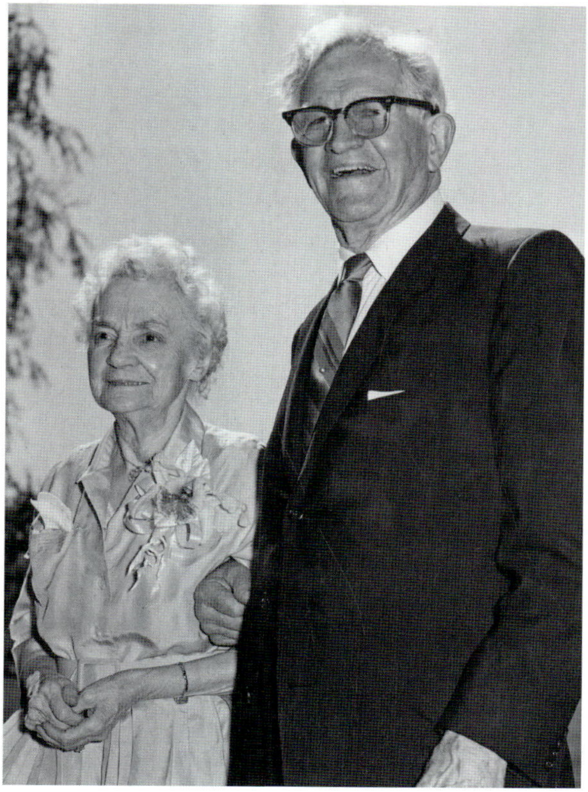

David O. McKay

David O. McKay was born in Hunstville on September 8, 1873. In 1902, McKay was appointed principal to the Weber Stake Academy. He was the ninth president of the Church of Jesus Christ of Latter-day Saints, serving from 1951 until 1970. During his presidency, McKay maintained his focus on education within the leadership of the LDS church. McKay died on January 18, 1970.

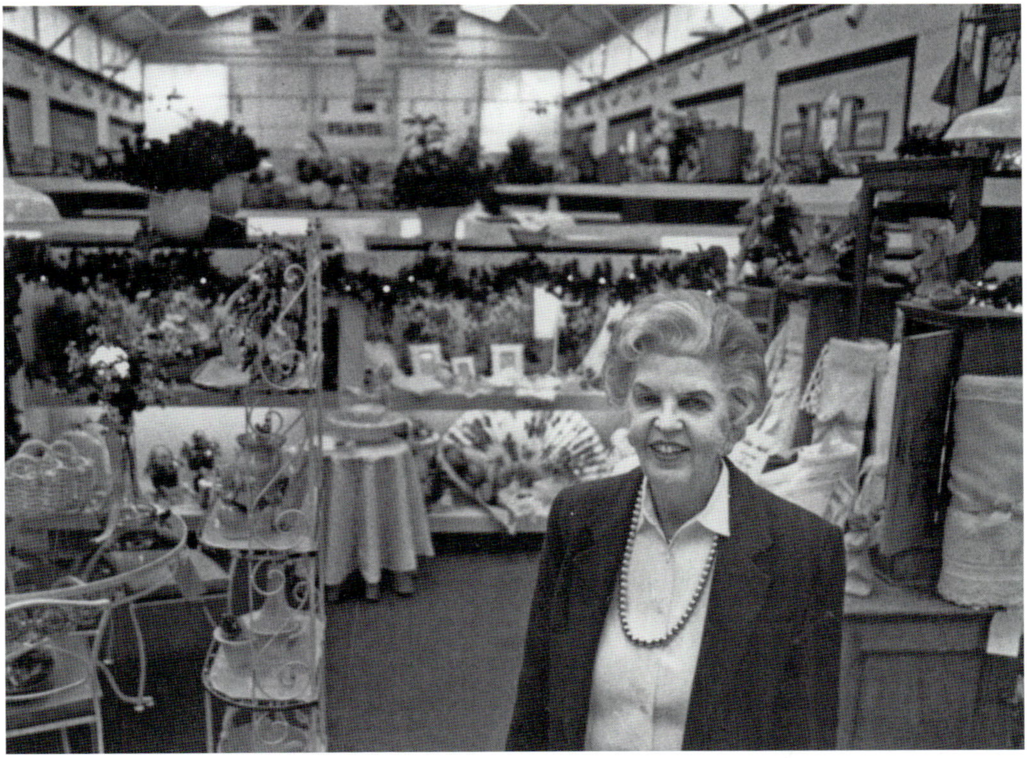

Rosanne King
Rosanne Peery King is the daughter of Mayor Harman Peery. In 1946, she and her husband, Robert, were given the resort Rainbow Gardens by Harm. For 25 years they operated as a resort, including indoor and outdoor swimming pools, a ballroom, and 18 bowling lanes. In 1977, King ran for Ogden City Council and was elected. (Photograph courtesy of *Ogden Standard Examiner.*)

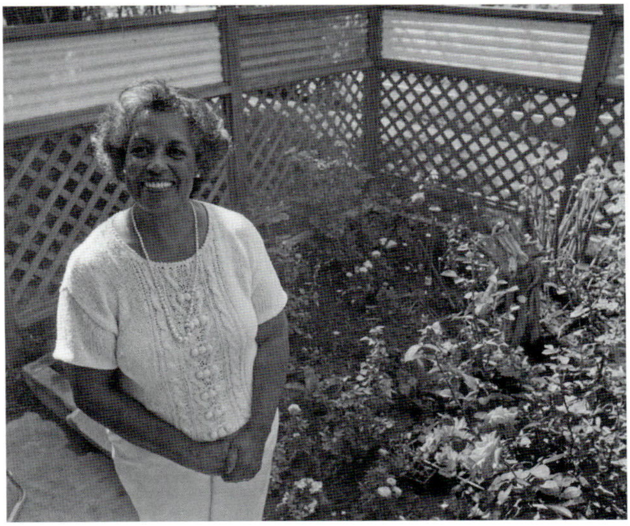

Betty Stewart Moore
Betty Stewart Moore is an Ogden native and grew up dealing with segregation during the 1940s. She remembers wanting to go dancing at Lagoon but not being able to because of a ban for African Americans at the dance hall and swimming pools. During her life, Moore worked at Hill Air Force Base as a race relations orientation specialist to try and break down some of these barriers. (Photograph courtesy of *Ogden Standard Examiner.*)

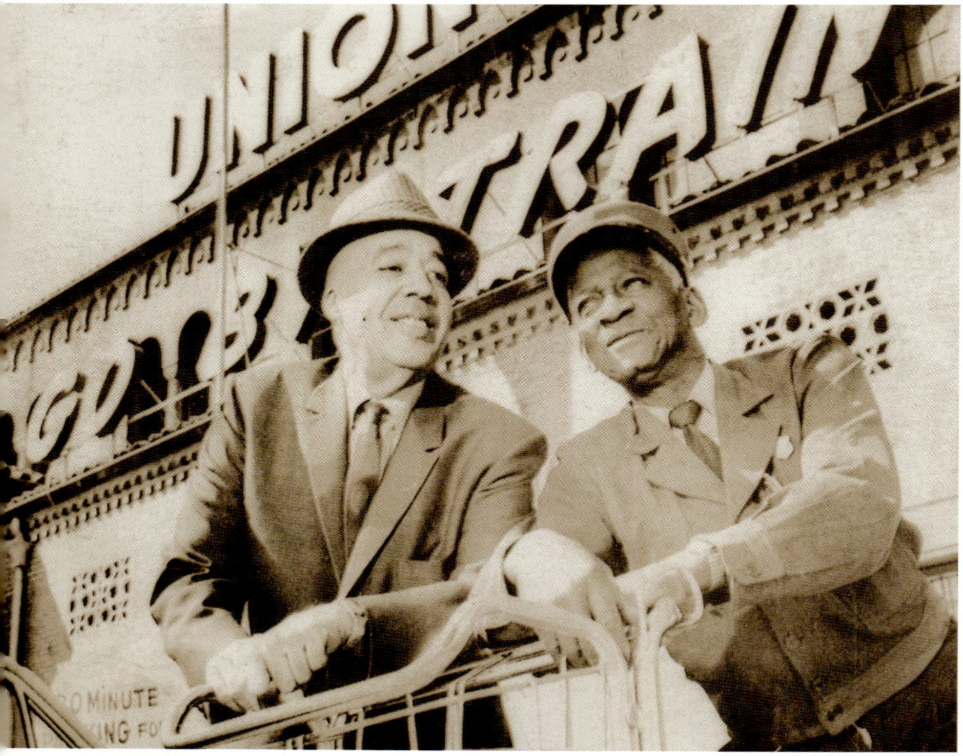

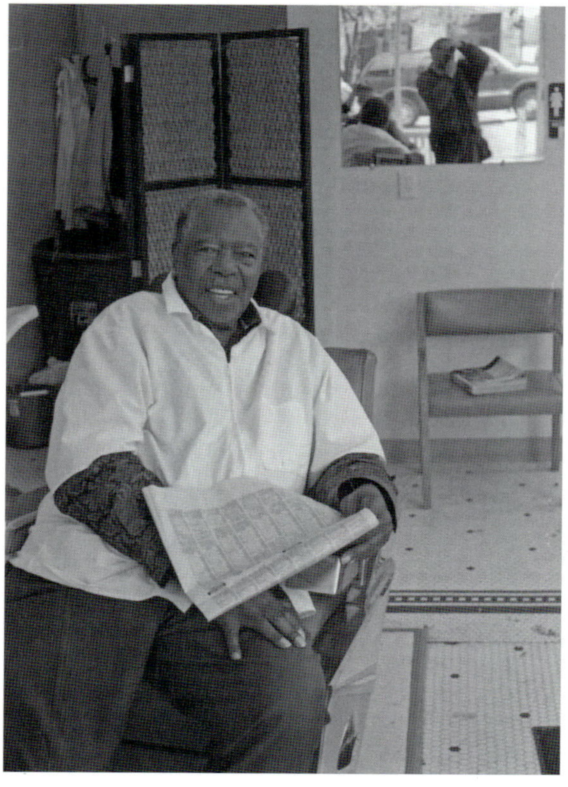

Last Two Redcaps
Johnny Hayes and Jimmy West were the last two redcaps at the Ogden Union Station. West started his career with the Union Pacific as a porter in 1942; Hayes started in 1937. Their retirement in 1970 came as train travel was declining, with passenger service just three days a week. Both gentlemen recalled a time when the train depot was so busy that the 12 redcaps could barely keep up.

Willie Moore
Willie Moore has been operating his barbershop in Ogden for over 40 years. He is the owner of Moore's Barber Shop on Twenty-fifth Street. Besides operating his business, Moore has been very active in supporting the Ogden community. In 1973, Moore was named the promotional representative for the Utah Stars of the American Basketball Association. He also sponsored delegates to Boys' State over the years and hosted an annual golf tournament. (Photograph courtesy of Charlie Trentelman.)

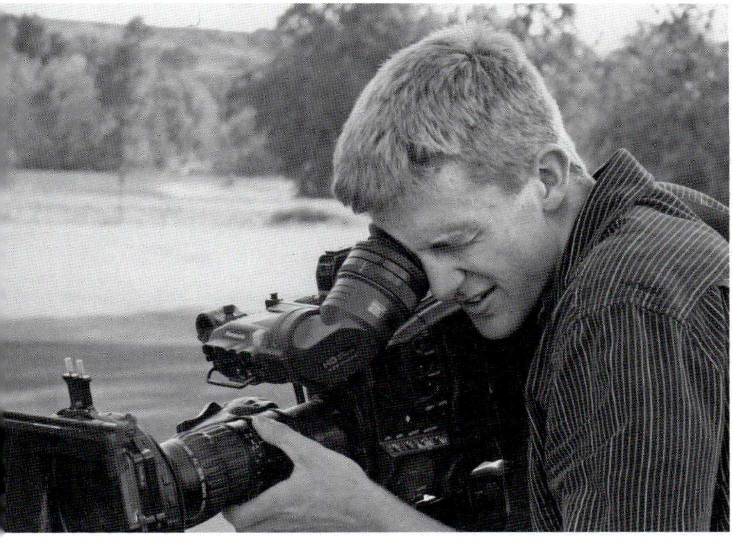

Issac Goeckeritz
Issac Goeckeritz is a local documentary filmmaker. While still a student at Weber State University, Issac began to make local history films. His film titled *Ogden: Junction City of the West* was awarded the 2008 Best Documentary at the Utah Best of State Awards. Goeckeritz has also completed a film on Uintah which won the 2009 Best Documentary award. Issac states that "as a filmmaker, I record to inspire." (Photograph courtesy of Issac Goeckeritz.)

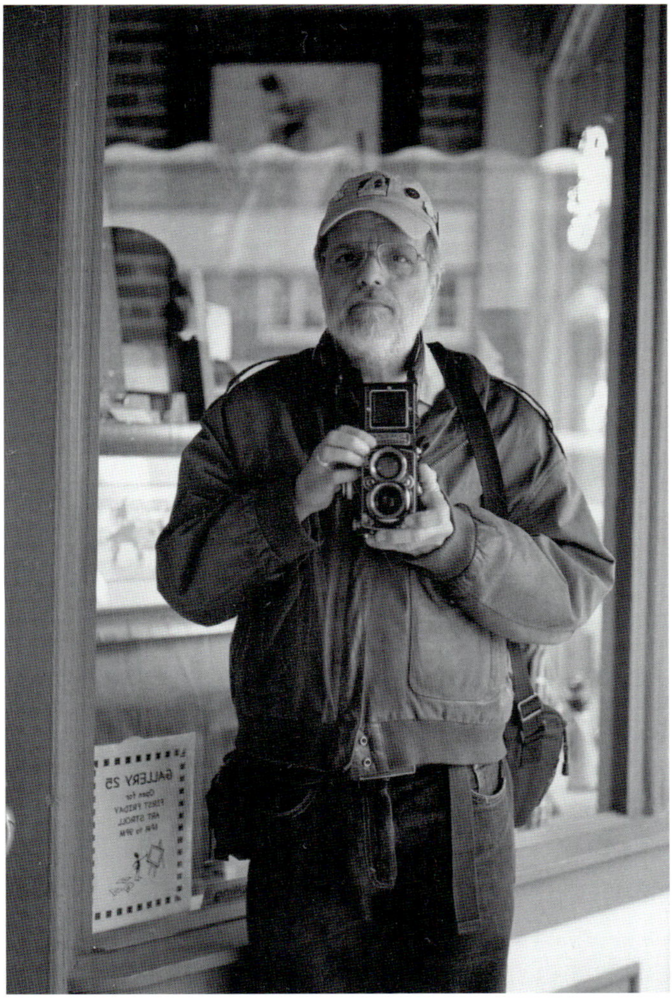

Charles Trentelman
Charles Trentelman is a newspaper reporter for the *Ogden Standard Examiner.* He focuses not only on the hard-hitting news stories of the day but on the local flavor surrounding Ogden. Trentelman is happy when he is talking to local Ogden citizens or digging through the history of Ogden looking for the truth. He is also an amateur photographer documenting his surroundings. (Photograph courtesy of Charlie Trentelman.)

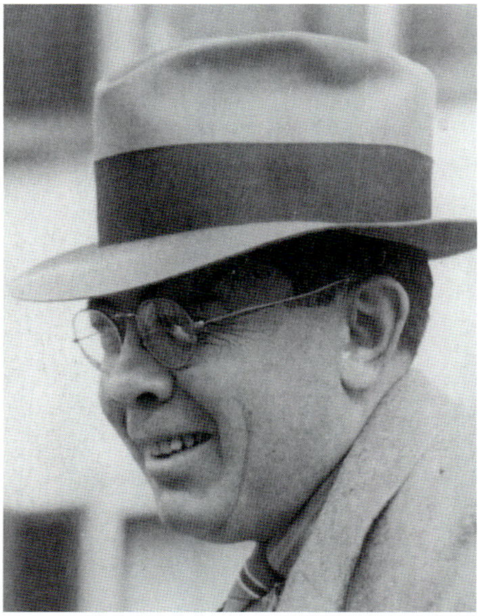

Bernard DeVoto
Born in Ogden in 1897, Bernard DeVoto had a distinguished career as a historian, critic, and commentator, receiving several prestigious awards including the Pulitzer and the National Book Award. He was also well known for his *Harper's* column "The Easy Chair." Though he had deep Ogden roots, his 1926 *American Mercury* article "Utah" angered many local residents when he stated that "civilized life" did not and would never exist in the state.

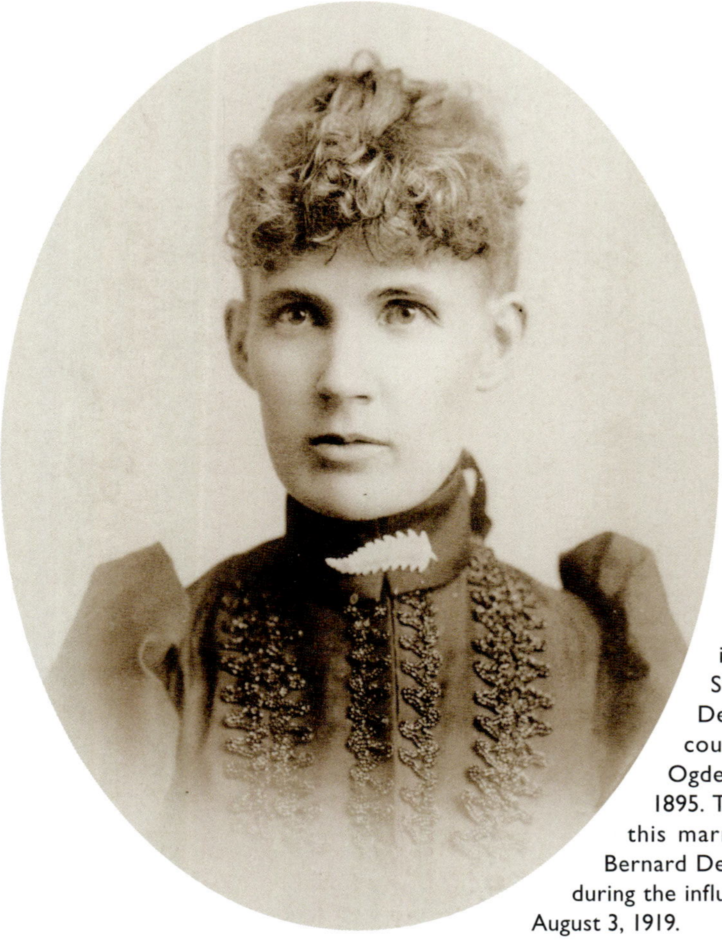

Rhoda DeVoto
Rhoda DeWolf DeVoto was born in 1867 to Samuel and Rhoda Dye in Uintah, Utah. She married Florian DeVoto, the deputy county recorder for Ogden, on October 6, 1895. The only child from this marriage was author Bernard DeVoto. Rhoda died during the influenza outbreak on August 3, 1919.

Sandy Santoro

C.J. "Sandy" Santoro was originally from Ohio but settled in Ogden after his discharge from the US Navy. He became the hotel manager of the Ben Lomond Hotel in the 1960s. His passion was playing jazz around Northern Utah. Here, he is pictured on the drums with other members of his jazz trio. Santoro was responsible for the celebration of Ogden's jazz great Red Nichols's 100th birthday party in 2005.

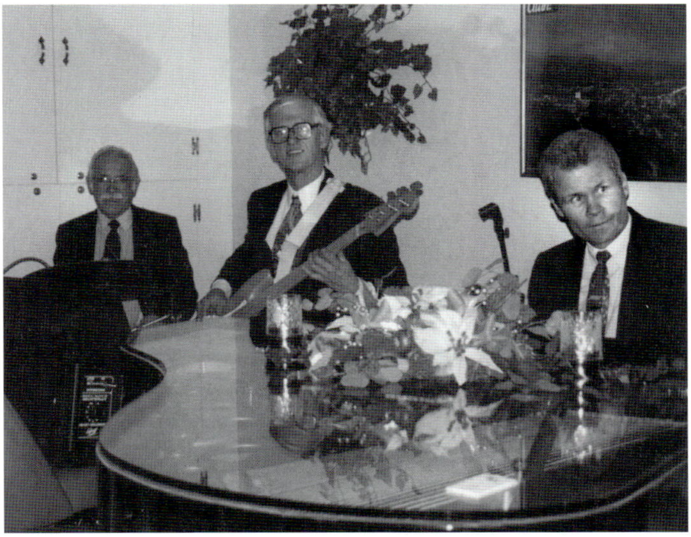

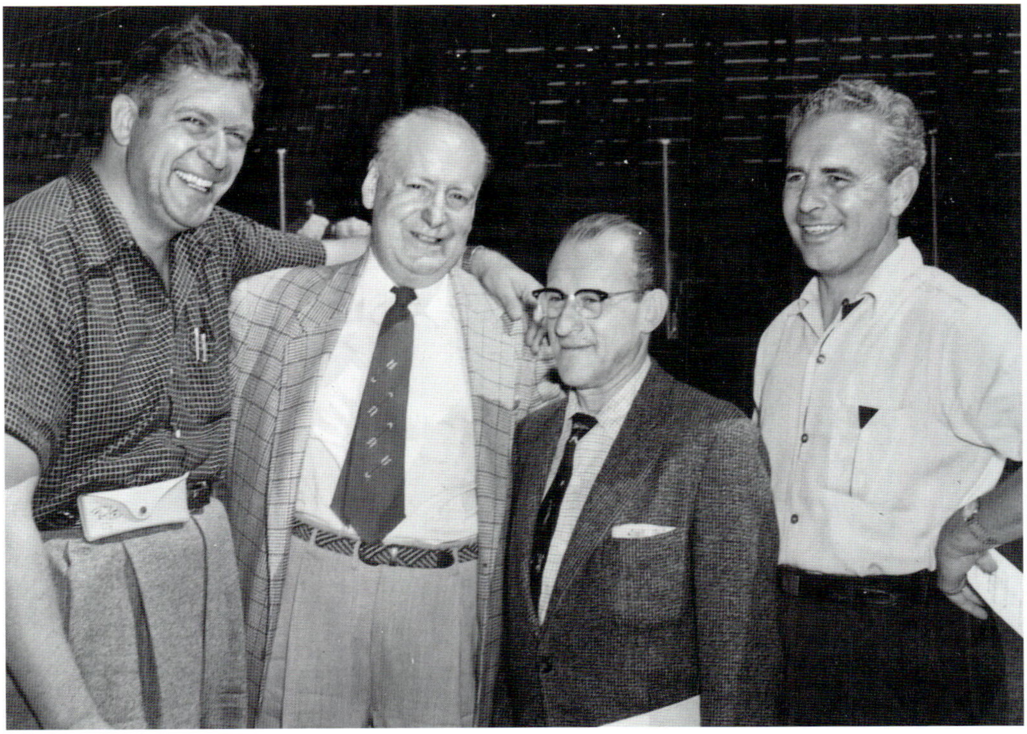

Al Warden

Al Warden, second on left, came to Ogden in 1919 to work as a reporter for the *Ogden Standard*. During his time in Ogden he promoted various sports events from the 1920s to the 1950s. He worked with the ski races at Becker Hill and Snow Basin and the winter sports events. He helped organize baseball's Pioneer League and brought famous athletes to Ogden, including Jack Dempsey.

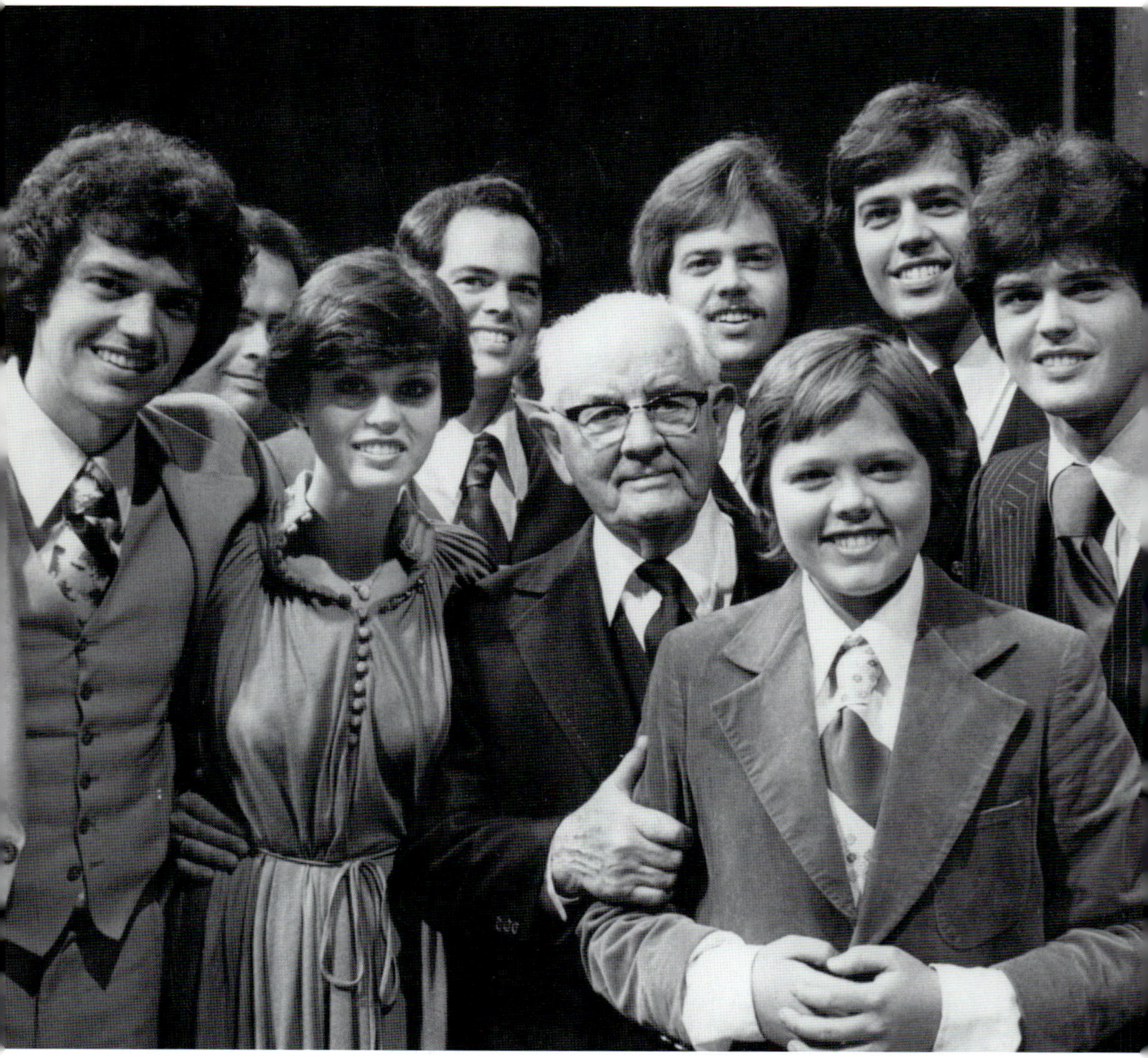

Osmond Family

All of the Osmond children were born in Ogden except the youngest, Jimmy. The group started as a barbershop quartet with Alan, Wayne, Merrill, and Jay Osmond. The Osmond brothers performed as regulars on the *Andy Williams Show* from 1962 to 1969, after being discovered performing for a televised Disney special. The Osmonds landed a record contract with MGM and a short-lived Saturday morning cartoon series from 1972 to 1974. Donny and Marie's solo careers emerged with different levels of success, each having No. 1 hits. In 1976, the older brothers began producing *The Donny & Marie Show*, which was a hit from 1976 to 1979. In 2003, the Osmond family was honored for their achievements with a star on the Hollywood Walk of Fame.

Moroni Olsen

Moroni Olsen was born on June 27, 1889, in Ogden. In 1923, Olsen organized the Moroni Olsen Players, who performed from Ogden to Seattle. After having worked on Broadway, Olsen made his film debut in a 1935 adaptation of *The Three Musketeers*. One of Olsen's most famous roles was the voice of the Magic Mirror in Walt Disney's *Snow White and the Seven Dwarfs*.

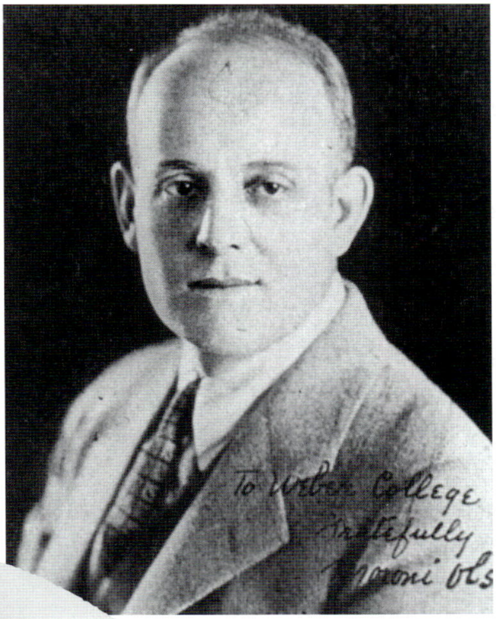

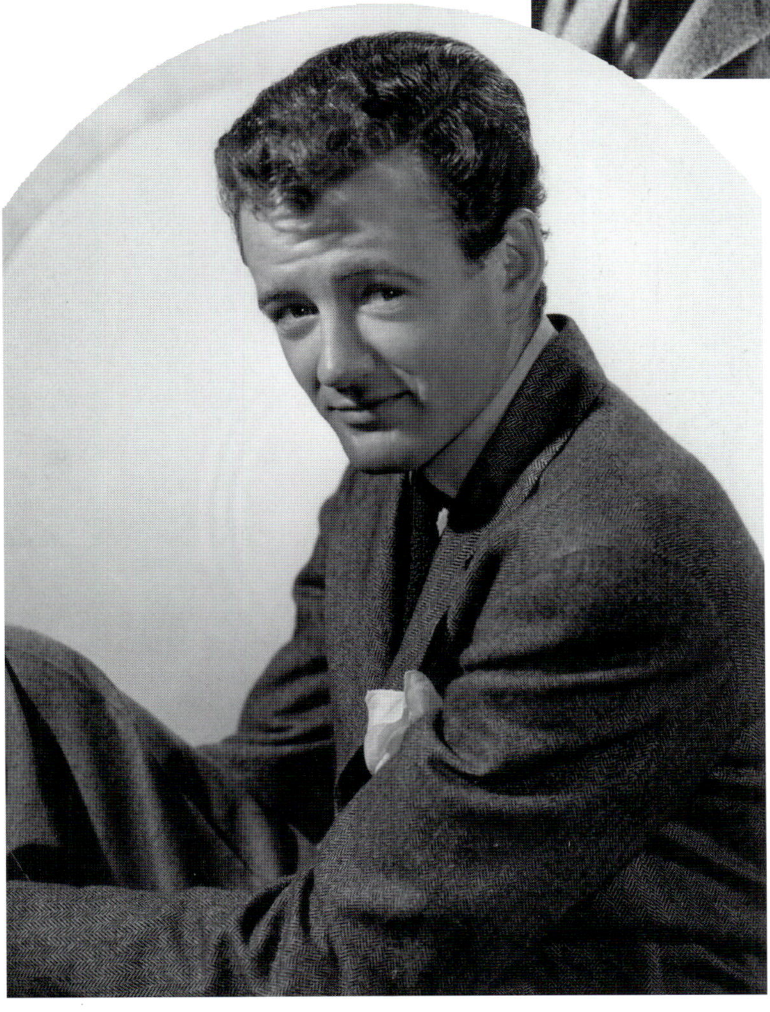

Robert Walker

Robert Walker was born on October 13, 1918. When he was 12, his family moved to Ogden where he lived before attending the American Academy of Dramatic Arts. Walker started acting in the film *Baatan* in 1943. He had roles in *See Here, Private Hargrove*, and *Her Highness and the Bellboy*. Walker worked opposite actresses Judy Garland and Katharine Hepburn. Walker died on August 28, 1951, at the age of 32.

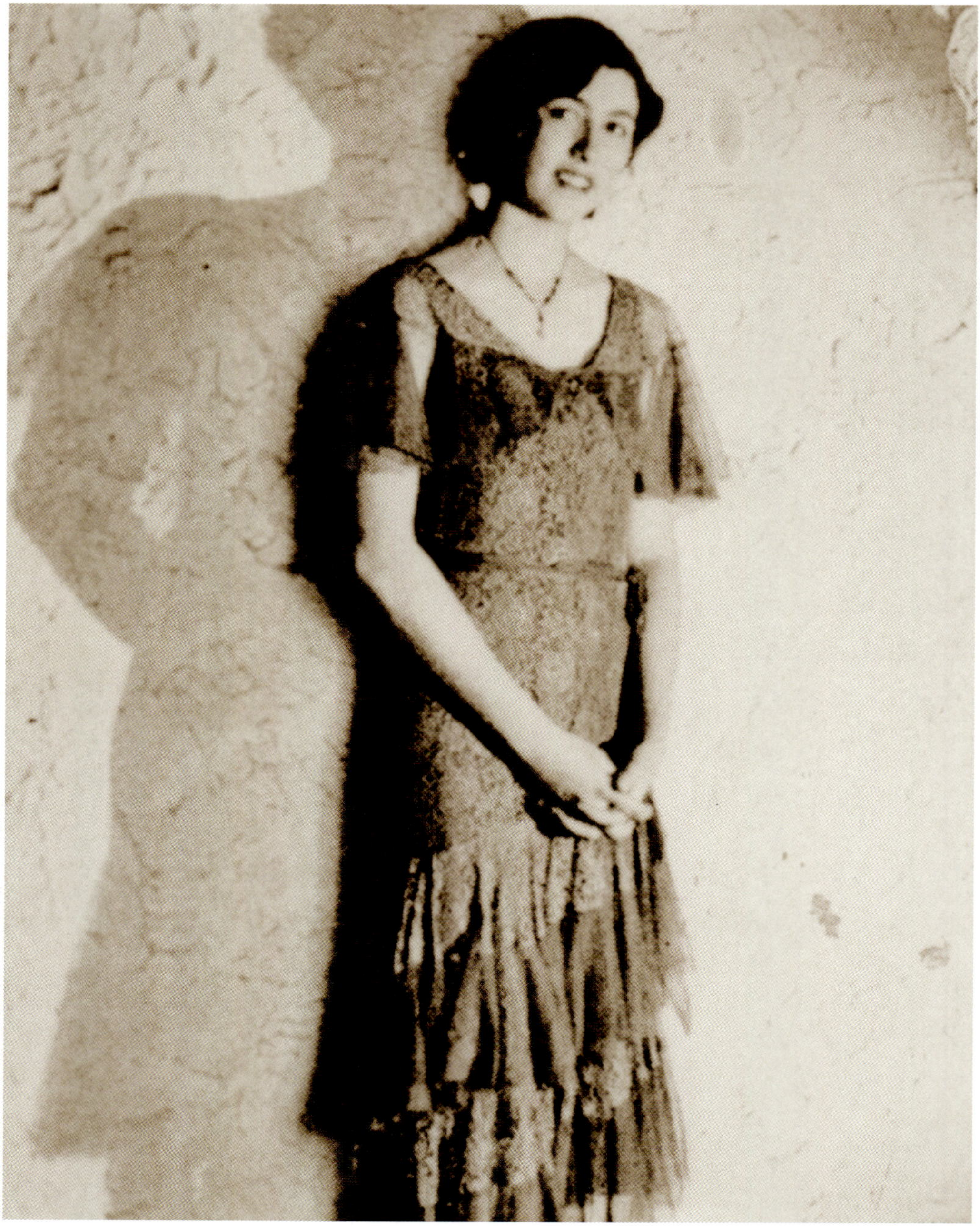

Fawn McKay Brodie

Fawn McKay Brodie was the second of five children of Thomas E. McKay and Fawn Brimhall. Born in Ogden in September 1915, she grew up in Huntsville. From 1930 to 1932, Fawn attended Weber College, where she became an accomplished public speaker and participated in intercollegiate debate. She then completed her bachelor of arts degree in English Literature at the University of Utah in 1934. At the age of 20, she completed a master's degree in English Literature from the University of Chicago. She taught for several years at UCLA. In 1945, Brodie's biography of Joseph Smith *No Man Knows My History* was published. She followed that with biographies on Thomas Jefferson and Richard Nixon.

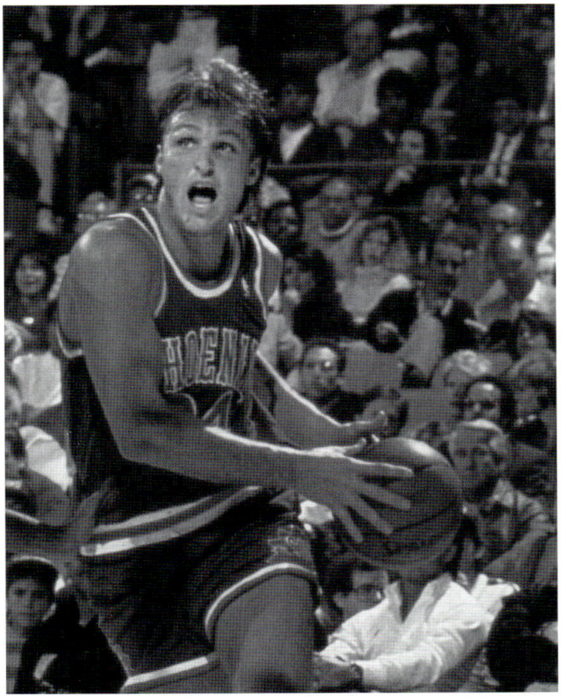

Tom Chambers

Tom Chambers was born in Ogden on June 21, 1959. Throughout his career, Chambers played for the San Diego Clippers (1981–1983), the Seattle Super Sonics (1983–1988), the Phoenix Suns (1988–1993), the Utah Jazz (1993–1995), and the Charlotte Hornets and the Philadelphia 76ers in 1997. After retiring from the NBA, he became a community relations representative for the Suns and owns the Tom Chambers Shooting Star Ranch in the Ogden Valley.

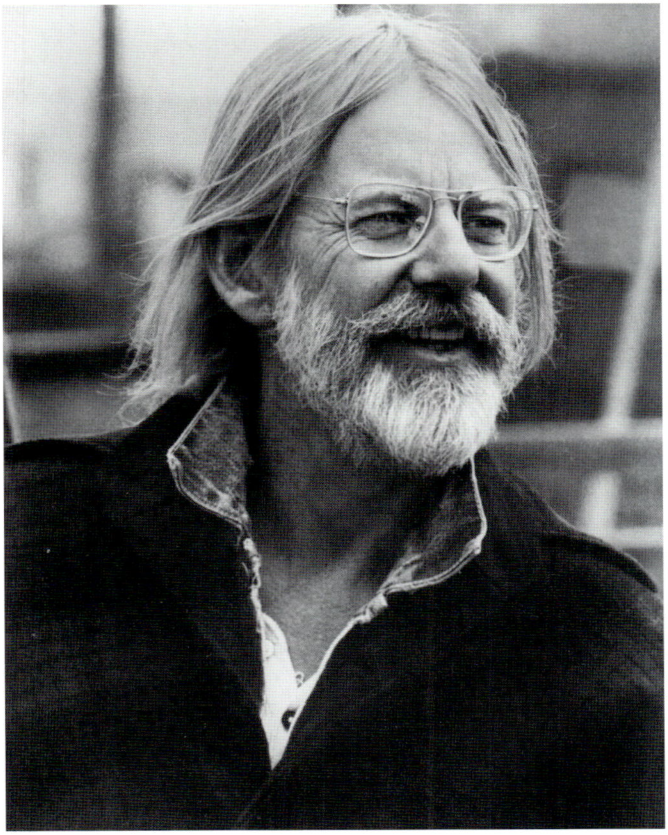

Hal Ashby

Hal Ashby was born in Ogden on September 2, 1929. As a young adult, Ashby moved to California. In 1967, he won the Academy Award for Film Editing for *In the Heat of the Night*. He went on to direct *Harold and Maude* and *Being There,* and his two great commercially successful films *Shampoo* and *Coming Home*. Ashby died of cancer on December 27, 1988.

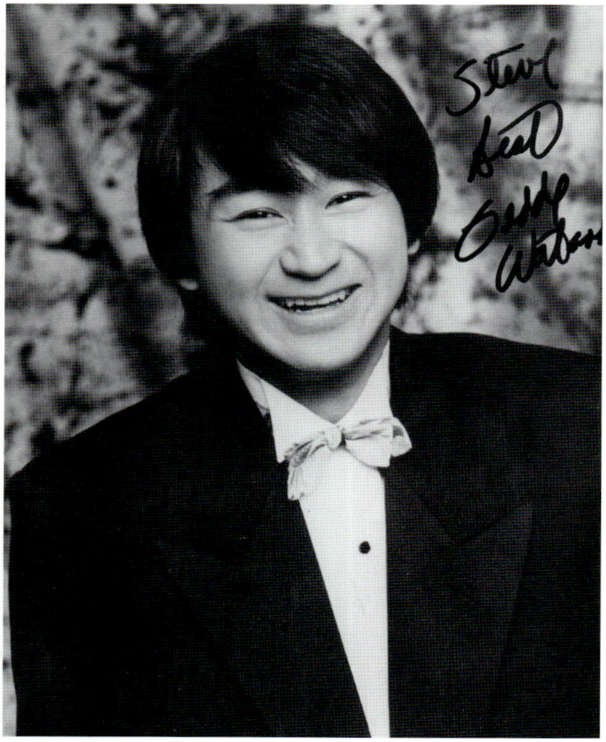

Gedde Watanabe
Gedde Watanabe was born on June 26, 1955, in Ogden. After graduating from Ogden High School, He moved to San Francisco. Watanabe appeared on *Sesame Street* for a few years, in *Gung Ho* with Michael Keaton, and had a recurring role on *ER* from 1998 to 2002. The character Watanabe is most remembered for is Long Duk Dong, the clumsy foreign exchange student in *Sixteen Candles.*

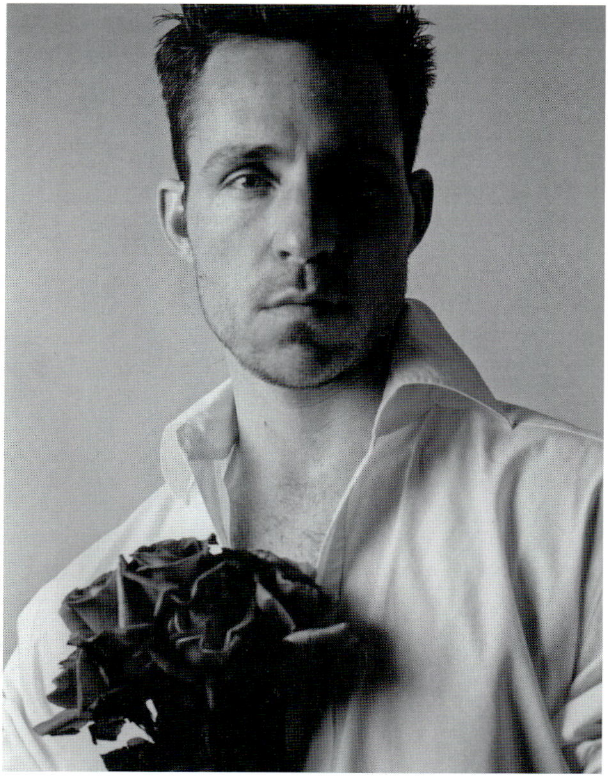

Jeff Leatham
Jeff Leatham, artistic director of the Four Seasons Hotel George V in Paris, has been creating sensations with his floral designs. He was voted Best Hotel Florist in Europe for three consecutive years. Leatham's clientele has included Kylie Minogue and Bill Clinton. He also starred in his own television show *Flowers Uncut with Jeff Leatham* on TLC. Leatham is originally from Ogden and is the son of Larry and Janet Leatham. (Photograph courtesy of Larry Leatham.)

BIBLIOGRAPHY

Alexander, Thomas G. "Ogden: A Federal Colony in Utah." *Utah Historical Quarterly* 47 (Summer 1979): 291–309.

Doxey. Clifford. "The History of Ogden Public Schools." Masters Thesis. University of Utah, 1944.

Hunter, Milton R. *Beneath Ben Lomond's Peak: A History of Weber County, 1824–1900, Fifth Edition.* Salt lake City, UT: Quality Press, 1995.

Kotter, Richard. "An Examination of Mormon and Non-Mormon Influences in Ogden City Politics, 1847 1996." Masters Thesis, University of Utah, 1967

Ogden Sesquicentennial Committee. *Ogden City: The First 150 years, 1851–2001*. Ogden, UT: Ogden Sesquicentennial Committee, 2002.

Ogden City Council Office. *Ogden City Councils and Mayors, 1851–2001.* Ogden, UT: Ogden City, 2000.

Peterson, F. Ross, and Robert E. Parson. *Ogden City, Its Governmental Legacy: A Sesquicentennial History.* Ogden, UT: Chapelle Limited, 2001

Roberts, Richard C., and Richard W. Sadler. *Ogden: Junction City.* Northridge, CA: Windsor Publications, 1985.

———. *A History of Weber County.* Salt Lake City, UT: Utah State Historical Society, 1997.

Roybal, Linda. Ogden's "Twenty-fifth Street: the spaces of which Legends are Made." Masters Thesis, Utah State University, 1997.

Sadler, Richard W. *Weber State College: A Centennial History.* Salt Lake City, UT: Publishers Press, 1989.

Sillito, John and Sarah Langsdon. *Ogden.* Charleston, SC: Arcadia Publishing, 2008.

Strack, Don. *Ogden Rails: A History of Ogden Railroads from 1869 to Today.* Ogden, UT: Golden Spike Chapter, Railway and Locomotive Historical Society, 1997.

Tillotson, Elizabeth. *A History of Ogden.* Ogden, UT, Ogden City, 1960.

White, Jean Bickmore. "The Right to Be Different: Ogden and Weber County Politics, 1850–1924. *Utah Historical Quarterly* (Summer 1979): 254–72.

INDEX

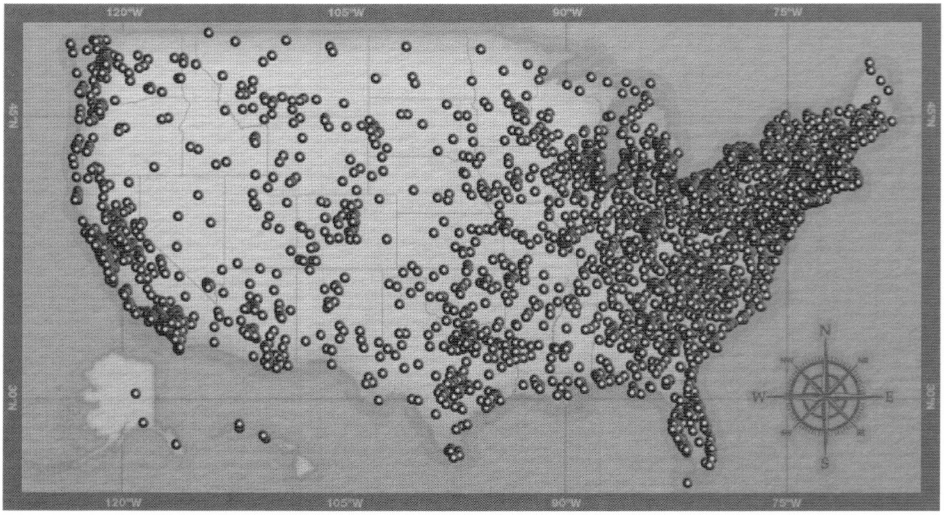

Consistent with our mission to preserve history on a local level, this book was printed in South Carolina on American-made paper and manufactured entirely in the United States. Products carrying the accredited Forest Stewardship Council (FSC) label are printed on 100 percent FSC-certified paper.

MADE IN THE USA